The Secret Lives of Adults

About the author

Allison Keating is a Chartered Psychologist with the Psychological Society of Ireland who has been practicing at her own clinic for the last 14 years. For four years prior to that, her first role as a trauma counsellor to asylum seekers with PTSD was an insight into growth through immense adversity. She also managed mass redundancies and saw the casualties of the recession first hand.

Making a difference to people's lives through compassion, therapy and learning are her core values. She has a keen interest in destigmatising mental health issues, taking evidence-based theory mainstream, and is a major advocate of positive psychology. She has been the resident psychologist on TV3's *Ireland AM*, *The Morning Show* and is currently on *Saturday AM* and *Sunday AM*. She also co-presented RTÉ2's *Then Comes Marriage* six-part series. Allison is a regular on *The Ray D'Arcy Show* and also contributes to programs with Dave Fanning, Matt Cooper and Ryan Tubridy as well as many other shows, magazines and newspapers.

www.bwell.ie

The Secret Lives of Adults

of Adults

Your seven key relationships
— and how to make them work

Allison Keating

Gill Books

Gill Books

Hume Avenue

Park West

Dublin 12

www.gillbooks.ie

Gill Books is an imprint of M.H. Gill and Co.

© Allison Keating 2018

978 07171 7956 5

Design and print origination by O'K Graphic Design, Dublin

Edited by Rachel Pierce

Proofread by Ellen Christie

Printed by CPI Group (UK) Ltd, Croydon CRO 4YY

This book is typeset in Minion 11/16 pt with chapter headings in Advert.

The paper used in this book comes from the wood pulp of managed forests. For every
tree felled, at least one tree is planted, thereby renewing natural resources.
A CIP catalogue record for this book is available from the British Library.

5 4 3 2 1

Dedicated to Thomas, Alannah, Hayley & Brooke,

my Mum & Dad, Barbara, Carol Ann & Sarah-Jane and all the kids

Contents

'Every story is us'

RUMI

Understanding Adulthood

Knowing is not enough; we must apply.
Willing is not enough; we must do.

Johann Wolfgang von Goethe

For many adults, life is tough. There are a lot of plates to keep spinning, from work, to parenthood, to being the child of ageing parents – and an underlying pressure to do it all flawlessly. People have been sharing their life stories with me for the past fourteen years in my practice at the bWell Clinic, and for four previous years in many challenging and purposeful roles. I hear and see all kinds of lives, but when it comes to talking to adults, the words I hear most often are: '*I feel overwhelmed.*'

Many people have a belief – whether they know it or not – that being an adult means having everything figured out. We think we leave our youth behind and become older and wiser. In fact, the only certainty is that things will remain uncertain. It's a difficult and demanding stage of life, and numbing out mental noise has never been easier to do. I see the look of dread on clients' faces when I ask them to just 'sit and be' with themselves, their thoughts and feelings. Checking in online has become easier than checking in with ourselves. So even though we are trying to do so much and be so much, we have trouble examining our roles and challenges. It's often easier to look the other way rather than confront and be with ourselves.

This is what *The Secret Lives of Adults* is all about: understanding yourself and the complexities surrounding all the important roles you play in life. We encourage change and development enthusiastically in children, but are more fearful of it in adulthood. This is the key premise of this book: to ask you to challenge and, if necessary, to change the core beliefs you have about who you are and how you behave in your relationships.

Where do those core beliefs come from? They are the secrets we carry within ourselves, often unknown even to ourselves – the secrets of our inner lives. Our behaviour is rooted in past experience. Your connection to yourself and to all your relationships began the day you came into this world. Knowing yourself, and yourself in relation to others, is an experiential life lesson, with each social interaction weaving and stitching the fabric of your adult relationships and making you the person you are today. We don't have access to the unconscious part of ourselves, most notably from ages one to three years, and yet this is an extremely formative and influential time. It can often hold many of our secrets of our unknown selves.

There are seven key relationships in adulthood, reflected in the chapters of this book: with yourself, with your parents, with your siblings, with your partner, with your children, with your friends and with your work. You are like a Russian doll: you contain layers of separate selves within the one 'me'. The outer Russian doll is the first representation of yourself, with each of your inner selves connected yet separate – a kaleidoscope of multifaceted reflections of all your inner selves. Taking each self and looking at it individually helps you to understand yourself better in this complex experience that is adulthood.

One of the key tools offered in this book is the pause. *The Secret Lives of Adults* asks you to pause, stand back and examine your patterns of behaviour and typical reactions, which you have learned and inherited primarily from your parents and other influencers. These make you the sum of many parts. They are the result of conditioning (whether you know it or not). I am asking you to look closely at these motivations and triggers and say, '*Hang on, is there a better way to respond here?*' This 'pause and think' approach will enlighten you to become aware of when you are being reactive and doing things habitually – responding to your secret triggers.

This book is an invitation to improve the quality and kindness in your relationship with yourself. The book provides you with guidelines on how to cultivate self-care and self-compassion among all the noise and constant juggling in each of your inner lives. In childhood your needs were hopefully met by your parents. They made the daily decisions, took responsibility and minded you. This book asks you to take responsibility for yourself, and to mind yourself.

My aims are to:

* ask you to make yourself a priority, because your wellbeing won't magically occur;
* ask you to seek out and find your strengths, and nurture them;
* bring back that childlike gregariousness, to be curious and bold;
* recognise and appreciate the good, work on and contain the bad, and actively cultivate more of what you actually want in your life;
* pause and rest when you feel worn out;
* plug yourself in and tune back into yourself every day, just like you do with your phone;
* use your Diary to check in with yourself daily using this one sentence: 'What have I done for myself today?'

The Secret Lives of Adults is a book full of hope. Grounded hope, as it is grounded in evidence-based practice. The Psychological Toolbox (p. 243) gives you the practical know-how to mind yourself across all the roles you must play. When you finish the book, you can come back to the toolbox again and again.

My hope for you is that this book will act as a gatekeeper that unlocks and opens the questions you have about yourself. Opening your mind and heart in a bid to genuinely understand who you really are is the first step in knowing yourself. Then, and only then, can you change. As an adult you have the power to do this, you just need the tools and the know-how, which is the focus and aim of this book.

My hope is that when you put this book down, you feel inspired to want to make changes and that, crucially, you will know how to make those real changes that will impact the quality of your day-to-day life. To that end, I'm asking you while reading this book to let down your walls, be vulnerable, be honest and be open to revealing your authentic self.

Regardless of what life is throwing at you, I will ask you to notice, to become aware and to change how you react. If you work through the book carefully, engaging with the questions it poses and asks you to answer, you will acquire the self-knowledge that is necessary for understanding and change. You will unlock your own secrets, and by doing so you will be able to create a more fulfilling and happier life. The aim of this book is to move you from existing to thriving, maybe not all of the time, but certainly more of the time.

The case studies are composites of issues and themes that have been presented at the clinic. I am also fully aware of issues of fertility, blended and single families, and other relationship types. Each of us is an unique individual in our own right, but the case studies may help highlight the overarching themes.

Psychologists love a good joke, especially when it contains a simple truth, so I ask you: How many psychologists does it take to change a lightbulb? Only one, but the lightbulb has to want to change.

This is your beginning, your moment of change.

Wishing you the best of luck,
Allison x

The secret of change is to focus all of your energy,
not on fighting the old, but on building the new.

Socrates

CHAPTER 1

Me, Myself & I

The most difficult thing in life is to know yourself.

Thales

INTRODUCTION

For all your years alive, do you really know yourself? Do you know what drives you, repels you or what makes you happy? With highly scheduled lives, the constant routines of adulthood can leave people feeling trapped in a cognitive and emotional hamster wheel of life. And sometimes it's easier to keep pushing and going round, rather than stopping and really thinking about your life.

This chapter is your starting point in getting to know you: your public *me*, your private *myself* and, deep undercover, your unconscious self or *I*. My aim is to help you identify and become aware of any large gaps between your public and private self, and to cultivate more peace of mind for you as one person. If there are patterns of behaviour you want to change, you must notice them, become aware of them and then understand them.

Let's take a typical morning. *Me* was your public face that walked out the door, that chatted to the mums at the school gate and interacted with colleagues pleasantly, even when you felt awful. You need this *me* to function publicly, even if you didn't want to get dressed that morning.

Myself was the private you, the one that felt exhausted that morning and really didn't want to get up. The private *myself* may have been worried about the kids, your parents or your job. The private you may have felt strong inner emotions and private worries, but the public *me* got you up and out. The public *me* knew the boss would see you coming in late, so it told you that you 'should' get up, even though the private, tired *myself* wanted to stay beneath the covers.

And where was *I* in this morning struggle? *I* was there, but was working away in the background, unseen, shaping your reactions and feelings and driving many of your behaviours without asking you for any instructions or input.

These inner selves can bring up a mixture of joy and disharmony, conflict and guilt for adults. By working through this chapter, you will work towards revealing who you really are, what you really want and how to make changes to allow you to experience a more harmonious inner and outer life.

This chapter comes first for good reason. It is a crucial first step because understanding the relationship you have with yourself is the key to understanding the relationships you have with others. If you don't know yourself, your triggers, your thought processes, why you react as you do in certain circumstances, then you will continue to repeat damaging patterns of behaviour. It's only when you know yourself that you can begin to improve or change the other relationships in your life.

COMMON ISSUES

In my practice, I have found that it is often during an unexpected crisis in our lives that we start to wonder about who we really are and how we have ended up at this particular point. That crisis may come in the form of grief, job loss, affairs, break-ups, trauma or sickness – unfortunately, the list is long. You and your worldview become irrevocably changed, leaving behind a trail of emotional chaos. Crisis robs you of certainty, and uncertainty breeds fear. Such events rip the rug of certainty from under you, take your confidence and create an almighty crack down the centre of your core identity, leaving you wondering: *Who am I now?*

To answer this fundamental question, you need to gain an understanding of all your dynamics, relationships and experiences from the past. These events have shaped you, but often remain hidden from you. However, these processes play a large role in how you live, think and feel today. That's why this chapter aims to help you understand your personal triggers – the things that make you unhappy, uncomfortable, angry or anxious. When you have identified these triggers, you can catch them in advance and work on alternative responses.

So the first question is: what are your common triggers? Do you have specific times that these core triggers are activated, such as in times of stress, like Christmas, exams or deadlines? Or do you find yourself triggered by people, perhaps your mother, boss or teacher? Or does it stem from a specific feeling, such as embarrassment or fear of failure? If you reflect back for a moment, has there been a personal theme to what triggers strong emotional reactions within you? Times when you find yourself incredulously saying, 'I can't believe this is happening to me again.'

Examples of common triggers are:

* Criticism
* Rejection
* Conflict, arguments
* Isolation
* Blame
* Judgement
* Fairness
* Being needed
* Not feeling good enough
* Abandonment

Triggers are often old and hidden. A negative thought, such as *I can't believe she said that to me*, is often underpinned by a personal insecurity, a feeling of not being good enough or comparing yourself to everyone else and finding yourself feeling a lack, or a sense failure. In order to understand yourself, you can't lash out or jump straight into the blame game. You have to sit with what the trigger has brought up for you. At the base of it you may find an emotional need that wasn't met in your childhood, and that you now seek to

fulfil through your relationships, whether at work or at home.
Take the example of Sarah:

Sarah felt her cheeks flush as she felt ignored in the boardroom. Before she knew it, she could feel a wave of fear wash over her and tears welling up. Oh no, she thought, please don't let this happen here.

This is why triggers are your best clue to understanding the pain that may have been long deferred but has not been forgotten, at least not by your hidden unconscious. Through therapy, Sarah learned that this old feeling of rejection came directly from her childhood. It would have been easy to have just stayed with the feeling of being mortified and not really look at what underpinned the triggered feeling. But through discussion in therapy, Sarah was able to identify the root cause of her unhelpful reaction.

In terms of the importance of really understanding and being compassionate with yourself, this is how you tune into your feelings, rather than getting swept away in the 'he said, she said' drama that will never resolve the issue, or your feelings. Once acknowledged, your trigger then moves from being an unknown to a known, at which point you can do something about it. Even though triggered vulnerable feelings are unpleasant and uncomfortable, use them as a mechanism, like pain, to signal you to listen, acknowledge and take action.

KEY THEORIES

The hidden place where your inner, undiscovered feelings, beliefs and values come from is your *I*, or, as Freud called it, your unconscious mind. It will remain unknown to you, but by exploring your triggers and reactions, you can discern old patterns of behaviour that may need to be changed as an adult. The Johari window is useful in showing who knows what and to get a sense of the public, private and unconscious selves.

	Known to self	Unknown to self
Known to others	**OPEN SELF** Information about you that both you & others know	**BLIND SELF** Information about you that you don't know but others do know
Unknown to others	**HIDDEN SELF** Information about you that you know but that others don't know	**UNKNOWN SELF** Information about you that neither you nor others know

The Johari window tells us that:

- Your public self is known to you and others.
- Your private self is private to you.
- Your personal blind-spots are known to others, but not to you.
- Your unconscious is unknown to you and everyone.

Can you see how hard it is to get a handle on your selves? At any time, you don't have access to the whole picture. You just have pieces of the puzzle, and you will always be missing a few pieces. This is the reward of striving to know yourself: the more you know yourself, the easier it is to see the bigger picture. Self-awareness gives the control back to you.

I'm sure you have been taken aback over the years when a close friend or family member has told you something about yourself that you really didn't think was the case. Once you've been told, it seems incredible that you hadn't seen it before. It is worth keeping in mind in this chapter that everyone is blind to parts of themselves. Your personal perspective creates a lens through which you can only look out from within yourself. It is much easier for others, objectively looking in, to see what you can't. The clarity of those objective others is a direct result of their thinking not being clouded by all the subjective feelings you experience, and that obscure your view of yourself.

Research shows that strangers can have a more objective and earlier insight into you than you have. This can lead to contradictions, like the boss who thinks he's a real 'people person' but the team doesn't like him at all. Or the friend who thinks she's an amazing listener, but talks incessantly about herself. You may be nodding your head, thinking of someone you know like that, but does anyone read the above and go, 'Oh yes, that's me'? It's pretty unlikely.

It's an unsettling truth, but people who feel they know themselves well and consider themselves self-aware may be unpleasantly surprised to learn what others think of them. You have blind-spots, we all do, but while we can't see them, other people can. One of the most common concerns I hear from the couch is: '*I wonder what they really think about me?*' This is a concern and a matter of curiosity for everyone, maybe even more so for those who protest, '*I don't care what people think about me.*'

This doesn't have to remain a puzzle forever. Through exploration of the inner selves and roles within the core you, you can get to know yourself better – even your blind-spots. In the Introduction, we touched on the idea of the 'Russian doll', whereby our different selves are all slotted one into the other inside us, separate but connected. The first Russian doll we will look at is the trinity of *me, myself* and *I*, which makes up the first of your secret life of adulthood: public, private and undiscovered, which is your 'inner child'. The Russian doll is a Matryoshka doll, meaning 'little Matron'. The outermost doll is usually brightly painted and wears traditional clothes. The dolls within can be either gender and are ornately decorated. The last, innermost doll is a baby made of plain solid wood. I love the idea of the baby, a piece of uncarved and unexplored potential. All of the experiences and events in your life etch out the essence of you as a person. This reflects a dual process of life changing you from outside and within.

The 'inner child' is a term originating from Jung's concept of the Divine Child archetype and is used frequently in therapy. You were that child once, and that child still lives and acts out through you. Signs of your inner child's presence can come from fears of abandonment or rejection. Your inner child, or *I*, drives powerful feelings in your present-day relationships, unconsciously influencing your actions and reactions. The *I* holds your core beliefs about the world, and its childlike ways – rather than its childishness – need to be nurtured by your adult self.

The positive side of the inner child is that it can be full of love, joy, fun and playfulness. The inner child has innocence and an ability to feel awe, and is very present and mindful in nature. Try bringing a toddler for a walk and you'll know what I mean! The unconscious takes a lot of disapproval for all its negatives, but I feel an essential part of being an adult is the ability to stay connected to the fun, joyful, creative, childlike aspects of yourself.

The difficulty with the *I* is that it lies deep within the dark recesses of your unconscious, which makes it so difficult to access. Adults become mature by age, but in order to become an adult psychologically, it really helps to connect back to a time that is not now within your conscious possession. Many people feel they have outgrown childish ways and left that inner child, – and its hopes and fears – far behind. But this is not the case. Imprinted in your unconscious are vital clues to your genuine self. Those clues often become evident when triggers release quick, strong and powerful reactions that leave you spinning, with the queasy feeling of not knowing where that reaction just came from.

Part of the experience of uncovering our true identity is to connect, talk, nurture and support your inner child, with the intention of gaining more insight into why you feel the way you do. It involves breaking down old, redundant and perhaps childish ways of dealing with conflict, rejection, shame and fear, and then consciously cultivating a sense of who you are and acting in ways that work for your life. You must acknowledge patterns that trigger strong feelings and actively soothe them, as you would an upset child. In other words, you must be an emotionally responsive adult to yourself. Otherwise you'll remain at the mercy of old patterns of behaviour that do not serve you well in adulthood.

How do you do this? You need to learn to compassionately catch yourself when your reaction far outweighs what has just occurred. For example, if you find yourself feeling deeply upset or hurt over a comment made by someone about your character – *'you are always so untidy'* or *'that is so like you, you'll never change'* – these statements feel pervasive, personal and unchangeable. This tricky situation can often occur in a romantic relationship as it carries

7

the heavy emotional baggage of triggers that you were 'told' as a child by a parent or teacher – *'you are so disorganised, what is wrong with you?'*.

In these sorts of situations, many of us immediately dismiss our feelings as an overreaction because we know that we shouldn't be as upset as we are, so we feel embarrassed and frustrated with our own reaction, even though we really feel that way. This is often immediately compounded, and confirmed to us, by being told that we are too sensitive or that *'you are having a complete overreaction, this is ridiculous, all I said was that you need to be a bit tidier'*. To get to the root of what has really upset, annoyed or angered us, we need to ask the question: *Why did that upset me so much?* Pause and give yourself a moment to really think about it. Take a deep breath, then you will be able to identify what just came up for you, minus the stomping feet.

A deep insecurity, originating in the home or in school, of feeling stupid or not being good enough, of being compared to siblings or classmates, is often at the root of a deeply distressed response to a fairly innocuous comment. You hear, internalise and personalise these comments into *'you are so disorganised'*, *'you are such a mess'*, *'you are not good enough'* because they hit upon old emotional wounds. I ask you to stop minimising real emotions, especially when you know it's an overreaction. Say to the other person: *'I'm sorry, yes, I know I overreacted, I want to get to what I'm actually upset about.'* This is then a chance to connect, not just to yourself, but to them as well.

As adults, feelings of shame and embarrassment that occur when we feel we have acted like a child can lead us to miss the emotional wound that has just been activated. The feelings usually come up rapidly and can feel all encompassing. Please do not chastise or criticise your inner child for being 'silly'. Stop berating yourself when you rationally know your reaction doesn't warrant the very strong response you felt. Stop giving out to yourself. Stop thinking, *'I shouldn't feel like this, this is ridiculous'*. Otherwise you will miss what the emotion is trying to tell you.

If you take notice of your emotions and reactions with compassion, you'll be amazed at the insight you'll gain into what has just triggered your reaction. You need to learn how to do your own 'emotional first aid', as described by psychologist Guy Winch. If it hurts emotionally, treat it in the same way as you would a physical wound: pay attention, do something to soothe the pain and heal it.

How can you apply this in your own life? The 'how' lies in the process of paying attention, acknowledging the feelings and emotions that have come up, and perhaps, if you are lucky, being able to pinpoint when this feeling occurred before. Don't get stuck on this, though, because a simple acknowledgement of the feeling is immensely powerful and cathartic by itself. In terms of healing, I am much more interested in the how than the why.

Many of my clients feel they can't move on unless they understand their past and know what happened or why. Sometimes it can be hugely beneficial to know the why – however, similar to physical ailments, knowing you have the 'flu won't change the fact that you have the 'flu. It's through the subsequent acknowledgement and active self-care that you can address the emotion and heal the old emotional wound.

THE PRACTICE

This is where you get to assess where you are in relation to your inner selves and the emotions they hold and behaviours they trigger. I recommend that you use a notebook or this Diary to record your answers as you work through the book. There are regular Diary segments, like this one, to get you actively thinking and evaluating your own life – and it's a very useful and powerful exercise that thinking alone won't provide. Writing is hugely cathartic, in terms of being able to identify your own thoughts, feelings and behaviours.

DIARY

Who am I?

Sample answer: I am Lucy. I am kind, stubborn, happy! I am a mum, a wife, a daughter, a sister, a solicitor and a good friend.

Your answer: _____

_____

_____

How do I know who I am?

Sample answer: I know how I feel, I know who I am within all my relationships and they know me. But now that I ask myself this question, maybe I only know it from my perspective and from what I've been told. Like, I'm the organiser with my friends, the tough one at work, but I am mum at home and yet I'm the eldest with my siblings and the responsible one of the family. They are all very different and yet there is the true me who I show only to one close friend and my husband. Maybe, I need to think about this a bit more...

Your answer: _____

_____

_____

Name three things that make you 'you':

Sample answer: Your answer:

◇ *Honest*   ◇ _____

◇ *Fair*   ◇ _____

◇ *Funny*   ◇ _____

How would you describe yourself?

Sample answer: It depends on who I am with. I am flexible to the role or people I am with, it depends on the level of trust. I would describe myself as optimistic and strong. I think people see me as confident and yet if I was tired, I would let some people see another part of me, I suppose the private part, that is full of doubts, fears and concerns about the kids or my relationship. It's really interesting if I divide this between the public and private me, it is quite different. And as for the unconscious, I have no idea what impact that has in my daily life.

Your answer: _____
_____
_____

What was the last thing you said about yourself to your:

Sample answer: Your answer:

◇ Mother: *'I'm fine, stop worrying.'*   1. Mother:_____

◇ Friend: *'I'm stressed.'*   2. Friend:_____

◇ Acquaintance: *'It's a beautiful day.'*   3. Acquaintance:_____

◇ Boss: *'I'll get it done.'*   4. Boss:_____

◇ Partner: *'How will I get it done?'*   5. Partner:_____

Me

Me is your public face. It is you, but at a surface level. It is the you who knows how to act socially and in public.

The public you is aware of physical boundaries, so you know, for example, that hugging the postman wouldn't be appropriate. It's the you who says 'Hi' on the school run, or who talks about the latest Netflix binge over coffee with a co-worker. This *me* knows how to wait in a queue and knows and abides by social cues and rules.

Me is surface, but not superficial. It wouldn't be appropriate to tell your innermost thoughts to the woman in the post office queue. Sometimes oversharing is not caring.

Problems occur when the gap between your public face and your private face becomes too wide. This is a serious problem and should be treated as such. For me, when people say, *'I don't feel like myself'*, I know they are feeling a really deep disconnect from the *me* that they know. If the public you is projecting a happy, confident façade while underneath you are struggling with inner conflicts of doubt, despair and anxiety, it can feel difficult to open up and allow yourself to be 'seen' as you are, and not as how you think you are perceived. This is especially relevant to people who identify with or have been told that they are the strong, calm one. No one is strong and calm all the time. Be mindful not to get caught up in your public persona or in the role of being, or perceived as being, in control all the time. I say this with a warning: expect resistance from family, partners, work and friends. When you decide to make changes, other people haven't acclimatised yet and often it won't suit them either. But when the gap between your public and private self is continually at odds, it wreaks havoc on your ability to be your authentic self. Be bold, have courage, 'to thine own self be true'.

The consequences of allowing the gap to be too wide can lead to a fear of being caught out, known as impostor syndrome, an erosion of self-esteem, an increase in stress and anxiety and, ultimately, a feeling of depression if it continues unchecked. We need congruence in our thoughts and behaviours. Acting against those leads to deepening discrepancies and further alienation from yourself. Don't let the silent despair of acting as who you think you are supposed to be, erode the quality of your life and joy.

If you don't feel like yourself, take action, and the earlier, the better. You know when you don't feel like you. Acknowledge that feeling, then use these psychological cues in the same way you inherently use pain cues to drive yourself to make changes. Start by talking to someone you trust, honestly. If the feelings of frustration, anger, irritation, low mood and tearfulness, or changes in sleeping or eating patterns persist continuously for more than two weeks, seek professional help.

DIARY

Describe three things people may say about you from what they see in public:

Sample answer: Easy-going, confident, aloof

1._____

2._____

3._____

Name three things about your public *me*, from your perspective:

Sample answer: 'Feel misunderstood' or 'don't actually know what they think about me' or 'want to fit in'

1._____

2._____

3._____

Name the differences between the public *me* and the private *myself*:

Sample answer: 'I am a worrier', 'I am very deep and sensitive'

Your answer: _____

_____

_____

_____

What would surprise people to learn about you?

Sample answer: 'No one would ever know how shy I am'.

Your answer: _____

_____

_____

_____

You can tell a lot about the public person by their energy and how they speak about themselves and others. Here's the thing, people really worry about how they are judged by others. It makes them feel exposed and vulnerable. Some people can hide their feelings, too well, unfortunately, while others struggle to not let their true feelings be shown even though their expression reveals their true feelings. The middle ground is a nicer place to be, when possible.

I know people worry constantly about what others think of them, but remember, everyone does. No one is invincible. Other people are so concerned about what you think about them, they aren't thinking about you. I wish people knew this. Be aware of how much time you waste on things you can't ever know. The more important question is: how do you think about you?

If your self-esteem is low, others may see you in a much more positive light than you see yourself. That lack of self-esteem can emerge in different ways. For example, it's the immediate personal minimisation when someone pays you a compliment and you say, *'Oh this? I got it for a fiver in Penneys'*. With a negative filter in place, your self-perception will look for, accept and take on the bad and discount the good. You dismiss the compliment because it does not fit with your own inner negative self-perception.

Other people only have access to the surface you, your public face. It is you who has access to the whole you, and there's a rich inner world in the private 'you'.

Faulty thoughts start with phrases like *'I always'* or *'you never'* and they become ingrained as a fixed mindset. Holding on to familiar ideas and maintaining the status quo can result in you feeling in control and secure. But this is an uncomfortable illusion. In reality, it will keep you trapped and frustrated. People do not like uncertainty, so they hold on tightly to old, familiar, unhelpful ways of thinking and behaving to offset the 'cost' of change. But the cost of staying the same is so much higher, led by frustration, anger and inner conflict. Change is vital to growth.

DIARY

What changes have you been avoiding? _____

_____

_____

_____

Why have you avoided making these changes? _____

_____

_____

_____

What has it cost you so far? _____

_____

_____

_____

How long have you felt like this? _____

_____

_____

_____

What needs to happen for you to change? _____

_____

_____

_____

Imagine you have made the change. Describe what is different in your life. _____

_____

_____

For all of us, change is uncomfortable and hard. This is why I ask my clients to sit with themselves, to be kind and to listen to how they are feeling. So many people struggle with this. The harsh inner critic can be so corrosive. If I said to you the things you say to yourself, you would be utterly horrified.

The public self has never had as many platforms to display and curate a positive version of itself as it has now. Thanks to social media, your public self can appear as its best version and receive positive affirmation for that. From a psychological perspective, this makes neurological sense. It is ingrained in us at an evolutionary level to want to be 'liked'. Without getting into the positive and negatives of social media platforms, understand this: at the core of it all, people want to connect and to feel that they belong. It is normal to want to present a public face that heightens your social 'status'. As social animals, we want to display and show off our best features. At the tender core lies a primal need to belong. To belong, we need to feel valued and lovable. When public and private selves are in conflict, it's very difficult to feel a sense of belonging. That can be a very isolating experience, which is why it's so important to tackle and resolve any public versus private inner conflicts.

Myself

Myself is the private self, the one known by you and your trusted inner circle. A place in the inner circle is earned through a deep connection born of sharing intimate information about one another. Who makes it into the inner circle? Various things earn your place there, such as genes (your family), time and mutual openness/vulnerability (friends), intimacy (partner) and trust.

DIARY

Describe your private self. _____
_____
_____
_____

Name three aspects of yourself you keep private. _____
_____
_____
_____

Why are they private? _____
_____
_____
_____

How would you feel if people knew this about you? _____
_____
_____
_____

Who is in your inner circle? _____
_____
_____
_____

How did they get in? _____
_____
_____
_____

What happens if someone breaks your trust? _____
_____
_____
_____

Is there any major gap between your public and private self? _____
_____
_____
_____

Does this gap cause you any conflict or frustration? _____
_____
_____
_____

In the therapy room, I have seen the surging fear of people 'finding out' there is a sizeable gap between their public face, i.e. who others think they are, and their private self. I see this specifically with 'strong' people. You will know the strong person – they are kind, helpful, considerate, happy, confident-looking people who say, *'Yes, sure, no problem'*. They are the first to say 'yes' and the last to ask for a favour in return. They say 'yes' even when they know they don't have the time or energy. They are so dependable, reliable and 'easy-going' and never look stressed. On the outside.

'Ask, Joanne, she'll do it no problem, she is so organised and in control'. Meanwhile, Joanne is crying in the bathroom, exhausted and overwhelmed.

If you recognise yourself as Mr/Mrs Dependable, please try 'no' sometime, but soon, because your mental health and relationships will thank you for it – and you may even enjoy it. You will instantly know when 'yes' is wrong for you because as 'yes' is emerging from your mouth, the private *myself* will have that immediate gut feeling of irritation and resentment. To help you identify why you do this, ask yourself the following questions.

DIARY

Who do you say 'yes' to when you want to say 'no'? _____
_____
_____
_____

Think of the last time you said 'no'. How did it feel? Did it feel uncomfortable? Where did you feel it in your body? _____
_____
_____
_____

Was it so uncomfortable that you said 'yes' instead? Or did you say 'no' only to revert quickly back to 'yes'? _____
_____
_____
_____

Now try to identify the origin of that thought or feeling of being uncomfortable with saying 'no'. _____
_____
_____
_____

Mr and Mrs Dependable need to know that by saying 'yes' to everyone else, they say 'no' to their own their needs. I would very much like you to take this from this chapter: you have a finite amount of energy and time. Ask yourself, do you take on too much responsibility because it fits with how you think everyone sees you? If so, you need to find your inner 'no'.

Joanne was so tired she could barely think and yet she had said yes again. 'What is wrong with me, why did I say yes?' In her therapy session she was asked, 'Can you remember a time when you said no that felt significant or painful? Where was it, with whom and what happened?' Joanne was surprised by the intensity of feelings that came up immediately. 'I was fifteen years old, my mum was sick, but I wanted to go out with my friends. She asked me for help with the younger kids, I chose to go out with my friends. When I was out a neighbour ran up to me and said there was an ambulance at my house. When I got back my mum had collapsed and was being taken to hospital, and my younger brother and sister were hysterical. I felt so bad, and swore I would never be selfish again.' Joanne stopped, and whispered, 'I haven't said no since.'

Joanne felt subdued and reflective for days. She realised that guilt was the primary driver behind why she never said no. She wrote out the experience she had that day and spoke with her mum. Her mum was shocked as she had never blamed her, she knew that she had a bad cough but hadn't gone to the doctor and it turned into pneumonia. Her mum asked her to mind herself as she recognised that she never minded herself and Joanne would have also taken that as her norm.

Joanne made up two simple questions to ask herself before she gave an answer: 'Do I want to do this? Do I have the energy or time to do it?' She would make herself answer with a yes or a no.

She created a new rule for herself and stuck it on her bathroom mirror: 'I am allowed to say no.' She knew this might look silly to other people, but she knew she needed that visual prompt to get her to stick to it.

....

I is your unconscious self. Enter from stage left Freud, Jung and all the misconceptions we have about the very large and yet inaccessible side to us, made up of our motives, desires and fears. Leaving aside the complexities of Jung's personal and collective unconscious and Freud and his oedipal complex, the question I am interested in is: How does your *I* affect your day-to-day experiences?

Before we venture into the unknown, I'd like to introduce a concept by Daniel Wegner, a social psychologist, called the 'illusion of conscious will'. This describes the common occurrence whereby people make many mistakes in how they make decisions, perceive that they are in control, and then make mistakes in how they put those decisions into action. This brings us to self-distortion. This occurs when thinking you are wrong is unimaginable, and you will 'prove' that you are right at a cost potentially to you and others. When you don't have access to your unconscious but it's influencing your decisions and actions, it is like you are driving blind-folded. And yet you can self-delude as the mere contemplation of being wrong is unfathomable. The alternative, and better, way to proceed is to be self-aware, mindful of your thoughts and behaviours and then consciously choose better actions and reactions. Recent research shows that your conscious and unconscious mind work together, simultaneously and collaboratively. Your conscious mind does the driving, while your unconscious mind is the engine, which means both are necessary and inseparable.

Your unconscious mind works very hard. A lot of essential automatic and background work is carried out here on your behalf. It is there to serve and protect. The problem is that when it sees danger, it can be somewhat trigger-happy and kick into action whether you are in danger or not. The unconscious is an 'act now, think later' kind of process, but that very quality has no doubt gotten you out of many a scrape.

The limbic brain doesn't have much of a sense of humour, and its primitive goal is to protect. Its primary goal is survival: it activates your behavioural and emotional responses to ensure this occurs. As part of this function, it can create defence mechanisms that are triggered when you feel threatened. These may have worked in the past, but are no longer the most efficient way of doing things and don't fit in with your adult life. So whenever you come in contact with a person, object or situation that felt dangerous or uncomfortable for you in the past, your unconscious hits the trigger button.

....

Jake realised that he was intensely worrying about a presentation he had to give at work in a month. Rationally he knew he would be OK, but emotionally he felt crippled, even the thought of standing up made his mouth go dry. He knew this anticipatory anxiety was as a result of the last disastrous presentation, where he panicked and his mind went completely blank. He started using the ABC method.

He wrote out:

Activating event – the presentation.

Belief – 'I'm going to make an idiot of myself.'

Consequences – worry, abject fear, terror, not sleeping, irritable and so on.

He worked on changing his reaction, even if it was simply to breathe through the panic, and to set out how he wanted the presentation to go. He wanted to go from feeling highly anxious to neutral. He set about identifying the triggering thoughts and actively began to soothe his immediate response to one that reduced the perceived 'threat'.

Now, this is the science bit. I won't give you too much detail, but it's enough to know that your unconscious autonomic nervous system is divided into:

1. the sympathetic nervous system, which speeds things up, like hitting the accelerator; and
2. the parasympathetic system, which puts on the brakes to slow things down.

These systems are 'unconscious', which means they do it all for you. You don't have to tell yourself to breathe or ask your heart to pump. You don't have to tell yourself to digest food and you certainly don't have to tell yourself to run from a menacing dog, thank you. Your sympathetic system is your 'fight or flight' response, while the parasympathetic system is your 'rest and digest' response. Their primary, primitive goal is to keep everything going and to keep you safe.

Your unconscious mind needs really clear instructions, and these instructions must:

- be given in the positive;
- say what you want to happen.

When was the last time you got into your car and said, *'I don't want to go to town'*? Oddly enough, you wouldn't get very far. No, you get into your car and you say, *'I'm going to ...'* and then you make a plan to get there.

But when we are talking to ourselves, we often say what we don't want to happen. We say things like, *'I don't want to have a panic attack'*, or *'I don't want to blush'*, or *'I don't want to look stupid in front of these people'*. This doesn't work for your brain because they aren't messages it can process and understand. Your wants and desires must be neurologically translated into instructions your brain can follow and act upon.

What you say	What actually happens	Instructions your brain needs
'I don't want to have a panic attack'	Triggers a panic attack	*'I want to feel in control'*
'I don't want to blush'	You blush	*'I want to look comfortable'*
'I don't want to look stupid in front of these people'	You feel really uncomfortable	*'I want to look confident and at ease'*

This isn't just semantics. For your unconscious mind to understand you, your instruction to it must be specific about what you want and how you want it to happen.

Something I would love to challenge is how people feel about their emotions. The avoidance of painful and uncomfortable emotions causes a lot of distress. Your emotions of fear, joy, sadness and anger are exquisitely good at delivering the message about how you feel. But can you decipher what these emotions are telling you? Do you listen, or block them out?

The word that often prevents us listening is *should*. I hear people say, *'I shouldn't feel as upset about this as I do'*. The problem with this is that you respond by stopping or repressing the feelings, thereby missing out on what they are telling you. This may be compounded by others saying, *'you are being too sensitive'*. None of this is helpful. I encourage you to ignore the two worst concepts for your mental health: *Should* and *What if?* Ban these loathsome words, or at least notice when you say them and note what situations trigger them. They genuinely should carry a health warning as they impact every aspect of your health.

Should is often deeply embedded in a sense of misplaced duty, often at a cost of not listening to your body's natural cues, cries of fatigue or your mood. *What if?* is the precursor to anticipatory anxiety by catastrophising all the awful things that could happen in the future in a feigned attempt to feel in control of the uncontrollable.

Often present issues trigger old wounds deep in your unconscious through your adult relationships. This is where you need to pause, reflect and stay in the moment, to notice a historical wound being brought to life again.

If you step back, having noticed the triggered emotion, and ask how it made you feel, then ask yourself: When was the first time I experienced a feeling like this? This question can lead you directly back to strong belief systems, memories and feelings of fear, abandonment, rejection, failure and shame that lie deep in your unconscious. Why? Because they hurt, and your brain remembers how it hurt and it tries to protect you from feeling those very strong feelings again. These old defence mechanisms are trying to help you. You need to be aware if they are holding you back, and think of a new plan to change them. (For more on this, see 'Mind the Gap' in the Psychological Toolbox, p. 243.)

If you avoid pain, you can't process it. It just sits there, like an emotional grenade, ready to be triggered at any moment. These painful moments allow you to glimpse inside yourself and gain a sense of self-awareness that can heal old wounds. When you have done this, you can live consciously and begin to recognise when wounds are old and need to be let go. This is the basis of a healthy adult: to acknowledge your inner child and the pain they felt, soothe their fears and reassure them that everything is going to be OK.

When the present 'you' bestows this kindness on your inner, frightened child, it can unravel long-held patterns of frustration and pain. It is such a freeing experience. It boosts your self-esteem and resilience, and engages forgiveness and self-compassion.

DIARY

You can use 'Soften, Soothe, Allow' to guide you through this. See Psychological Toolbox, p. 246.

Notice

◇ Can you think of an event that has impacted upon you that you would like to release? _____

_____

_____

_____

◇ How did it make you feel? _____

_____

_____

_____

◇ What emotion comes to the surface when you think about it? _____

_____

_____

_____

◇ Where can you feel it in your body? _____

_____

_____

_____

◇ If you could rate the pain out of 10 (10 being the highest intensity), how would you rate it? _____

_____

_____

_____

Acknowledge

◇ What did it mean to you? _____

_____

_____

_____

✧ How does that make you feel? _____

_____

_____

_____

Reflect

✧ Are you surprised by what came up? _____

_____

_____

_____

✧ Now that you have identified the feelings, are there any other or different feelings now? _____

_____

_____

_____

Self-awareness

✧ What have you learned from this? _____

_____

_____

_____

✧ What would you like to do differently next time? _____

_____

_____

_____

✧ Can you see how you may have grown through the adversity or bad experience? _____

_____

_____

_____

✧ Acknowledge and list the strengths that came from this experience.

_____

_____

_____

It may sound odd that such important things can remain hidden from you, but your unconscious self likes order and files away all your memories carefully. Some adults say they have very few memories of their childhood, and this can sometimes be a result of a difficult childhood, sometimes not. What is interesting to me is the variety of memory, the perception of those memories and the variances between the two. Sit down with your siblings one day and recount one shared memory together and see how the stories differ.

Your unconscious makes connections and associations. The ability to keep noticing and reflecting on which present-day situations have triggered you, allows you to become more self-aware of outdated and destructive defence mechanisms that may have run their course. Ask yourself the following questions.

DIARY

✧ What makes you feel defensive? _____
_____
_____
_____

✧ What made you feel 'attacked' as a child (verbal, physical, emotional, sexual)? _____
_____
_____

✧ Are there present-day triggers that bring this up for you? e.g. *'Come on Paul, you are just being difficult', 'you can be so cold', 'sensitive', 'moody'.*
_____
_____
_____
_____

✧ Are there specific words, tones or situations that trigger this? _____
_____
_____
_____

✧ Were your parents authoritarian? What type of parenting style did they have? _____

_____

_____

_____

✧ How do you deal with criticism? _____

_____

_____

_____

✧ Did you have a critical mother or father? _____

_____

_____

We will explore these questions in detail in Chapter 2, but it is essential to know that the answers to those questions are imperative to understand how you now operate within all your relationships.

Socrates said, *'know thyself'*, and as beautifully simple as this is, I know it requires great courage and commitment to unveil inner truths about yourself and that it will not be without pain, and even surprise. This is where the growth happens, as you identify the triggers and put the change into action.

Your frame of reference dictates how you will react physiologically to any new idea, ranging from cautiousness to excitement. If I said the word 'holiday', for some there is great anticipation, and yet for others it brings fear and stress related to the thought of the preparations and packing, or a fear of flying. Priming our mind to change how we feel about change takes the conflict and sting out of moving forward. People say they want to be happy and healthy, but until you get your mind to know the specifics of what it needs to do, that won't happen. With clear intent, your drive and ability to change become a step-by-step process that you can follow.

So let's explore your frame of reference, that inner voice that dictates your response to yourself and to change. This is the story of you. The most important thing to realise is that you are the narrator. Please stop and listen to your voice, and to the narrative you tell yourself.

DIARY

✧ Is your inner voice a kind, encouraging voice, or is it mean-spirited and a confidence-knocker? _____

_____

_____

✧ When are you encouraging to yourself? _____

_____

_____

_____

✧ How do you react when you are under stress, pressure or feel overwhelmed?

_____

_____

_____

✧ What do you want the narrative of your life to be? _____

_____

_____

_____

✧ What story do you tell people about you every day? e.g. are your stories optimistic, hopeful, energised, or full of tiredness, frustration and stress? (Note: they can be a mixture of both, life is never a tick-the-box exercise.)

_____

_____

_____

✧ Do you like your story? _____

_____

_____

_____

✧ If you don't like it, how could you change it? _____

_____

_____

_____

> ✧ How can you effect that change in reality? _____
> _____
> _____
> _____

Is this the voice you want to guide you through your life? Is this a nice story to be part of? Well, you are the narrator, which puts you in control. If you don't like how your life is, what can you do to change it?

Lori saw in slow motion her hand knock over the 20mls of expressed milk that had taken over an hour to pump out. 'You idiot,' she screamed inside her head, and a haze of exhausted fury coursed through her body. Her husband tried to make a joke that she was actually crying over spilt milk, but this was the proverbial last straw. That was it, she was giving up breastfeeding. Other mothers were telling her they couldn't store their milk as they had so much, but Lori felt she might have better luck squeezing some out of a stone. She slumped into the chair and sobbed, she felt like such a failure, and quickly she started down into a negative spiral of thoughts dragging every personal 'failure' into the mix: 'I knew I wouldn't be able to do it. Why is it so hard for me? What am I doing wrong? This is supposed to be the most natural thing to do in the world', on and on and down and down she went.

Her husband recognised what was happening and called her mum, and they all had a talk about what was going on. Lori set up an appointment with her therapist. As they discussed the 'spilt milk', they looked at how Lori spoke to herself. It was so harsh, so unkind and unsupportive. They looked back at the life narrative she told herself. Underpinning it all was a huge sense of insecurity. The session finished and Lori was asked to rewrite her story. She started small and kept to an idea they had discussed in therapy to help her stay calm and connected to herself and that was to ask herself: 'What would I say to someone else?'

Lori's new story started with the idea of her being in charge of her own 'hero's story'. It began with how brave she had been to become pregnant again, as she had experienced PND the first time. It continued with praise that she had managed her stress and anxiety before the birth by going to therapy and taking time for herself. She let go of her high expectations of how she thought everything 'should' be and stopped comparing herself to other mothers. Part of this was to stop going to the mother and baby group that at this point was too much for her. She asked for more support and help from her family, and she saw that she would be delighted to help if someone asked her. It was like a light went on, instead of seeing herself as a huge burden, she began to see how interconnected she was and how everyone depended upon each other.

CONCLUSION

As you build self-awareness, the way you live, love and react will become much clearer to you. You will recognise with more clarity that this matters to you. You will be able to identify that you are not being overly sensitive. You will feel old feelings or emotional wounds that have been triggered by something someone has said or not said. It makes me very sad when I hear people describe themselves as 'sensitive'. Years of untreated emotional wounds create a high sensitivity, like if you injured your knee and kept playing sports on it, even when it hurt. No one says to the person whose knee is dislocated that they are being overly sensitive. They are told they have an injury that needs attention and are given a plan of action to heal it.

You may have heard you are *'too sensitive'* for a long time, so it has become internalised and part of your own narrative. The issue is that you then minimise how you feel, and those old emotional wounds become entrenched. But they are still raw because they haven't been treated properly. When a new trigger hits, it sets off the emotional pain again.

We need to change how we view treating and managing emotional wounds. I often ask clients to place their hands on the body part that the pain is coming from. It is instinctive, and if the feelings are of sadness, they will often place their hand on their chest and the feelings flow out, literally and physically. Bringing self-compassion into your daily life is so easy. The number one difficulty in this regard is that it's so much harder to be objective about yourself, therefore 'seeing' the issue is incredibly hard.

I hope that you feel you now have some tools to help you notice yourself and become more self-aware, as this is the start of the process of making changes to improve your life.

CHAPTER 2

Mum & Dad

A baby is born with a need to be loved — and never outgrows it.

Frank A. Clarke

INTRODUCTION

This chapter investigates the psychodynamics of your relationship with your parents, the impact of your childhood attachment and how it relates to you as an adult. The emotional and mental processes developed early in childhood are often unseen, but they drive you and motivate your behaviour. This is your first relationship, your first attachment experience, and it influences everything that comes after.

The selves we examined in Chapter 1 were the uppermost branches of your family tree. Getting down to your *I* brings you much deeper into your primary roots, to your 'family of origin'. Down at this level, you'll find the psychological seeds of who you are, hidden in your unconscious. The aim of this chapter is to help you see why you think, feel and react the way you do. To really forge ahead with mental wellbeing, you have to get into the trenches. You have to go back to the start and explore where you learned who you are and how you expect the world and others to treat you.

The goal is to examine, as objectively as possible, your reactions and triggers in adulthood that stem from your family experiences. Some were good and provided a sense of security, which now guides your decisions from a secure model of the world. Some were not so good and may have left vulnerable sore spots, and those old wounds can be reopened and retriggered in your adult relationships.

No relationship is perfect, so let's start there. No matter how much you love your parents, they aren't perfect, because there are no perfect people.

Not only is that OK, but it's integral to recognise within others and yourself. At the same time, good, bad or indifferent, your parents have been the pivotal influences on the person you are today. This is because the quality of care you experienced with your parents shapes who you are and how you conduct yourself in all your relationships.

Psychoanalyst John Bowlby believed that behavioural and emotional issues could be traced back to experiences in early childhood. He felt that babies were born pre-programmed to attach themselves to their parents, to ensure their survival. These needs weren't about crying out for food, but about the child's emotional need to feel responded to, loved and cared for, from an emotionally responsive parent.

Bowlby defined attachment as a 'lasting psychological connectedness between human beings'. Attachment is one specific aspect of the relationship between a child and its caregiver and is involved with making the child feel safe, secure and protected. A good attachment is a strong predictor of how they will develop, emotionally and socially.

There are four key types of attachment: secure, ambivalent, avoidant and disorganised. If a parent is consistent and loving, that creates a secure attachment. A child who experienced an emotionally distant and disengaged parent may have an avoidant attachment style. A child whose parenting was inconsistent, sometimes sensitive to their needs and sometimes neglectful, could develop an ambivalent attachment type. A child who experienced unpredictable, erratic or frightening parenting may have a disorganised attachment type. Whatever your attachment type, you are carrying it with you today, right into adulthood. The question is: is it a helpful attachment type, or is it hindering your adult relationships and life?

You may have a predominant secure attachment style most of the time, but you may take on insecure attachment traits when you feel threatened by the idea of a partner leaving, or when you feel fear, separation or insecurity, just like you did as a child. These primary 'threats' that babies are programmed to protest about, such as separation anxiety, are still active in your adult attachments. Your parents are your prototype of 'how to do relationships 101'. That prototype created a fairly stable internal working model. Bowlby describes this model as a framework made up of mental representations for understanding yourself, others and the world. What is vital to note is that you may not be consciously aware of these.

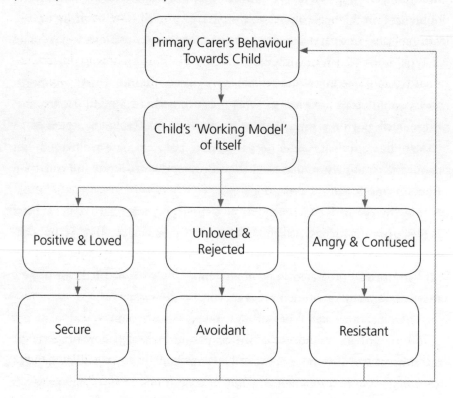

There are three main features of Bowlby's internal working model.

1. A model of others as being trustworthy.
2. A model of the self as valuable.
3. A model of the self as effective when interacting with others.

Can you see how your internal working model is integral to every thought, feeling and reaction you have in each of the roles you play, from home to work? From trust issues at work – *'I knew I couldn't trust anyone in management, when will I ever learn?'* – to every relationship you interact within – *'I knew they'd let me down'* – to feeling secure in knowing that you can rely on the support of your partner – *'it is so wonderful to know that you are always here for me, thank you'*. It infiltrates every aspect of your thinking.

You may be unaware of the importance and daily relevance of this model until you are triggered by your adult romantic relationships, and then double-triggered when you become a parent yourself. The other legacy of learning from your parents is a set of rules called procedural memory, which is a type of long-term unconscious memory of knowing how to do certain things without needing to consciously think about them, such as tying your shoelaces. Procedural memory stores the memories of how to do specific things, such as ride a bike or drive a car. Once something is stored as a procedural memory, it feels automatic.

In terms of how this plays out in your day-to-day life, you can see how difficult it is to change habits or automatic responses to specific situations, especially when you are not even aware that you are being triggered. You may feel that your response is *'it's just the way I am'*, rather than seeing the possibility that these are learned emotional and behavioural responses, and are therefore within your ability to change. This is what I hope you will begin to notice and identify. These responses come with a helpful clue: your reaction may far surpass the incident to which you are responding.

Your procedural memories can make themselves clearly known, especially in child-rearing. This can create problems as your partner will have their own procedural memory, which could lead to fundamental differences in opinion regarding the 'right way' to do the basics of sleeping, eating and reprimanding. You implicitly learned how to do things a certain way and in your mind this is the right way, and you don't consciously question if it is helpful, or even useful, and this can be exacerbated when you come up against your partner's 'right way' of doing it.

You learned many wonderful ways of doing things that work for you and your life and that make you who you are. The aim is to pull out what's not working for you. In order to understand the weight of carrying this excess emotional baggage, made all the more difficult by its secret nature, you need to cultivate a high level of self-awareness. This sounds simple, but it's not, so keep self-compassion as a forethought in your mind. You need to notice and tune into what you do and how you react. This is not an exercise in self-flagellation. Keep the criticism, judgement and regret in check. This is a time of growth and exploration. Bring a sense of curiosity to your search.

This self-awareness will teach you about your inner child, and also teach you what you need to get rid of now, as an adult. There is a simple but wonderful line from Marie Kondo's book, *The Life-Changing Magic of Tidying Up*, that asks one brilliant question: *'Does it bring you joy?'* This is the question I need you to ask every time you are struggling to let go of some of that emotional baggage.

COMMON ISSUES

Each experience you have leaves a psychological marker on you. None of these markers is as significant as those from the first three years of your life when 90 percent of the hardwiring occurs. Certain behaviours and events can directly impact the development of attachment, such as trauma, death, illness or separation through hospitalisation, parental mental health issues, any type of abuse, substance abuse and/or neglect, including emotional neglect. However, in my experience, even clients who have experienced deeply traumatic childhoods have been able to recover. I have seen many adults who now have healthy relationships with their parents notwithstanding a very difficult start in life. You need to remember that your brain is adaptive and even though the hardwiring has long been in place, life is one long learning experience. New experiences create new neural pathways, which means change is always possible. This is the grounded hope I gently ask you to remember.

One common impediment to attachment in life today is technology. In our connected-disconnected society, I feel our empathy response is under threat. Babies know exactly how to get their parents' attention, with the goal of getting their needs met. Deprivation of those needs being met as an infant leads to social, emotional and intellectual deficits in development. As adults, those social cues can be hampered by the new 'heads-down' phenomenon of the smartphone era, with many 'missing out' on new, vital messages being relayed by their children, parents and partners. Listening and nodding is only getting half the memo because the most important part is written on the other person's face, which your brain knows how to pick up and decipher. If you aren't looking, you really are missing out. That need to connect, belong and be accepted never leaves. A deficit in this feeling of belonging and being important can be seen in the ever-growing rates of distress in adult mental health, which suggest that need is often not being met. As we look across the board at rates of loneliness, isolation and relationship break-downs, it raises the question: how do you get your protests or bids for attention heard? Perhaps the answer lies in how you ask for it.

Adult attachment bids for attention may come in the form of being anxious and clingy, reactions of intense anger or hurt, feelings of low self-esteem and self-worth, difficulty in regulating your emotions and calming down, high levels of insecurity, leading to demands being placed on partners, parents, children and friends. On the other hand, avoidant forms of protest would include being overly self-reliant, with an intense fear of intimacy and being 'dependent' on others.

Can you see yourself in any of these reactions? How do you go about getting your emotional needs met? Do you go quietly, do you lash out in anger and protest loudly, or do you detach and think, *'I don't really care, anyway'*?

What response do you get when you cry? Who do you let in when this occurs? Do you feel safe doing this, knowing that your needs will be met? Or do you feel scared that you will be dismissed or diminished – *'For God's sake, what are you crying about now?'* or, *'I can't believe you're reacting like this, you're so overly dramatic'*? The original blueprint or 'rules' of your life were set in the everyday exchanges between your parents and you as a child. The key to change is to recognise how they continue to play out now. Can you identify some key attachment triggers that result in responses such as *'you are never here for me'* or *'I can't depend on you'* in your relationships now?

From my perspective, one of the main issues for many people is a lack of knowledge as to how their attachment has conditioned their response to themselves and to the world. That's logical because we can't remember when these 'rules' were laid down. The task for you is to attune to your own needs, listen to your body's cues, stop minimising your feelings and be emotionally responsive to yourself.

KEY THEORIES

From the moment of conception, the magic of full dependence on your mother for survival begins. Then you are born, and the cry of separation is heard. The immediate importance of bonding with the mother is well understood. As quickly as possible, the cord is cut so that mother and baby are reunited. The baby needs to feel that physical and emotional attachment to its mother to feel safe and calm. It's important to note that attachment reaches beyond the initial bonding between parent and child.

But what does attachment mean to you now, in your adult life? When you have a feeling of belonging and connectedness within your significant relationships that leads to a sense of self-worth, that you are valued and safe, feeling at 'home'. Believing that you are lovable is vital to your psychological wellbeing. This is why it's so important to get to grips with your attachment style, what it means and how it impacts your life.

How does attachment actually occur? Attachment itself happens naturally as a result of interaction between the parent and child. But the infant's attachment system is 'activated' when their feelings of safety and security are threatened. This happens when they are sick, or when they think you are leaving, or when they hurt themselves either physically or emotionally and, most specifically, when they are frightened. It is the quality of the primary caregivers' response to those activated needs that leads to the subsequent attachment style.

Secure attachment occurs when the parent responds to a child's needs in a sensitive, appropriate, loving and consistent way. Its characteristics are as follows:

As Children	As Adults
Can separate from parent	Trusting and stable relationships
Look for comfort from parents when frightened	Stable self-esteem
Are happy to see the parent come back	Are open about how they feel with friends and partners
Prefers parents to strangers	Are able to look for social support

(Source: Attachment tables adapted from Main and Cassidy, 1988.)

Avoidant attachment occurs when a parent responds to the child's needs in an insensitive and rejecting manner, such as ignoring or ridiculing. Its characteristics are as follows:

As Children	As Adults
Avoid parents	May have issues with intimacy
If upset, does not go to parents for comfort	Holds back emotionally in social and romantic relationships
Has no preference for parents over strangers	Doesn't share thoughts and feelings with others

Ambivalent attachment occurs when the parent responds to the child's needs in an insensitive, inconsistent and involving way, whereby the parent may involve the child in their concerns or issues. Its characteristics are as follows:

As Children	As Adults
Somewhat wary of strangers	Reluctant to get close to others
Become very upset when parents leave	Worry about whether their partner loves them
When the parents return they are not comforted	High distress when relationships end

Disorganised attachment occurs when the child doesn't know how to get the parents' attention to reduce their stress or distress. It stems from the parents responding in a 'frightening, frightened, dissociated, sexualized' way, or there may also be a history of unresolved mourning or unresolved emotional, physical or sexual trauma. It can occur where the parent is traumatised, such as a victim of domestic violence. Its characteristics are as follows:

As children	As adults
Fears close proximity to parents, who can be physically or emotionally abusive	Fears close proximity or intimacy in relationships
Mixture of avoidant, resistant or aggressive behaviours in proximity to parent	Fears showing vulnerability

As children	As adults
Little or no sense of safety in relationships	Extreme rage or anger response to confrontation or threat
Complete inability to self-regulate emotion	Little or no understanding of personal boundaries
Seems dazed, dissociated or confused	

(Source: Adapted from Main & Solomon, 1990

It can be a lot to take in that the first three years of your life would have such a long-term impact. Finding out what your attachment style is and how it relates to your life is key to having a quality relationship with yourself and others. It is important to feel hopeful that, once you have identified it, you can then take steps to change certain 'rules' you have in your life that need to be broken. There is an immense freedom in that.

Going back to the beginning and seeing where some of these rules came from can allow you to resolve old wounds. This can be very powerful as you process emotions and feelings, from insecurity to fear. Becoming consciously aware now gives you the ability to make a choice based on what would serve you best as an adult. And identifying how you get 'activated' within your relationships will open up a window of opportunity to grow and develop.

Let's look at some examples of attachment styles to understand this important concept fully.

1. Secure attachment – Parental style: appropriately responsive, caring and secure.

Lucy ran in, crying really hard. Nicky, her mum, walked over to her and picked her up.

'Ah, Lucy, what happened?'

'I fell outside, and everyone laughed at me.'

'That must have been really hard, show me that knee, ah yeah, I can see where it's sore. Will I put a plaster on it for you?'

Lucy nodded, still crying but calming down.

8

Nicky cleaned her knee and smiled at Lucy and gave her a big hug. 'Which plaster would you like?'

Lucy pointed to the spotty one. Lucy had stopped crying and Nicky sat her on her knee.

'Is your knee better?'

'Yes, but I'm too embarrassed to go back outside'.

'Lucy, hun, we all fall, we all feel silly sometimes, and that's OK, I remember something like that happened to me.'

'Really?' said Lucy.

'Sure, but I went back outside. I remember my best friend asked me if I was OK and we played doctors and nurses then.'

'OK,' Lucy said as she jumped off her mum's knee. 'I'm going to bring my doctor bag and they can look after me!'

Nicky validated Lucy's two hurts: one physical, the other emotional. She showed Lucy she could come to her for comfort and that her emotions were acceptable. By doing this, it shortens the time a child will be in distress as they don't have to protest for you to take notice. This will help her learn how to regulate and recognise her own emotions. By giving words to her feelings she becomes emotionally aware, and in time will learn how to articulate strong feelings. Lucy will take this lesson into adulthood and have a belief system that she can depend on someone she trusts when she feels upset. She will express her emotions in an appropriate way. Her bid for attention, whether in her partnership or standing up for herself at work or with siblings, will draw empathy and encourage her to set appropriate boundaries in her relationships.

2. Avoidant attachment – Parental style: insensitive, unavailable, rejecting. Let's take the same scenario, where Lucy runs in crying.

'Oh my God, Lucy, what now? You need to grow up. So what if they laughed at you? I'm really busy, you are fine, go back outside.'

If this was the consistent type of response Lucy received, in adulthood she would model the same level of intolerance to herself and others. She would avoid forming close relationships and perhaps find herself rigid and critical in relationships, preferring to remain distant and not feeling comfortable with emotional connection.

3. Ambivalent attachment – Parental style: unpredictable, sometimes intrusive and over involved, sometimes caring.

If Nicky was caring one moment and not the next, that would lead to Lucy not knowing what reactions she would get. Here, Lucy runs in crying:

'What happened?' Nicky asked, in a panic. 'I told you to wear trousers today, you never listen to me. This wouldn't have happened if you had just done what I asked you to do in the first place. I'm not able for this today, you are stressing me out! Who laughed at you? That's it, I'm going to tell them what I think.'

If Nicky's consistent response was unpredictable, intrusive and all about her, then in adulthood Lucy may feel anxious and insecure. She may find she has outbursts of anger that she finds hard to control. She may try to blame and control the people in her life – *'It's all your fault'*, *'If it wasn't for you I'd be fine'*.

4. Disorganized attachment – Parental style: angry, overreact, frightening.

Lucy runs in.

Nicky screams, 'I told you never to come into my bedroom unless you knocked. Get out!'

Someone Lucy doesn't know throws a shoe at the door and just misses her head.

'But Mam, I–'

'GET OUT!'

Lucy runs back out to the street, terrified.

In this sort of scenario, often there can be major issues from substance abuse, physical, mental, emotional and sexual abuse, and domestic violence. As an adult, trust will be a major issue for Lucy. Even if she wanted to connect with someone, fear, inner conflict and self-sabotage can create an adult life filled with chaos, major difficulty managing anger, self-destruction and a lack of empathy for herself and others.

Regardless of attachment type, there are two needs or feelings I see with my clients time and time again:

* the need to belong; and
* the need for purpose and meaning in life.

It's common for clients to present in therapy with anxiety and panic attacks as a motivation to seek help, but when we look a little deeper and examine early attachment, it often reveals the underlying reasons for these outward signs of stress.

Gerard categorised himself as a 'worrier', but it seemed to have become worse, with stress at work mounting. Worse still was the fact that no one else seemed bothered by the growing demands and some were even calling it a 'challenge'. This resulted in Gerard feeling even more frustrated with himself. The panic attacks were getting worse, so he decided to do something about it. He was very surprised and felt initially annoyed when the discussion kept reverting to his childhood.

'What has any of this got to do with my panic attacks now?' he demanded angrily. Then, to his great discomfort, he started to cry. His therapist responded gently and patiently. Gerard realised his feelings had always been minimised and ridiculed. 'You're such a worrier,' his mother used to say with great disappointment and frustration. 'Where did I get you from?' So Gerard started to bottle up how he felt. He learned that his feelings were unacceptable, and not only was no one listening but he would be openly criticised for being 'weak'. He had found the root cause of his feelings, and he could then begin to work on them.

When people are showing physical signs of stress, they are often ashamed of this. They believe that, as a functioning adult, they should really have their life together by this stage. Ask yourself: where does that internal wagging finger come from?

DIARY

✧ Who was your first critic? _____

_____

_____

✧ What were you criticised for? _____

_____

_____

✧ Have you replaced your first critics? _____

_____

_____

I often have to remind clients that *I'm not a parent basher* when I see them cringing on the couch as they look over one shoulder, clearly feeling like Judas the betrayer as they talk about their childhood or their adult experiences with their parents. It's a difficult thing to do. With that in mind, let's take a breather before we plunge into those questions.

I met a yogi who had a great saying: *'Every time you breathe, you become a new person.'* So, stop momentarily, lift your shoulders up to your ears and drop them gently down, placing your shoulders blades a little closer together and breathing in through your nose. Release. Do this three more times, and be aware of how different it feels when you engage in conscious posturing and breathing. The simplicity of this exercise doesn't take away from its effectiveness as a readily available tool. I'm going to call this exercise 'brain space'.

Now that you've had some brain space, let's continue.

As a natural part of growing up, our relationship with our parents changes a number of times. As small children, our parents are the most important part of our lives, then our friends are added to this mix. As teenagers and young adults we attempt to separate from our parents, seeking our individuation. As we grow into adult life, become part of committed relationships, potentially have children, our relationship with and view of our parents changes again. We see them as people as well as parents and gain an understanding of all parts of them. This may be positive or negative, admiring or disappointing, or a mix of all these parts.

The key fact here is that you are an adult. You have choices and the ability to make your own decisions about how you want the relationship to be, moving forward. I have seen some clients choose to cut contact with very toxic parents where there is ongoing dysfunctionality. I have also seen many clients who repaired past hurts, even when they had described awful childhoods. They expended a lot of work and effort, as did their parents, but as a result they now enjoy a good relationship with their parent. The best choice for you depends on you. You know best. Parents make mistakes, but when parents continue to engage in destructive patterns that everyone is aware of, you need to decide what a healthy boundary would be for you. Setting boundaries and maintaining them can be the beginning of a whole new chapter in cultivating a healthy relationship with your parent/s. (You can see how to put this into practice in the Psychological Toolbox, under 'Boundaries', p. 247.)

The key thing to remember is that this does not mean you are hardwired beyond change. You can activate your brain's neural plasticity, which is its ability to learn, adapt and change. Change is hard, but also possible. Your brain's neural plasticity just needs clear instructions on what to do.

THE PRACTICE

This is where we move from theory to action. The questions here are designed to help you identify your attachment type, and how it influences your behaviour as an adult. I would like to invite you to review the narrative of your own childhood, as a first step towards healing past wounds or changing course. The key point to remember is: when you discover your attachment style, you are not stuck with it. The point to consider is whether it helps or hinders you, and then change it if you discover that it's an unhelpful influence on your life.

The process of uncovering child attachment issues can start by following these steps.

Diary

◇ Remember, reveal and recall your experiences as a child. Are there any specific situations that activated you feeling threatened, e.g. fear of abandonment?

_____

_____

_____

◇ Acknowledge and validate your experience. What did that experience mean to you? _____

_____

_____

Look within your narrative to find the themes, the emotions, the scars and wounds that were inflicted intentionally and unintentionally. Listen with compassion to your inner child.

◇ What would you like to tell that frightened child now? _____

_____

_____

_____

Let any feelings come to the surface, and if you can, connect with them physically. You may experience strong feelings in your chest or throat. If you can, release these emotions.

These questions should help you to discover your attachment type. Do you:

✧ Sometimes pursue and then retreat in relationships? _____

_____

_____

_____

✧ Expect people to let you down? _____

_____

_____

_____

✧ Trust people? _____

_____

_____

_____

✧ Feel comfortable with intimacy, self-disclosure or letting people in?

_____

_____

_____

✧ Feel comfortable or uncomfortable with sharing your vulnerabilities?

_____

_____

_____

✧ Feel loved? _____

_____

_____

✧ Feel worthy of love? _____

_____

_____

_____

✧ How much do you like yourself? _____
_____
_____

To bring this back to the experience you had with your parents, answer these questions:

✧ Describe your mum in three words. _____
_____
_____

✧ Describe your dad in three words. _____
_____
_____

✧ When you were a child, how did your parents react when you were sick?
_____
_____
_____

✧ What stressed out your parents? _____
_____
_____
_____

✧ How did you know they were stressed? _____
_____
_____
_____

✧ How did your parents argue/fight? _____
_____
_____
_____

✧ How did your parents get on together? _____
_____
_____
_____

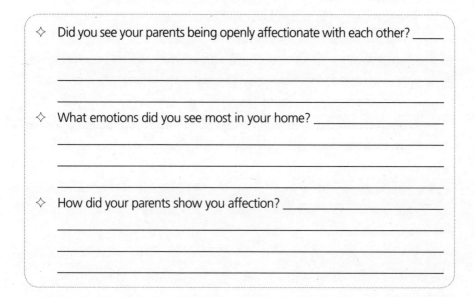

◇ Did you see your parents being openly affectionate with each other? _____

_____

_____

◇ What emotions did you see most in your home? _____

_____

_____

◇ How did your parents show you affection? _____

_____

_____

These questions may open memories for you. You can free associate in your Diary for any images, thoughts or feelings that arise. Take your time, be kind to yourself.

It is very interesting that, according to various studies, your *perception* of your past is a critical factor in your understanding of any given experience. In other words, it is about first validating the experiences you had. Even within one family, each sibling will have different versions of shared histories. There are many factors that influence this, such as different temperaments and personalities, different parental reactions/relationships with each child. Positive or negative experiences shape the lens through which you view subsequent experiences, affecting how you interpret them. Your own perception is how you stored and filed away the memory. But there should be an innermost respect to listen to and validate your experience, which is unique to you.

This is tough but worthy and rewarding work.

Now, it's time to introduce you to Norm. From all the knowledge we have of relationships and how we learn, the phrase 'Monkey see, monkey do' holds a lot of sway. It's quite simple:

- you watch;
- you learn;
- you copy.

As you copy, something insidious and covert happens: Norm comes in. Norm has lived in your house for years, he was there before you were born. He lived with your parents and their parents. Norm saw how everything was done in your home, he saw how your parents dealt with conflict, he saw the hidden looks of support, love and *'don't even go there'*. He quietly walked in, like a silent observer, pen and paper to hand, and watched and learned from everything that was happening in your home. Norm was like your family culture correspondent.

So, who is Norm? It is your 'norm' – your learned idea of how things are meant to be. Psychologist Gillian Fournier defines norms as: 'The implicit (not spoken of … you learn about them through violation of the "rule") or explicit (openly talked about) rules of a group concerning the appropriateness or inappropriateness of certain values, beliefs, attitudes and behaviours'.

Everyone has a Norm that lived at their childhood home. You carry Norm everywhere you go, and your norms are formed through the practice of them every day. If you stepped outside of the norm, you were told about it, and fast. Your parents chastised you, both in words (*'I cannot believe that you did that'*) and/or implicitly (through guilt, silence, shame and disappointment). Norm was strongly reinforced to ensure you didn't step outside of it again.

What are the norms you have taken from home?

This is a very hard question to answer because you unquestioningly accepted these implicit and explicit rules about what was acceptable and unacceptable. These unwritten rules of what behaviours were acceptable and expected were observed and followed, and violation met with swift retribution. If we take it to a cultural level, handshaking between men and women is considered 'normal' in Western society, and yet in some societies this would be a completely unacceptable practice. The two norms can come into conflict when people from two different cultures meet and greet. At home, conflict often ensues when the norms of the family are questioned, as it can bring up huge resistance from parents: *'This is how we have been doing it in our family for years!'*

In order to discover your norms, start with small things, like how you celebrated Christmas, birthdays or anniversaries. Was there always a cake, a present, a card or none of the above? Did each celebratory day have some rules, like breakfast in bed for the special person or going out to dinner? Or was the norm not to 'make a big fuss' and let the day go by? It isn't about right or wrong, the main point is that your norm will influence you in your other relationships in terms of how you expect things to be done. This is not an exercise in judgement, it's merely an eye-opener to see how those rules still play on.

How was emotion expressed in your family? Norm will have keenly observed this.

Norm 1:

Maureen had been feeling overwhelmed lately, but she kept tight-lipped about it. When her husband asked, a quick 'Nothing's wrong' was her reply. The children could feel the tension building, and they knew what would come next: the same pattern of a silent but tense build-up would ultimately end in tears, anger and a very big argument between their parents. They knew that anything that they said or did could be the proverbial last straw. It was in this low but constant level of hypervigilance that Jack's anxiety took root.

Norm 2:

Johnny came in and went straight to his room. His dad followed him up and knocked on the door. 'Hey, Johnny, can I come in?' He could hear him trying to stop crying. 'Hey, what's going on, fella?' 'Ah, nothing,' Johnny said with a pained smile. 'I'm grand.' His dad sat on his bed. 'I can see that something has happened today. You're home, I'm here for you buddy, I don't like seeing you upset. What can I do to help?' The tears came again, and his dad gave him a big hug. As Johnny went through what had happened, his dad listened and acknowledged how tough that must have been for him. As an adult, Johnny remembered this day so clearly, he understood what it felt like to be heard and understood. He felt safe and comforted. When his friends and girlfriend spoke of how open and caring he was, he knew that he had witnessed and experienced it first-hand from his dad.

Norm 3:

Luke knew what mood his dad was in when he heard the key in the front door. There was a difference in his step, and the mood was set: it felt threatening and ominous. These nights the kids never had to be asked to go to bed, they would run to their rooms. The anger would turn to rage in an instant and Luke would feel a despair that was conflicted between minding his siblings and seeing if his mum was OK. Later, in therapy as an adult, Luke began to see how this fear was triggered with his wife when she showed any level of anger. The anger was a specific trigger and immediately those old feelings of fear would kick in and he would freeze. His wife thought his 'non-response' meant he was not bothered, and this made her angrier still. But he couldn't find the words to respond. He had to learn how to change his automatic response, moving the perceived 'threat' to what was happening in that argument with his wife in that moment and staying connected to that moment.

DIARY

Explore and reflect on your trigger points by answering the following questions.

◇ What was the most common emotion you saw your mother express? _____

_____

_____

_____

◇ How did you know when your mother was sad? _____

_____

_____

_____

◇ How did she express anger? _____

_____

_____

_____

✧ How did your mother deal with conflict? _____
_____
_____
_____

✧ What was the most common emotion you saw your father express? ____
_____
_____
_____

✧ How did you know when your father was sad? _____
_____
_____
_____

✧ How did he express anger? _____
_____
_____
_____

✧ How did he express joy? _____
_____
_____
_____

✧ How did your father deal with conflict? _____
_____
_____
_____

✧ How did your parents greet each other at the start and end of the day, or
when returning from being away from each other? _____
_____
_____
_____

✧ Did you feel your mother/father loved you as a child? _____
_____
_____
_____

✧ How did your parents argue? _____
_____
_____

✧ What is an important memory for you as a child? _____
_____
_____
_____

✧ What were your family's values? _____
_____
_____
_____

✧ What was something of great importance to your mother, e.g. religion,
home, honesty? _____
_____
_____
_____

✧ What beliefs originated with your parents that you still have today? ____
_____
_____
_____

✧ How did your parents deal with stress? _____
_____
_____
_____

✧ Did either or both your parents ever experience anxiety? _____
_____
_____
_____

✧ Did either of your parents ever experience mental health issues? _____
_____
_____
_____

◇ Could you openly discuss topics, emotions, deal with conflict? _____

_____

_____

_____

◇ Were there any taboo subjects? _____

_____

_____

_____

◇ How were difficult emotions dealt with? _____

_____

_____

_____

◇ What emotions were considered unacceptable, e.g. anger, being upset?

_____

_____

_____

◇ Was guilt used in your family, e.g. as a mechanism of control? _____

_____

_____

_____

◇ Was shame present in your family? If so, how did this manifest itself? ___

_____

_____

_____

◇ Were your parents physically affectionate with you? _____

_____

_____

_____

◇ What are the negative memories you have of either or both your parents?

_____

_____

_____

❖ How did your mother and father deal with you when you were angry? ___

_____

_____

_____

❖ Were you allowed to express your emotions and feelings? _____

_____

_____

_____

❖ What are your expectations of your parents as an adult? _____

_____

_____

_____

❖ Do you seek their approval? If so, how? _____

_____

_____

❖ Do you vie for their attention with your siblings?_____

_____

_____

_____

❖ If you have siblings, is there adult sibling rivalry?_____

_____

_____

_____

I know it's hard to sit down and write out answers, but it's incredibly helpful. A study in UCLA found that when you write down your feelings, it activates the right ventrolateral prefrontal cortex in the brain and reduces the response in the amygdala. In other words, by putting your feelings into written words, it is like putting the brakes on as your emotional response.

So, if you can, ensure that you do complete the questions above. I know people are time-starved, but when creating space to heal old wounds, engaging with the exercises will allow you to get as much out of this as possible.

Your inner voice was most likely formed by your early interactions with your parents. Your mum and dad's voice and the narrative it told you, was it kind or cruel? Was it encouraging or exasperated if you made a mistake or failed? There's a good chance your parents were in the middle ground, as that's the most common, but it can be so liberating to listen to your adult inner voice and ask the question: Who spoke to me like this first?

If you want to get to what your inner voice sounds like, do something stupid or embarrassing, heck, do both. What's the instant reaction of your inner voice? Does it tell you that you're *'an idiot'*, *'you're so stupid!'*, *'you always do this!'*, or does it say, *'Ah, mistakes happen, it's OK'*. Your instant response will give you a very good insight into the words, tone and the real essence of the message you absorbed in childhood. Your parents may not have said *'you're an idiot'*, but as a child you may have interpreted that from the tone. This is what psychologists mean by 'internalising'.

This is also why I am pedantic about the words used with kids. The words that come from your mum and dad become your internal narrative.

Step back and think about this for a moment.

Question your belief systems (BS), and you'll probably find it is quite unbelievable when you do. Go back to the information funnel and know that as children, there is no filter, you let it all flow in, especially the negative. To be honest, most adults do as well. Often this acceptance is implicit and you will be unaware about what your 'Norm' is, but it will be reflected in what your family's norms were and are.

Your world view starts at home. Your parents' comments, opinions, beliefs and actions spoke volumes to you. Their attitudes to sex, religion, parenting, relationships, work and money were woven into your open mind and heart. Often during the important teenage years, a rebellion against family norms can occur as you try to find your own identity, separate from their family of origin. But those norms are usually buried deep.

Did you ever wonder why stereotypes prevail in the face of factual evidence to the contrary? I imagine it as a stack of words and thoughts, balanced one on top of the other. Most are rigid and dogged. Each new experience and accepted thought are handpicked to ensure they will slot into place within the existing thought system, and not threaten the delicate balancing act.

The problem is, when you start digging and find major holes in your beliefs, the foundations can become unstable and, quite quickly, they can all come tumbling down. That crash cannot be undone. Complete worldview annihilation. In order to avoid this, you hang on to your BS with a fist clenched around all your faulty cognitions and belief systems.

This is why family dynamics are so powerful. This is why people can stay openly deluded about the state of play in their family. You can't just question a bit, because it's all interconnected. Once you start to question, and patterns and behaviours come out of the shadows of shame, guilt and fear, years of toxicity and dysfunctionality unravel before your eyes. This can be a very disorienting experience, which is why many people choose to navigate it under the guidance of a mental health professional.

So if we go back to our Russian doll, deep within the layers is the baby – the beginning. That is your inner child, and it was moulded and shaped by your parents and everything they did and didn't do.

The baby is the only part of the Russian doll that is a solid piece of unadorned wood. It is life, your genes, your own personality and every experience you have that will colour who you are and how you come to be. With each inner self, the primary relationship and attachment between the parent and child set up the rules that govern it. It is up to you now, in a hopeful way, to make some necessary adjustments.

In my experience, I still see adults adhering to childhood gender stereotypes. The idea of 'being a good girl' dies hard and perhaps can be seen within the office, while 'big boys don't cry' is a pervasive idea that orders men to never show perceived weakness and ultimately impacts their mental health. These two stereotypes still have a strong pull on many adults.

How does it start? Mostly in a fairly innocuous, yet deeply insidious, way. The majority of parents will have uttered these words at some point: *'Aren't you a very good girl?'*, *'Come on, you're fine, get up, big boys don't cry'.* These words can so easily slip out because these stereotypes are so deeply ingrained. The 'good girl' is compliant, always puts the needs of others first. The 'big boy' sees emotions as irrational and something to be controlled, or fear losing face. Even if we are taking steps towards being more gender-neutral, there's still a long way to go to dispel the long spectre that casts a shadow over how you express your emotions and needs. A quick remedy is to imagine changing gender: would the same request or task be asked of you? For example, a woman may be comforted by friends when she cries about her relationship break-up, but how comfortable would male friends be with a guy in this scenario? These are very generalised examples, but do they play out in your roles. Every now and then, just ask yourself: if I was the opposite gender, would this be asked of me?

Dr Brené Brown is a research professor, and she coined 'the 3 Ps': please, perform and perfect. These are often the cornerstone of a girl's childhood, stalking her long into adulthood. For example, as my female adult clients become carers to their elderly parents, the 3 Ps can place huge strain on their already heavily laden shoulders. It's a story I have heard too many times, told the same way: lots of capable siblings, but 'the girls' do the lion's share of the caring. This is the 3 Ps at work, making the woman believe she must say 'yes', she must take on the burden alone, and that she must carry it perfectly and without complaint. This is a very damaging expectation to pass on to our daughters. Did your parents pass it on to you? Brown also asked, do we allow men to be vulnerable? Does the cultural narrative say, yes, of course we do, but in reality are men taught to suppress and repress their real feelings?

DIARY

The 'good girls' need to consider and answer the following questions.

◇ Who do you want to please? _____

_____

_____

_____

◇ How does this translate into your life now? _____

_____

_____

_____

◇ What attention did you get from your parents when you did any of the 3 Ps? _____

_____

_____

◇ At home, at work, as a friend, as a mother, how does being the good girl work for you? _____

_____

_____

◇ When does it work against you? _____

_____

_____

_____

◇ How do you feel about saying no? _____

_____

_____

_____

◇ How do you deal with conflict? _____

_____

_____

_____

The good girl's most frequently used word is 'yes'. You will know her by her can-do attitude, and people marvel at how she does it all. She does it all because she doesn't feel she can say no. Casey's story provides a good example.

If Casey heard one more person telling her she was 'easy-going', she might just throttle them. She flew in the door, shopping in hand to make cakes for the class the following morning because her cakes were 'so delicious' and the words 'not at all, it only takes a minute,' had come flying out of her mouth. Exhaustion had set in, as had a lack of joy. She talked through how she felt: 'misunderstood, used and taken advantage of'. The therapist asked her a question that blindsided her: 'Who are you trying to please?' She was about to say the usual but stopped. 'I don't know. I actually don't know why I do it.' She had a sister and brother, both of whom had caused a lot of turmoil in the family, while Casey had been labelled 'the good one'. She had a great relationship with her mother and they were very close, but maybe it was too much on Casey as she was her mother's confidant. Her mother often said: 'I don't know what I would do if I didn't have you'. The role of the good, helpful daughter began early and it became her defining role. The problem now, since she'd had her own family, was that she was run ragged. She knew it needed to change and, even more so, she didn't want to teach her kids the same lesson she had been taught. Being 'the good girl' wasn't helpful to Casey anymore.

Boys have it tough in a whole other way. One of the most damaging stereotypes to which boys are subjected is the idea put forward above, that 'big boys don't cry'. There are generations of male damage in that one sentence alone. So many sons have been emotionally stunted by strict ideas of what it means to be a boy. The idea of a non-emotional human is as daft as it is damaging. We all have emotions, and ordering someone to suppress theirs doesn't make them go away.

It's a narrative that can lead to adult feelings of shame and fear. Many boys react to this expectation by shutting down any normal expressions or reactions to challenging situations. The idea that emotional reactions, such as crying, are a sign of weakness can drill deep into the unconsciousness of boys, impacting and shaping who they feel they can be as a man. It's a hugely limiting idea.

The flipside of this emotional limit on sadness or anxiety is the praise of anger and its associated expressions. Anger is the one emotion deemed acceptable in boys. While girls are being burdened with the good girl stereotype, boys are allowed to express anger with it seen as, '*Ah, they are just being boys*'. Those same behaviours are viewed as less acceptable in females.

DIARY

Consider and answer the following questions.

◇ How did your dad and mum express anger? _____
_____
_____
_____

◇ As a girl/boy, were you allowed to be angry? _____
_____
_____
_____

◇ What happened when you were sad or cried? _____
_____
_____
_____

◇ Did you feel these were acceptable 'boy' or 'girl' feelings? _____
_____
_____
_____

◇ How did you express your emotions, such as fear, sadness, joy, disgust?
_____
_____
_____

◇ Can you remember any specific events that had an impact upon you about what it meant being a boy or a girl? _____
_____
_____
_____

◇ Did you feel the treatment of boys and girls in your family was equal? ____
_____
_____
_____

◇ If not, what was different for you as a boy or as a girl? _____
_____
_____
_____

◇ As a man/woman how has this impacted you at work, and in your relationships with your children and your partner? _____
_____
_____
_____

If you happen to be working through this book as a couple, comparing your answers will be hugely interesting and insightful. The result is often that the female and male adult are not equipped to deal with their shameful emotions because they don't fit in nicely with being 'a good girl' or 'a real boy'.

There is another factor here: your attachment style. How you handle and express emotion relates back to your attachment to your parents as well. In *Seeing Through Tears: Crying and Attachment*, psychotherapist Judith Kay Nelson showed that people who are securely attached feel more comfortable expressing how they feel and allowing themselves to cry. Insecurely attached people seemed able to cry very quickly, but it took a lot longer to calm them down. From watching and learning first-hand as a child how you *should* behave, clear psychological markers were laid down to tell you how you *can* or, my taboo word, how you think you *should* react as an adult.

This tends to continue through generations. You are a product of a collective of your family, community and culture. So when a client sits in front of me and they speak about their father and/or mother, I imagine a double mirror behind them, where I can see the lineage of their parents' parents and so on, reaching back in time. Each and every family has its Norm. The norms changed in different times and social contexts, but belief systems, like DNA strands, have a way of getting the instructions across as to what is acceptable and unacceptable behaviour. That look from your mother that said *'wait till we get home'* or the warm gentle squeeze of her hand when you did well in your spelling test communicated loud and clear what gained positive attention, and what didn't.

We have learned a lot about being a child and the role of parenting in our emotional lives. Attachment is an essential element in our psychological makeup. But how do you use what you've learned about your relationship with your parents to make changes in that relationship? Psychotherapist Tina B. Tessina gives a very simple piece of advice: 'Feeling and acting like an adult around your parents is the cornerstone of having an adult relationship with them.' If you want your parents to treat you like an adult, be a grown-up.

In what seems an unnatural twist of advice, I recommend that you talk to your parents, husband, wife, siblings and/or child as you would to a stranger. You would not speak to a stranger as abruptly or with as little patience as many of us do in our close relationships. And of course, you are often your worst self with your parents. At a psychological level, this is because we feel safe to be 'ourselves', albeit ruder, less tolerant selves, with the ones we love. It is a really useful strategy to take the same civic courtesy you have for strangers back into the home.

Let's work this through in an example. Picture this scenario: Maria arrives at her parents' house to tell them she has decided to buy a particular house. Immediately they start questioning the wisdom of her choice.

'Do you really like that area? Do you not mind that the garden is tiny?'

Maria immediately feels under attack and reacts crossly. 'Seriously, Mum, why do you always do this?'

'What do I do? We're just trying to help you.'

'You have absolutely no idea how hard it is to get a house, you are making me feel like a child. I know what I'm doing, just back off.' Maria bit her lip, gathered up the kids and left.

When Maria got home she felt conflicted. Her mum really had annoyed her and her 'advice' had really grated on her nerves. She realised that she was really stressed, there was so much to think of on top of the normal day and time was running out. When talking it through with her therapist she was asked, 'What do you think your mum's intent was?' This softened her annoyance as she knew that her mum and dad were also worried about her. Then she accepted that the garden was bloody tiny, but what could she do? It was near to the kids' school and it was a bit disappointing as a choice, but she needed to move on this. She met her mum two days later.

'I'm sorry for storming out the other day. I'm under a huge amount of stress. I mightn't find the perfect house, but I know I could do with your support, I'd really appreciate that.'

Pause when that conversation with your parents is turning quickly down the road to resentment. Pick up your emotional baggage and 'adult up'. Whatever the trigger is – it could be your mum's unsolicited advice or 'opinions' on your childrearing or finances – follow these steps for a better result.

1. Step back and stop.
2. Take a deep breath.
3. Ask yourself: what is his/her intent?
4. Think before you talk.

Number three will be like a guiding light, even if the comment is intensely annoying. The parent's intent is to say/do what they think will help you – regardless of whether you agree and whether you asked for it or not!

Your parents built a home with you in it. Over time the quality of that 'psychological' home requires renovations and clear-outs. This chapter is about letting go of the emotional baggage you absorbed implicitly from how your needs were or were not met as a child and learning how to meet your needs as an adult. It is time for a major decluttering as you identify which primary threats, such as feelings of insecurity, require a spring-clean.

Holding on takes a lot of energy. I am reminded of a great illustration I saw with a character holding a huge rock over its head with outstretched arms. Another person walks by and asks, *'Why are you holding onto that?'* The rock carrier responds, somewhat surprised, *'I don't know'*. This next exercise offers you the opportunity to release and let go of emotional weight that no longer serves you.

For this emotional decluttering you will need three boxes:

1. One filled with what you want to let go of.
2. One to recycle the old into something new.
3. One holding everything you want to keep and cherish.

Here are some tips to help you declutter:

* Be honest about who you are and what you want from your relationship with your parent/s.
* Tell them what bothers, upsets or infuriates you.
* Write this list out for yourself first. Make two columns, one where change can occur with you and your parents, and one where you can work on your reaction to their responses.
* Pick a good time to talk – there's never a perfect time, but some are better than others.
* Watch your tone. Remember the 'sticks and stones' rhyme? Well, words can hurt, choose them wisely.
* Check your child expectations at the door.
* If past events or pain need to be dealt with, do it, but with good intentions of repairing the damage rather than apportioning blame.
* Be clear about what you want to get out of the discussion.
* This may require a lot of work and personal reflection on your part before you talk with either or both parents.
* Recognise what you can and can't change about your relationship.
* Can you accept what you can't change? If not, what options are available to you?
* Dump the emotional baggage you have sorted into your three boxes, labelled 'Let it go', 'Recycling' and 'Keep: the good stuff'. The problem with holding on to it is that you are the one left holding it.
* Forgive, have compassion and move on.

There are all sorts of parents, but the one thing they all have in common is that they are getting older all the time. The changing dynamic from your parents being your carers to a possible role reversal can be quite unsettling for everyone.

Look at where your parents are in terms of age, health and ability to have difficult and emotive conversations. Sometimes having the big conversation is not the thing to do. In order to decide whether to broach this conversation or not, ask yourself the following.

1. Will you be heard? Does your parent respond rationally or irrationally? This is an important question as you need two rational people to have an adult conversation; this holds true in every relationship.
2. Health is a factor, I'm not saying it gives a free pass, but the difficult conversation needs to merit the fallout that may ensue. Health concerns impede the quality of the discussion. Your parents needs to be 'able' to have that type of conversation.
3. If you know you will lose before you even start, question the point of the exercise.
4. It is so important to recognise what can and can't change. Working through these issues yourself and accepting your own emotional wounds is a very powerful and freeing experience. You don't need anyone's permission to do that.

So even if you feel the time isn't right to bring up this discussion with your parent/s, it is hugely helpful to do this work on yourself and bring yourself to a new level of understanding and awareness. One of the most genuinely difficult yet cathartic aspects of therapy is when you address past hurts that did not get the 'ending' you were hoping for. This unfinished business sits badly in the gut and chest, generating a deep heaviness and sadness for the loss of an apology, or the lack of acknowledgement of the pain a parent may have intentionally or non-intentionally put upon you. This is where you need to extend compassion and forgiveness to yourself. If your inner child is wounded, you must have utter compassion for yourself.

The last practice is a lovely, simple exercise to soothe your inner child.

- Close your eyes.
- Imagine yourself as you are now. Softly, get down on one knee.
- With great kindness, open your heart and arms to your wounded inner child. Wrap your arms around the inner child and tell them it must have been so very hard to go through what they did.
- Tell them that you understand and are sorry for the pain they have felt and feel. Look them in the eye and tell them they are so loved and worthy.

We noted above that you need to park your child expectations of your parents and move on. This is crucial to developing an adult-to-adult relationship with your parent/s. Here are some tips for how to develop a mature relationship:

- Respect each other.
- Use criticism sparingly and humour in abundance.
- Behave like an adult around your parent/s.
- Accept your parents as two individual people, strengths, faults and all.
- Be kind.
- Be patient.
- Only ask for their opinion if you really want it.
- Cultivate an adult relationship together.
- Reminisce on the good of the past and create new good memories.
- Create a new shared meaning.
- Like every relationship, give it space to grow and time and effort.

CONCLUSION

This chapter opened out the Russian doll of your selves and delved deep into the earliest influences on your life: your parents. The quality of your parent-child relationship formed your first attachment and your subsequent world view, governing how you relate to yourself and other people. This chapter explored where those deeply ingrained, and often implicit, emotions stem from and how they can take root. It is hard to do the type of work I've asked you to do here, but if you ignore your inner child and schemas, you will keep repeating the same old patterns with your parents, and then with your own children, if and when you become a parent. This is how Norm becomes intergenerational.

But this chapter also comes with a message of hope: your parents and your childhood influenced you greatly, but they don't define you. There is still choice. You have the personal autonomy to be who you want to be and to decide how you want to manage your past. That's a huge comfort, especially for people who didn't experience secure attachment or an ideal childhood. Life is never about perfection, in fact that's when the rot sets in. You grow through adversity and challenge.

Examining your family narrative throws light on so much of who you are and how you conduct your relationships. It shows where you learned your rules and roles, because you recognised those that brought warm attention and those that were deemed less desirable. You may still be searching for that recognition, at work or in your relationships. Your inner child may be seeking to satisfy its emotional hunger of unmet emotional needs in childhood.

Once you are aware of this, you can start making changes as an adult. When you can see the patterns of quality and inequality within your family, that leads to an understanding of how to change, forgive and move forward. Look for patterns of perfectionism and drives that bypass your physical and emotional limits. When you have this information, you can then go about creating and maintaining healthy boundaries for your adult self.

Perhaps what you learned in this chapter has been difficult to accept, particularly if your parents are no longer with you. If you didn't experience secure attachment, this might be the first time you've thought about that or realised it fully. There might be hurt there now, but this realisation can be a turning-point in your life. You can now see the problems clearly, and their root cause. This means you can tackle them effectively. And remember, just because you are the child of an emotionally unresponsive parent, or an emotionally unstable parent, doesn't mean you are like them. If you become emotionally responsive to yourself, you can nurture yourself to be the person *you* want to be. Earning a secure attachment type is possible.

CHAPTER 3

Siblings

*Siblings: children of the same parents, each of whom
is perfectly normal, until they get together.*

Sam Levenson

INTRODUCTION

From start to finish, your sibling relationships are very often the longest relationships of your life. Given the pressures and demands of modern adult life, these complex relationships often evolve in very different directions. It can be a huge transition to move from the intensity of being siblings in childhood to being adult siblings. These tricky relationships are made all the more difficult by how easy it is to take your siblings for granted and forget that, like all other relationships, they require time, effort and a mutual willingness to maintain them throughout life.

There are shelves of books with advice for parents on how to promote good sibling relationships, but I see a huge gap on the book shelves, and in scientific research, on adult sibling relationships and how to conduct them. This chapter aims to address that balance and help you to nurture and protect this primary connection.

If I say the word 'sibling', what is the first word you associate with it – is it rivalry? Since the dawn of time there have been epic stories of sibling rivalry. Some siblings make us feel supported and understood, others make us feel like we are from different planets, never mind the same family. The far-reaching negative and positive influences of your sibling relationships should not be underestimated.

There is a key question for us to start with: Who are you with your siblings?

Are you connected daily on your sibling WhatsApp group, but hold your tongue in person when your sibling gives you advice *again* that you didn't ask for? Do you share cute pictures of your kids, but feel irritated when asked if you could mind their kids *again*, at short notice? When with your siblings, can you be your adult self, or do you find yourself behaving in old patterns that you thought you'd gotten rid of forever? This is the crux of the sibling relationship: whether you let each other move on into adulthood, and how you handle an adult-to-adult relationship.

It is helpful to approach this from the position of the roles we adopted in our families at a young age and that you perhaps find yourself falling back into with your siblings. I have found that adult clients get terribly frustrated with their siblings when they know they are a competent adult but their siblings insist on still seeing them as a cute eight-year-old or a stubborn fourteen-year-old. In order to understand the dynamics at play here, let's look at the twenty-fifth of December.

Let's do the Christmas Doorstep Sibling Test. Like the perennial poinsettia plant, sibling relationships at Christmas time can be a Pandora's box filled with the 'gift' of Christmas past and present. The magic of a family Christmas provides a perfect scenario for looking at how you can get stuck in a role that may no longer fit you. And, of course, add to this the basic sibling rivalry of scrambling for the coveted prize of the 'triple A': parental attention, affection and admiration.

Gentle note: the eternal search for the triple A hasn't stopped because you are an adult, it is just more subtle … sometimes. We'll come back to this later in the chapter.

So, what happens when you ring the doorbell of the family home on Christmas day? Are you somewhat taken aback at how snappy (read: irrational) you can be to a question your sibling asks you? Do you know all the while that if your best friend asked the same question, you would be civil and rational about it? Or do you find that you are surprised (read: annoyed) with yourself when a conflict erupts and instead of doing what you normally do – deal with it head-on in that professional, competent manner you exhibit at work – you shut down and feel small and answer meekly, while silently fuming very thinly under the surface?

If you recognise yourself in either of these scenarios, you are not alone. These are common problems afflicting adult sibling relationships. We'll examine the problems first, then look at ways to resolve them and change the dynamics of the relationship.

COMMON ISSUES

In *The Sibling Effect*, Jeffrey Kluger illustrates why there are more people in your home than you know of, or at least many more relationships. Each person in your family has a one-to-one relationship with each member of the family and these 'pairings', or 'dyads' (consisting of two parts), add up pretty quickly. In a family of five, for example, there are thirteen distinct dyads: mum and dad have a relationship (1), mum has an individual relationship with each of her children (2, 3, 4), as does dad (5, 6, 7), and then there are the inter-sibling relationships (8, 9, 10, 11, 12, 13).

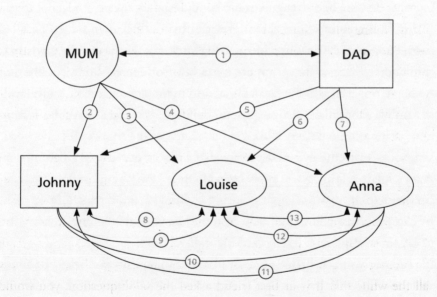

As *The Sibling Effect* theory shows, you have individual connections with each of your siblings, and each of these is related to but distinct from every other connection. Kluger helps to clarify how the threads of connection in each

THE SECRET LIVES OF ADULTS

pairing can become so entangled, so quickly. Adding past experiences, unmet needs as a child and adult, power struggles, sibling rivalry, parental influence and a host of other factors I will go into in more detail in this chapter, offers an insight into the level of complexity in the dynamics of just one family. The intimacy of the sibling relationship can bring joy and pain. You need to reach a place where you are mindful and hopeful about cultivating the type of relationship you would like to have with your sibling, coupled with the knowledge that you can't force this to happen. The grounded hope is that you can change your behaviour and reactions, which is fully within your control. For this to happen, you need to see each new interaction as a chance to foster an old or create a new connection. Your connection with your siblings is an ongoing relationship to which you contribute. For those who have a good connection with their siblings, it can be useful to write out what makes your relationship special and to identify the strengths you all have. It is so important to validate what you do well in your relationships because focusing on the good strengthens the bond even more.

While the connections themselves can bring their own issues, lack of connection also has a huge impact. Research studies have suggested that childhood sibling relationships are a predictor of depression in adulthood. A lot of this research looked at the origins of depression in adulthood stemming from the relationship of children and their parents, but a 68-year longitudinal study looked at the quality of the relationships between siblings as a potentially better predictor of a higher or reduced risk of major depression in adulthood. 'It appears that there is a strong connection between closeness to at least one sibling during childhood and having a lower risk of depression in adulthood,' said lead author Robert Waldinger, associate professor of Psychiatry at Harvard Medical School.

The study's participants were asked about the quality of their childhood relationships with their siblings and parents, marital discord and any family history of depression. It was found that the two key independent factors of a later diagnosis of depression were a family history of depression and poor sibling relationships. Siblings who get along well feel safe knowing someone has their back, no questions asked. This creates a feeling of being supported, validated and understood. No friend knows you as well as your sibling does.

The intensity and myriad of feelings and factors involved in your childhood relationship can provide a security in your adult sibling relationship that can buffer you from the strains and stresses of life. When a parent dies or gets sick, that connection is quickly re-established as the only person you want to talk to is your sibling(s). But what if you can't make that phone call? What if you haven't spoken in years? That lack of connection can be shrouded in shame because there is an expectation that you *should* be close to your sibling. But the truth is, this is often not the case. The loss and sadness of that lack of connection, and the conflicted feelings it produces, don't fade just because you are older.

There is no doubt about the influence your parents have upon you and yet, have you ever considered the influence your sibling relationships have had upon you? For siblings with a close connection, the value and importance of that relationship will be well observed. Similarly, if you have a deep-seated, ongoing conflict with a sibling, you will be very aware of its negative impact. How about those in the middle, with a more neutral relationship? Would you like it to be closer, or are you happy as it is? It is worth noting that each sibling's perception about the quality of connection is integral to how they feel about the relationship. For some, this may be a new concept that they never considered before, others pining for a deeper connection will be sorely aware of the loss of that bond.

These findings are surprising and yet helpful at highlighting how important and influential your sibling relationships are. The huge range between sibling relationships, from love to hate to utter indifference, shows that no one sibling relationship is like another. Intense feelings and reactions and internal and external influences add to the complexity of this relationship. The integral role siblings play throughout your life is in constant flux, with ever-evolving resetting of boundaries and roles, and the passage of time changing the context, coupled with times of closeness or lack of closeness. The one constant is that connection with your sibling impacts you mentally and emotionally.

Cicirelli (1989) studied siblings aged 61–91 years in terms of their wellbeing, their connection and perception of closeness, any perception of 'disruption' of this bond, such as conflict or rivalry, and any differences between those perceptions. They rated their closeness from feeling connected to feeling indifferent. Their wellbeing was measured by a depression scale. Separate analysis was undertaken to look at the four sex combinations of siblings, and the results correlated with Waldinger's research. Siblings, male or female, who felt close to a sister showed less depression. Sisters who perceived conflict or indifference in the relationship reported higher depression.

Nothing is ever simple in terms of the dynamics present in relationships. The word I find so interesting from this study is 'perception'. Your perception is your reality, and yet this perceived reality will establish itself, rightly or wrongly, within how you feel and think about your sibling. It will be made up of various factors, such as your place in the family, age, temperament and sibling rivalry stemming from parental attention or lack of attention. Many researchers would also add that sibling relationships are also influenced by in how your parents behaved, the quality of their marriage and the amount and intensity of family conflict'. Parents can play a large role in inter-sibling rivalry, through exhibiting open favouritism. All parents must divide their attention, whether real or perceived, and this can create and sustain a need in the adult-child to vie for that attention. Children are hyper-aware that their siblings steal a portion of that attention away. The adult version of this may be as simple as an awareness of preference, warmth, love or bog-standard attention. The question to ask yourself is: how do I vie for my parents' attention now? Is it through your successes, your skills, your children?

This idea may sound silly to you, that you could still be looking to your parents for attention, but as Freud noted, 'the unconscious isn't aware of the passing of time'. This is why you get stuck in a rut in your sibling relationships, not even knowing why you are so irritated by the fairly innocuous thing your sibling just said. Your perceptions and reactions are stuck in a time-warp, which is preventing you from progressing your sibling connections into mature, adult relationships.

....

Joseph had always felt like the underdog of the family, especially when in direct comparison with his champion brother, Liam. These weren't just feelings Joseph kept to himself, his parents proclaimed Liam's achievements loudly at every opportunity, while Joseph stood there, feeling awkward. Life seemed so easy for Liam, he seemed to be gifted at anything he turned his hand to, and everybody loved him.

When Joseph was getting married, he picked his best friend of twenty-five years to be his best man. This caused huge ructions with his mother, who was deeply upset. In a furious phone call, she told Joseph that he had always been jealous of his brother, that he was selfish, and what would everyone think when he didn't have Liam by his side on his wedding day?

This was the last straw for Joseph. Could he not even have one day that was his? A surge of anger and years of pent-up frustration erupted.

The funny thing was that Joseph liked his brother, and they got on well together. They sometimes shared a private joke that their mother had sibling rivalry for them and had put them in competition from day one. But Joseph was really hurt. He felt he had been patient for all the years of putting up with the obvious favourite, never uttering a word when his mother referred to Liam as 'the handsome one' or 'the bright one' as he stood silently by.

Joseph decided to talk to a therapist about his feelings. He talked it out in a safe space, but became worried as his anger towards his mother and father increased. It was tough work, but by acknowledging it and thinking about it, he realised that he had low self-esteem, which led him to bow out in social and work situations. Only recently he had let a promotion go to the popular guy in the office, even though he was more experienced. He began to understand why he kept a low profile in social situations and was painfully uncomfortable with compliments. It was because he never believed them. Therapeutically, he began to identify patterns that had been psychodynamic and rooted in his childhood. This allowed him to review his own ideas and behaviours and change the way he viewed himself.

We are more familiar with sibling rivalry than with the disruptive role parents can have upon those sibling relationships. If we go back to Kluger's dyads, or pairings, in a family and take it a step further, we see that the mother and father both had a relationship with each of their parents, as did their grandparents, and on and on it goes. Intergenerational beliefs, hurts and unmet needs are often passed on, sometimes unwittingly, and sometimes the pain is so searing it can lead to a polar response: *'I am such a good father, you have no idea what a childhood I had'*, *'Stop your whining, you don't know what a difficult mother is'*. Your parents were children too, and they had their own difficulties. Many parents' unprocessed grievances are triggered and re-enacted through their own children. This is not to give a carte blanche for unacceptable behaviour, but understanding their emotional history may help you understand their displaced feelings.

As an adult, consider this and ask yourself if it is something that can be improved through a conversation or not. Have a written conversation with yourself first, write out how hurt, angry or frustrated you felt and acknowledge how that was for you. Self-compassion can aid your own process, but be mindful not to minimise your feelings. This is especially relevant in the type of situation where your inner adult voice or harsh critic may quickly chastise you to *'stop being so ridiculous'* or *'get over it'*, but your harsh critic originated from the words of a harsh parent. Potentially, another helpful conversation could start between two siblings, especially in a supportive and emotionally responsive one like that between Joseph and Liam. The key in this conversation is being heard and emotionally validated, and this shared experience can strengthen the bond between siblings.

Often clients come to me very upset when their siblings tell them they are *'too sensitive'*. Not only does this block and minimise the feeling they are experiencing, the triggered emotion gets lumped on top of all the other old emotional scar tissue, and the cycle continues on. If your siblings' words are making you think, *'this is silly'* or *'I shouldn't feel like this'*, that is an alarm bell sounding. It means your feelings are not being listened to or respected. As mentioned above, change occurs when a wrong-doing is acknowledged. This can only start with you. Ask yourself: When have I felt like this before? This will enable you to chart the times when you felt dismissed, ignored or chastised for your feelings, which you were told were unacceptable. The idea is not to become a grievance collector, quite the opposite. By assessing the origin or source(s) of times or situations where you were upset, you may notice a theme. Did they find your anger or sadness difficult to accept or acknowledge? How did they express their emotions? In this mirror, often it is the siblings' inability to express their own emotions, which they then project onto you.

The common reaction to difficult sibling relationships is to create defence mechanisms to keep the sibling at bay and try to protect yourself. These mechanisms in turn affect how you respond to situations. You can identify your defence mechanisms by answering these questions.

DIARY

◇ How do you react when you come under verbal attack from your boss, friend or partner? _____

_____

◇ Do you take them on or retreat and run for cover? _____

_____

◇ Does it feel personal, or does it slide off your back? _____

_____

◇ Where did you learn this from? _____

_____

◇ Have you noticed if those learnings became conditioned responses, and if so, where are they triggered in your life now, e.g. in times of conflict, criticism, under stress? _____

_____

When you have identified your defence mechanism, you can then assess if it's working in your present-day life. If it doesn't work in the context of adult relationships, you need to change it. This was the task faced by Sue, who was being poorly served by her defence mechanism.

'You are too funny, Sue,' Leanne said as she laughed loudly in their open-plan office. To many this comment wouldn't have meant anything and they would have just kept working, but Sue could feel the redness coming up her neck and she felt so embarrassed. She silently wished she was at home, or anywhere else but here. Leanne said whatever she wanted, whenever she wanted. In fact, she reminded her of her eldest sister: strong, confident, mouthy. Sue was angry, she was sick of the nit-picking comments about everything from her clothes to her performance. She'd had enough. Normally she went very quiet and small, hoping it would stop, but now she thought back to her sessions and counselled herself: 'OK, just say what is in my head with an upbeat tone at the end.'

'Yeah, you're a bit of a comedian yourself, Leanne.'

Leanne looked slightly shocked. 'What?'

'Well, I'm so glad you find every little thing about me amusing, from the sandwiches I bring in to how I drink my tea.'

'What?' said Leanne.

'We should make a double act, and I'll start a running commentary on you.' Sue laughed, as did everyone else in the office.

'Oh, OK', Leanne said somewhat sheepishly, with an unsure laugh.

Sue couldn't believe it, she had done it. She'd stood up for herself. She pretended to work on her computer, but she was feeling utterly alive and vindicated. Leanne had been nothing short of bullying her and she had had enough. From that moment on, she was not going to let anyone walk all over her. She knew exactly where this came from and she knew her response was appropriate as her real anger was towards her sister. She started to write an email to her sister, it flowed out of her, the years of bullying, the years of publicly embarrassing her. She told her sister she had drawn a line in the sand and if they were to have a relationship, there would be new rules. She read over it and put it in her Drafts folder, as she wanted to make sure she wasn't been reactive. She would read it later and make changes, if she needed to.

That evening she looked it over and was really pleased that it was exactly what she needed to say. She pressed Send.

To her utter surprise, her sister wrote back that night and apologised. She knew that she was harsh on her, but she didn't realise the impact it was having on Sue. She asked if they could meet to discuss it and to hopefully build a healthy relationship for the first time in their life.

Another common issue among siblings is an ambivalence at the heart of their relationship. Psychologist Maryse Vaillant points out that sibling relationships have a duality that, as adults, you have to be quite mature about. She describes these relationships as 'multi-faceted mirrors', whereby you may recognise aspects of yourself, but also hold a distorted image. This can exacerbate long-held childhood jealousies as it can be hard to see clearly when you can only see things from your own perspective. This is only natural, but it's helpful to try to stand back and identify whether the habit in your sibling that drives you mad is something you also do yourself.

Recognising the ambivalent nature of how you feel is key to a healthy adult sibling relationship. It's OK to see that it is driven by love and hate. This sounds very dramatic, but as we gain insight into our unconscious processes, we can begin to recognise how long-held feelings, emotions and traumas are still hanging about, constantly retriggered by fresh experiences. Jessica's story, below, is a good illustration of this.

Jessica is 35 and has always had a 'Marmite' relationship with her sister Joan, whom they all call the 'boss'. The last straw came when Jessica was exhausted, depleted of energy and patience, and Joan 'told' her how to warm her newborn's bottles and 'not to mind what they told you in the hospital because this is how I did it on my four children'. She laughed at what a total 'first-time mother' Jessica was!

The normally composed Jessica, who was considered the laidback one in the family, cracked. 'Would you gimme a break, I am so sick and tired of you bossing me.' Joan was shocked. She choked back tears as packed up her bag and left. Twenty-five minutes later, their mother called. 'Why were you so mean to Joan? There was no need to be so awful to your sister, she was only trying to help you.'

For the first time in Jessica's life, she hung up on her mother. In the silence of her kitchen, she started to sob. Then she made an appointment to come to my clinic.

In the first session there were a lot of tears, a mixture of immediate physical and emotional exhaustion, long-held frustrations and unexpressed words. Jessica knew her sister would be hurting, but also that she would be giving out about her. She began to discover how this had stopped her from saying how she really felt over the years. If she stood up to her sister, she was guaranteed a 'mum distress call'. By exploring the relationship and dynamic between the three of them, she realised that was one of the major issues in her relationship with Joan.

Even though it looked on paper like the two sisters couldn't be more different, they were both vying for the same thing: their parents' attention.

Until Jessica started talking about it, she hadn't seen the underlying sibling rivalry that had impacted the choices she'd made. It wasn't until she became a mum herself that she began to really step into her own identity and, in a way, she was most upset with her mum for making it so obvious who her favourite was. She began to establish better boundaries by saying how she felt, even when this didn't go down well.

Jessica felt calmer, and accepted that her mother wouldn't change. By owning and expressing her feelings, she felt a freedom and peace she'd never experienced before. It was as if the struggle was over, and she realised she had been using a lot of energy in all the pushing and pulling. Becoming a mother helped her find her voice. She became really clear about the boundaries that she had to set for herself and for others. She accepted both her mother and sister and that felt good.

Ultimately, the person who can change is you. The change comes in the form of a new response rather than a knee-jerk reaction, which never sorts the initial issue. Often in sibling relationships it can be so easy to step into childhood roles of being the eldest or the youngest and the spill-over from both. In this case Joan felt like another mother and authority figure to Jessica. When that role continues into adulthood, the unsolicited 'advice' can be taken very badly from one adult to another. The tone will set the conversation. Becoming a mother is a major milestone, and it can challenge existing dynamics and roles. This can be very useful, but the initial transition can be difficult for all. Accepting people and situations as they are is very helpful. Frustration at things not being how you would like them to be causes a lot of pain. The mother-daughter dynamic is often changed after someone becomes a mother themselves because old feelings resurface as the first rush of love is felt for the child. Many new mothers are surprised by the depth of feelings they have about the relationship with their mother. It can be an immensely cathartic experience to acknowledge and process these feelings with or without your mother. As it is your experience that needs to be validated.

The examples used above – Joseph and Jessica – show the classic symptoms of off-kilter sibling relationships, but it's also vitally important to recognise that not all sibling relationships are good. Some are dysfunctional, and it's important to know when to draw a healthy line. Setting clear boundaries of acceptable and unacceptable behaviour is important for your mental health. It takes two reasonable and willing people to work through past and current issues. It takes huge maturity to be able to own the complexity of emotions within the sibling relationship. In dysfunctional sibling relationships, old traces of destructive behavioural patterns can hold sway. In situations where reason has left the building, I suggest you do as well.

Anger can be used to control the honest conversation that needs to be had. Sadness can be used to induce guilt and in that way push people away from a 'dangerous' conversation. This often pulls in all the family members. This is why families are such complex, multi-layered dyads and it can get messy, fast. Family therapy can really help, as can individual therapy. One unfortunate after-effect I see following individual therapy is that you can now see a lot of your patterns and other people's patterns, and it's impossible to unsee them. You may have worked hard to change, but that doesn't mean other people are able to see or accept that.

It can be painful and frustrating to see siblings acting in unhealthy ways, especially when they are bound to the past and when the impact is current and affects all the family. Adult siblings can become the protectors of their ageing parents against grievous and difficult behaviour from a sibling. This can place a heavy burden on the protector sibling's shoulders. This is something that is becoming more and more noticeable in our ageing society.

Be aware that patterns of silencing by siblings who habitually react with rage and fury force others into resentful quietness. Notice your own and others' conditioned responses – often the patterns are easy to see. Anger can be used as a weapon to shut people down. If you find you don't voice your real feelings because you know the reaction will not be worth it, that is a conditioned learned response. This leads directly to fear, which stops you putting healthy boundaries in place.

The issue of mental health can pose serious difficulties to the sibling and family dynamic. If we consider mental health statistics, it makes sense that in a family at least one in four will experience negative mental health either through sporadic bouts, episodes or with lifelong concerns. The impact of this on sibling and family relationships can range from frustrating, highly corrosive to irreparably damaging.

Leslie's story is a fairly typical illustration of how a family copes with mental health:

As a child, Leslie was happy and carefree, and got on with her sister Julie and brother John. From age 11, Leslie began to experience crippling anxiety. She worried about everything, she felt clingy to her parents one moment and then suffocated by them the next when they tried to help. But mostly, she felt rage, everything annoyed her, especially her older sister Julie.

John seemed unbothered by the tension in the house and was happy to play outside with his friends. Leslie would lash out verbally at Julie. She would feel dreadful afterwards, but couldn't bring herself to say sorry. This caused a lot of pain and upset in the family. Leslie felt her parents were always on Julie's side. Even though Leslie admired her sister, she also had strong feelings of resentment and unfairness. She felt so alone and misunderstood.

In her twenties, Leslie began attending therapy, and then the whole family engaged in family therapy. It was at this point that the destructive patterns of behaviour and the roles that everyone played became clearer.

John had also been experiencing anxiety for a number of years, but hadn't spoken about it as so much attention was given to refereeing the relationship between the sisters. He was very angry about this, but struggled to say this to his parents as he felt they already had enough pressure. John learned that he avoided conflict at all costs, and he began to see how he had become conditioned to fear anger, which meant he swallowed his feelings and got on with it.

The parents could see how they had enabled Leslie to impact the family. Anger had conditioned the rest of the family to not have those difficult conversations that needed to be had, for fear of the vicious verbal lashback.

That understanding helped Leslie to feel compassion towards her sister. For her part, Julie could see for the first time the pain, desperation and loneliness her sister had felt, and she felt empathy for her. This changed their dynamic. They began to talk honestly to each other, and that brought the start of real change.

If this has been the case in your family, ask yourself where else in your life you shut down or avoid conflict and anger. This is where the seeds of resentment and simmering anger are planted, sometimes leading to a disconnection from the sibling.

There isn't always a happy ending. This is real life, so it doesn't go according to plan all the time. Dysfunction is something that needs to be acknowledged, and it's healthy to stop trying to change the unchangeable.

It's necessary to accept the situation as it is. This acceptance is essential in terms of reducing the pain and frustration of the relationship not being the way you want it to be. This is real mindfulness in action.

If your sibling bond is beyond repair, there's a humility and humanity to understanding that each family member is an individual and makes their own choices, and it's not always helpful to assign blame. You can change you, but you certainly have no control over others. If you fail to accept this, it may only lead you to feel upset, hurt and frustration. The core message of this chapter is how you can learn to change your role and your reaction as a sibling. This takes time, effort and continual practice.

KEY THEORIES

Time, love, energy, praise and attention are valuable and precious commodities to be shared within a family. Your parents only have a certain amount of these commodities. Your family home provided the perfect natural habitat to test out sharing, compromise and conflict, and these lessons taught you how to interact with the wider world outside your home. It was a safe space to push those boundaries, where you found out pretty quickly what was acceptable and what was not.

The sibling relationships forged at home have three distinct characteristics, as set out by psychologist Judith Dunn.

1. Emotional power
2. Intimacy
3. Tone

We'll examine these three characteristics one by one.

Emotional power

The first characteristic of siblings, as described by Dunn, is the 'uninhibited expression of emotion'. You and I know how that really goes in non-scientific speak! Children speak their minds, and at volume – particularly with their siblings. However, this uninhibited communication may change as we become adults, but those strong feelings of anger, frustration or envy may still exist. In adulthood, they become stifled and more socially sophisticated. This suppression of true feeling can lead siblings who were close to drift apart, and to feel sadness for the loss of the intense relationship experienced as children.

Each time Lucy left her sister Ann's company, she had a tight lump in her throat, a sense of being physically, emotionally and verbally gagged, and it annoyed her so much. Why could she not say how she really felt? 'What the hell is wrong with me?' This was the type of self-scolding she'd give herself as she packed the kids back into the car, her head feeling like it was about to implode with irritation and anger. 'I can't believe she said that to me.' She then turned and smiled, as if she'd had a lovely time, and said goodbye to Ann – with Ann none the wiser.

The goal is to learn how to connect the old inner kid siblings with the adult siblings. So how do you go about doing this?

How much time do you choose to spend together now? If we discount birthdays, christenings, Christmas, Easter, funerals or any event organised by your parents, when was the last time you met your brother or sister just to spend time with them? If you're struggling to remember, ask yourself: why? Go back to your Diary and write in big letters: WHY? Free associate, doodle, make a list. Just write what comes into your mind.

If you know exactly when you last saw them, what did you do, where did you go, what was it like? Write these down as I'm looking for the good as much as I'm looking for the bad.

There is hope to build strong sibling bonds in adulthood with willing siblings, even if you did not get on as children. You need a baseline to measure your sibling relationship. This is provided by listing the good, the bad and the ugly about each of your siblings.

The Good – sense of closeness, support, deep intimacy, fun, sense of togetherness and understanding, feeling like you belong.

The Bad – conflict, conflict avoidance, sibling rivalry, interference from your parents.

The Ugly – power struggles, destructive relationships, long-term dysfunctionality.

How can **The Good** be strengthened?
How can **The Bad** be changed or accepted?
How can you stop **The Ugly**?

Adult siblings need to move away from the childhood 'uninhibited' way of communicating their real feelings with their siblings, and this in itself can be a challenge if it has never been done before. This can be one of the reasons adult siblings stop talking to each other. It is so interesting that it is within our intimate relationships, especially with family, romantic relationships and siblings that we don't hold back.

Real intimacy allows us to speak freely. The closeness of the relationship is a buffer from the outside world, where you have to be your public self. That task of being your public *me* is tiring, so when people get home they can sometimes let the public civilities slip a bit too far. Ask yourself how you would feel if someone at work or on the street heard you speak to your sibling in your normal way. If this idea makes you uncomfortable, a bit of caution and kindness could be warranted.

Navigating from uninhibited to a more thoughtful response will further strengthen your adult sibling relationship.

Intimacy

The second characteristic is intimacy, which refers to the deep knowledge of each other built up from living under the same roof, and sometimes in the same bedroom. You shared, witnessed and went through so many crucial experiences together, with so many firsts. This intimacy was so deep, personal and intense that many of those experiences imprinted on your belief systems of how to respond and act. The flipside of intimacy is that it means your sibling knows exactly which buttons to press and when to wind you up. Knowledge is power, and power can corrupt!

As psychologist Dorothy Rowe puts it: 'only a sibling knows innately how to trigger that sick, panicked feeling we experience when we've been humiliated, rejected or betrayed.' Dunn says even a two-year-old knows with great 'sophistication' what will upset and annoy their sibling. Every parent out there is nodding their head. The difference in the adult version is that it is by words, or the lack of them, that they know how to set off their sibling. In knowing each other so well, the intimacy can be a source of support or of conflict.

When a sibling attempts to push our buttons, we can sometimes self-defend our personal annihilation by forming an alliance with a parent or another sibling. In families, dyads can form out of necessity. Alternatively, we create an 'impenetrable bond' with another sibling. Think for a moment to see if there are any of these bonds in your family.

On the positive side, these strong alliances will provide emotional protection. Conversely, they can alienate other siblings. Power struggles and the lack of connection can be hurtful to other family members. A central tenet in this book is to *notice*, then become *aware* of how your alliance is affecting others. Is there anything you can do to change this, can you include the other siblings now, or can you protect them from the bond that you have by not brandishing your closeness to them?

Eoin was the youngest in his family, often still lovingly called 'the baby' of the family, even at the grand age of 37. Eoin was kind and thoughtful and yet somehow seemed to wrangle out of getting any jobs that were divvied out at family get-togethers. These jobs often fell onto his sisters' shoulders, even though they both had young children and he did not. When their dad got sick, again the sisters and their mum shouldered the day-to-day care, hospital appointments, etc.

After months of trying to juggle it all, and another sleepless night with one of her kids, Jean's last proverbial straw snapped as Eoin arrived at the house, much to his dad's delight, looking well rested albeit a bit red-faced having just come straight from the gym.

'Great to see you Eoin, you're looking well,' their dad said.

'Eoin, it's all very well for you! It's about time you grew up, you are not a baby anymore.' Jean burst into tears and stormed out.

Eoin, and everyone else, was flabbergasted. Jean was considered 'the strong one' of the family, everyone always commented on how calm and in control she was. But Jean was really struggling. She felt an immense mixture of feelings of anger and resentment and yet she also loved Eoin. It was hard to be angry with 'the baby', but she was. Even though the family considered themselves fairly modern and progressive, she could see how they had all fallen into their expected gender roles, and she was sick of it. But she also felt really guilty to have had that outburst in front of her parents as she knew there was to be no stress. This had really added to the problem though, as they were all pretending everything was OK, but it wasn't.

Through therapy, Jean found she had huge difficulty saying how she really felt because she was seen as the strong, competent one. She learned that strength is to know you are a human, and to be human is to be vulnerable, that she only had a certain amount of time and energy and had to assert herself and learn to say no. She found the reality of that really hard, even though she was exhausted.

They had all prepared 'the conversation' (see p. 102) before the first sibling meeting and even though it was difficult, upsetting and uncomfortable, they really felt a connection to each other that was very authentic and different. Even though there were a lot of tears and anger, everyone tried to recognise when they were getting really upset and would say they needed to press the 'pause button'. Sometimes this worked, sometimes it didn't. It's a skill they are working on. But they felt good, the conversation exercise gave them the framework they needed to have their needs met and to work collaboratively together as a team.

The explained how they felt. Eoin was sorry, and he finally noticed the struggle and tiredness on his sisters' faces. When he apologised, he said he wanted to help out, but felt left out of the decisions the girls made. He said he felt like this his whole life, he had never felt close to them and *didn't think he could because their bond was so strong. He agreed that he felt and was treated like the baby of the family and he didn't like his role either.*

His sisters were really taken aback. They hadn't realised he felt left out. But now they saw how they had never included him in their plans nor had they asked for his help. They had assumed the role of care-takers. They drew up a rota to share out caring for their dad and also to get time for their mum to get out with her friends. Small changes, but they made a huge difference.

They all started meeting for dinner once every three or four months and began to relate to each other differently. They saw Eoin in a new light and rather than the exclusive, impenetrable bond between Jean and her sister, it now included Eoin. Challenging times, such as sickness in a family, can provide a positive new way of relating with each other. Even though they 'knew' Eoin their whole life, they really were only seeing him as his adult self for the first time.

Intimacy and connection can be built, but sometimes siblings who have very close bonds can unintentionally exclude other siblings. Adulthood provides you with more freedom, maturity and the ability to cultivate new levels of connectedness with your siblings, even within well-established inter-sibling cliques.

Is there a conflict between how you think/feel and how you think your sibling perceives you? It is helpful to list out your feelings and how you feel they are interpreted by your sibling. Here's an example:

How the private, real me feels	What my sibling perceives/believes
I feel attacked.	I think she thinks I am strong.
Overwhelmed, can't say how I really feel.	I think he thinks my life is perfect.
Shut down emotionally, am scared of her being angry with me, again.	I think she thinks I'm unfeeling and don't care about her.

Tone

The third characteristic of siblings is the tone of the relationship, from love, hate and conflict, to indifference or ambivalence. It is not a given that you will look like, act like or even get on with your siblings. This is an important point to remember.

Having a good or a great relationship with your sibling(s) is a powerful protector. In childhood, as you were learning your way and being guided, influenced and influencing your sibling(s), you got to test out a lot of things in a safe way. An ongoing bond of connectedness and love is like having a built-in friend for life. The gift of childhood for many was that life had more certainty. Adulthood increases in uncertainty, and a strong sibling relationship is a great life buffer. It can be this reciprocity and responsiveness that provide the comfort when it all falls apart and, equally important, when you rejoice your wins and high points. The fun aspect of siblings is not to be overlooked. A supportive sibling relationship is one of life's great joys.

On the flip side, what if you hate your sibling(s)? Hate is a big word, but the sibling relationship can sour and curdle. The Cain Complex is a psychoanalytical term that means 'a destructive sibling rivalry, in which one of the siblings resents the other for perceived favouritism from a parental rivalry'. This definition leaves out the less sweet and very Freudian 'unconscious desire' to kill the younger sibling!

If you feel a strong level of dislike or resentment towards your sibling, try to honestly find out why. Do you still battle it out with your siblings for your mum and dad's attentive ear or eye? Do you always act like an adult, or does *'it's not fair, he always …'* fall out of your mouth every now and then? As we've seen, you're not obliged to like or love your siblings, but if the relationship can be salvaged, you owe it to yourself to try to do so.

What if you feel ambivalent towards your siblings? You need to ask yourself: what is the ambivalence born out of? Perhaps it comes from the starkness of opposing emotions that can range from feelings of love to hate, support to competitiveness and admiration to jealousy? This stems in part from your birth order, which plays a key role in understanding your conflicted emotions.

Birth order is a tricky one, and you might wonder how science can apply with any rigour to something that is so completely random. But birth order has been found to be quite an accurate predictor of future behaviour, attitude and relationships.

Your birth order made a tangible dent in what Kluger calls your 'temperamental templates', setting the scene for how you interact with the world as an adult. Were you the 'serious and striving' first born, or the 'democratically fighting through it' middle child, or the 'wild, adventurous and funny' last born? Your place in the pecking order has an impact on who you are and how you relate to others.

First born: the bossy yet compliant first born, dutiful to mum, dad, teachers and authority. Their aggressive 'go-getter' streak is tempered by warmth, having minded younger siblings. Conventional, risk-averse and willing to please, more likely to be a CEO, astronaut or in the medical or legal professions. Nobel Prize winners in science and American presidents are much more likely to be a first born. They are organisers, or, to say it another way, they are bossy!

Science backs up these 'temperamental templates' as first borns have higher IQs, are physically bigger, more likely to have their vaccines and occupy more CEO roles as adults. Why is this? Because they had more attention from mum and dad, were brought to the doctor more often and perhaps had higher expectations to succeed placed upon them. The first born occupies a dual role: they can have that authoritative tone from the top, but they can also be soft and maternal/paternal due to their responsibilities to care for and mind younger siblings.

Second born: the main goal of the second born is to be completely different from the first. They are also flexible, easy-going, modest and great peacekeepers. They can sometimes feel restless, and can find it hard to figure out a career path. Frank Sulloway, author of *Born To Rebel,* says 'the first rule of the sibling role is that first and second born will be different in personality, interests and achievement. Generally, the middle or second will be what the first born isn't'.

Sulloway's most important finding is that eldest children support the status quo by being traditional and conventional, adhering to mum, dad and authority, whereas the younger children rebel against it and look for innovative, creative new ways to live. Meanwhile, the middle kid may have to strive to be heard. This disadvantage perhaps moulds middle children to be great negotiators. They make deep, intense outside relationships if those needs aren't met within the home.

Last born: the baby of the family is warm, uncomplicated, fun, loving, open to new experiences, innovative, creative, charming-manipulative, sociable, affable and funny! Why? Because mum and dad were more relaxed and at ease in their roles at this stage so more lenient rules prevailed, as the others had already broken them in. The youngest is often smaller and funnier, which is a good defence mechanism. It's harder to hit the funny one who makes you laugh. These traits bode well for last borns in how they will experience adult life.

Michael Grose's book, *Why First-borns Rule the World And Last-borns Want To Change It*, explains the basics of the impact of birth order: 'We're in a Darwinian struggle from the moment we're born, fighting for scarce resources within a family – our parents' time, love and affection.'

The other factor here is the age gap between siblings. A gap of less than eighteen months will produce less sibling rivalry at the beginning because the older child isn't as aware of the baby getting its attention. However, sibling rivalry can be strong with an age gap between two and four years. This is a mixed situation: on the one hand, parental resources are stretched by a relatively short gap, but on the other, a two- to three-year gap may be ideal as a baby's and a toddler's needs are different. When the gap is over five year, it reduces the rivalry. But when there is a large age gap between siblings, it can create a sense of two families within the same family. Each family is unique, what is important is your perception coupled with the experience you had. It is important not to get stuck on ideals in a non-ideal world.

DIARY

Think about how your birth order has impacted your life.

✧ Are you surprised by anything you've read above? If so, what? _____

_____

_____

_____

✧ Is there anything you would like to change or strengthen based upon what you've just read? _____

_____

_____

✧ In terms of the sibling age gaps in your family, do you think it has made a difference to you? In terms of attachment, do you feel you got enough of your parents' attention, did you feel loved, valued and that you belonged?

_____

_____

_____

One of the fascinating aspects of siblings is their similarities, and their differences. There's a general idea that siblings should be alike, both physically and in terms of personality, but often the opposite is the case. What is the case in your family?

✧ How are you like your siblings? _____

_____

_____

✧ How are you different from your siblings? _____

_____

_____

_____

I find that it is more usual for people to feel they are different from their siblings. This, of course, brings up the nature-nurture debate, and it does seem to lend weight to the nature side and of course personality factors. There is another force at work, however, a process called de-identification, which is defined by Schachter *et al.* (1976) as 'the process in which one sibling defines their identity by intentionally attempting to be different from the other'.

Danny is the smart one, Lucy is the pretty one, Johnny is the funny one, Emelia is the sporty one – siblings often choose specific identities that are theirs and theirs alone. This is an excellent tactic as they will receive 100% attention from their parents for the role that they are specifically good at, and won't have to share any of that coveted parental attention with their very different siblings.

It's a good tactic for children, but it can cause problems for adults. If you get stuck in a role that no longer fits you, that can have an adverse effect on your sibling relationships. Your desire for parental attention doesn't end when you reach adulthood, so you are likely to be playing out some role to get your fair share. You need to consider this and ask yourself if your role is helpful or unhelpful. It could be time for a change and a new way of relating to your family.

THE PRACTICE

I hope exploring your relationships with your siblings will provide a safe space for honest evaluation, helping you to clarify how you think and behave together, and blending this with the knowledge of how birth order, family dynamics and sibling rivalry are major drivers and influencers in your everyday sibling experience.

However, I must open with a triple caveat:

- sometimes the biggest lesson is to accept people as they are and accept that we cannot change them;
- just because you want to change does not mean your sibling will;
- the only person you can change is you.

DIARY

The big question is: Who are you around your siblings? Take some time to think about this and answer it in your Diary, and then answer these questions. (If appropriate or you feel comfortable doing so, ask your sibling to answer questions 2 and 4.)

1. What role do you think you play in your family? _____
   _____
   _____
   _____

2. Ask your sibling(s) what role they think you play in your family. _____
   _____
   _____
   _____

3. What are you like as a sibling? _____
   _____
   _____
   _____

4. Ask your sibling(s) what you are like as a sibling. _____
   _____
   _____
   _____

5. Are you your true self with them? _____
   _____
   _____
   _____

6. If not, in what situations do you conceal your authentic self from your sibling(s)? _____
   _____
   _____
   _____

7. Why do you do this? _____
_____
_____
_____

8. Have you noticed any patterns or trends to this behaviour? _____
_____
_____
_____
_____

9. Are you more argumentative or conflict-avoidant with your siblings than
with other people? _____
_____
_____
_____

10. What do you want to change in the sibling relationships? _____
_____
_____
_____
_____

11. How can you change this? _____
_____
_____
_____

12. List three positive and three negative traits for each sibling. _____
_____
_____
_____
_____

13. How have each of your siblings influenced your life? List out noteworthy
positive and negative events or experiences. _____
_____
_____
_____

14. Do you have favourites among your siblings? _____
_____
_____
_____

15. Do you have a sibling who you don't get on with or don't have a relationship with? _____
_____
_____
_____

16. Do you feel there is any sibling rivalry now? _____
_____
_____
_____

17. If so, what and where do you think it comes from? _____
_____
_____
_____

18. Did you feel sibling rivalry as a child? _____
_____
_____
_____

19. Are there any 'elephants in the room' that no one dares speak of? _____
_____
_____
_____
_____

20. Rate each of your siblings in terms of how much you get on with them: __
_____
_____
_____
_____

THE SECRET LIVES OF ADULTS

Please circle where you are with each of your siblings:

1	2	3	4	5
Dysfunctional	No relationship	Poor	Somewhat indifferent	Neutral
6	7	8	9	10
Fine	Satisfactory	Good	Very good	Best friend

Have you gained any insight from answering these questions? Has it changed your perspective? Can you see where certain trigger points in your life may have originated from past family dynamics, such as sibling rivalry?

What conversation would you like to have with any or all of your siblings? What would you really like them to know, hear, acknowledge or apologise for? This exercise can be a game-changer in cultivating the adult sibling relationship you want to have, helping you find the words that will heal rather than hurt.

DIARY

Ask yourself what conversation needs to be had.

◇ Who do you need to have this conversation with? _____

_____

_____

_____

◇ Write out how you feel about it first, don't show anyone. _____

_____

_____

_____

◇ What is your intention in the conversation? _____

_____

_____

_____

◇ What do you hope to achieve? _____
_____
_____
_____

◇ What are you feeling? _____
_____
_____
_____

◇ What are you upset by? _____
_____
_____
_____

◇ What would you like to change? _____
_____
_____
_____

◇ What outcome do you want from the conversation? _____
_____
_____
_____

While doing this exercise, it is important to:

- be mindful of harmful words and phrases, such as *you always*;
- check and challenge how you perceive your sibling – remember they are not your little brother or sister anymore;
- stop the labelling – old roles die hard, your sibling may have worked really hard to change;
- see your sibling with 'beginner's eyes', as if you have never met them.

First, do the exercise above yourself, then – the scary part – broach the subject with your sibling(s).

How do you broach 'the conversation'?

- Find a good time to have a talk with your sibling(s).
- Start gently: *'I would like to have a chat with you about something that is really important to me.'*
- Make it about both of you: *'I hope this could be beneficial for both of us.'*
- Invite your sibling to be a participant: *'I've been thinking about how we can change certain parts of our relationship and I'm wondering if you would like to try something that will hopefully be of help to us both?'*
- You may need to give the person some time to think about this, seeing as this is the first time they've heard about it.
- You could share your process with them: *'If you like, I can send you on something we can each do on our own first, it's called The Conversation.'*
- Make it a joint venture: *'I find it helps me to write out how I feel first and I'm asking if you would like to do the same, with the intention of then having a conversation together?'*
- Point out what you admire or like in your sibling to soften the invite and to show your intent is for a mutually beneficial outcome.
- Acknowledge their role: *'Thank you for listening to me, it was hard for me to say this, I hope you know how important you are to me in my life.'*

CONCLUSION

Your relationships with your siblings are the longest and most influential in your life. Your siblings can make you laugh and they can make you cry, thanks to your intense intimacy with them. Your siblings are part of you and you are part of them. This role, minus the heavy emotional baggage, can be a great source of joy; the threads of your sibling relationship connect you to your sense of self within your family and the world. If you take this relationship for granted, you could miss out on a very important part of your life that could enhance and enrich your adulthood.

These are the key lessons we've learned about nurturing sibling relationships:

- Take the time to get to know your adult siblings.
- Stop assuming you know everything about them.
- Stop treating each other like children.
- Reminisce about the past and create new experiences.
- Create clean boundaries and be consistent in them.
- Not all sibling relationships are healthy. Stop blaming yourself.
- Be willing to forgive and grow; equally, be willing to let go.
- Be kind, caring and thoughtful. Move from the intensity of saying anything you want to being considerate of your sibling's feelings.
- Enjoy each other's differences.
- Laugh together.

Acceptance is a word you hear a lot in therapy. It does not mean giving up. It is a beautiful word. It is a powerful word. It is a widely misunderstood word. There is a compassion in accepting things as they are. A phrase I find incredibly helpful is: *'it is what it is.'* A lot of frustration arises from things not being the way we want them to be. But if you keep living in frustration, it's like trying to hold back the tide. You are putting all your energy into pushing against something that isn't yours to move. It's exhausting, and pointless. The best approach is to accept the situation as it is. Have compassion for the feelings of irritation, frustration and anger that are coursing through your body. Try this lovely mindfulness exercise by Thich Nhat Hanh, called the 'half-smile': 'When you realize you are irritated, half-smile at once. Inhale and exhale quietly, maintaining the half-smile for three breaths.'

This chapter asked you to do deep work to identify and resolve old rivalries, to sit in the uncomfortableness of ambivalent feelings. Your sibling relationship is constantly changing and evolving. Sometimes, we have to let go of the idea we have of someone. Be kind to yourself, and with a compassionate heart see what you can do and change, and accept what you cannot change.

Here are some ideas for building stronger sibling relationships:

- Stay in touch regularly. Use technology such as WhatsApp and Facetime to cultivate a sense of connectedness in between your in-person meet-ups.

- Plan new experiences together. Again, technology can be a great help here. Make a plan, communicate it to everyone, put it in the Diary, and do it.

- Allow your sibling(s) to change. It can be very upsetting and frustrating for the adult sibling who has grown up and left behind childhood roles, such as being the silly, loud or moany one, when these old roles are constantly referred to and thrown at them. Try to see your adult sibling with 'beginner's eyes' – notice the preconceptions you have of them, or the assumptions you make about them. These might have applied in childhood, but could be outdated now.

- Christmas is the best time to see the old roles manifest among siblings. You will be frustrated with yourself when you find yourself turning back to being seven, or eleven or thirteen years old again. Notice when you are reverting back – what triggers it? Stay calm and don't react. You may be pleasantly surprised by the results. Also, use humour, not only will it disarm but it's also a different reaction that could break the old dynamic.

- We are guided by social inhibition to hold back on saying inappropriate things to other people. However, knowing your sibling so well can blur these important lines. Be aware that cruel words can never be taken back. In a nutshell: think before you speak.

- Use your 'pause button'. Pause for a moment, as you would with a stranger or colleague. Being completely uninhibited and being honest are not one and the same. Being open and mindful of what you say will move your relationship to new levels of connection.

- It may seem daunting, but I urge you to complete the conversation exercise, above. It will give you a much clearer picture of the health and status of your sibling relationships, and this will allow you to mind them properly.

Romance

Gravity is not responsible for people falling in love.

Albert Einstein

INTRODUCTION

I n a world that has become deflated and cynical about love, with daily accounts of yet another relationship breaking up, affairs and the seemingly inevitable loss of 'spark', the idea of love can seem a foolish, naive ideal. Perhaps unexpectedly, science has weighed in to show that love is essential for our survival. Love is a primary human instinct, which is why you are propelled like a magnet to connect. Love and the desire to connect is as natural as breathing. It isn't always easy, of course, but as the neurologist Viktor Frankl said: 'What is to give light must endure burning.'

You have been learning to love your whole life. Your first teachers were your mum and dad. They were your first 'attachment', and that first experience of love influences all the rest. Adult romantic relationships continue this attachment – you transfer all of those needs you had as a child to be minded, cared for and to feel connected to your parents onto your romantic partner. You don't grow out of the need to be loved. The difference in adulthood is that you don't need your partner to be physically near you, like a child does, which is a good thing as it may look a little bit strange if your partner comes to the office crying because you went out to work! No, the need I am talking about is an emotional one: the need to feel loved, cared for, supported, safe and understood.

The journey from fear to love runs by a mighty chasm, wherein lies the fear of being unlovable and alone. That deeply buried, private, painful shame that whispers, *'if they really knew me, they mightn't really like me'.*

The horrid voice of being *'not good enough'* that fills so many hearts and minds. Ironically, it is the act of holding back some of your heart and hiding parts of yourself that makes it impossible to make a wholehearted connection. It is a cruel irony. There may be valid reasons for you to hold back, as you may have banked up experiences from rejection to painful heartbreak. The problem is, you can stay being right, but it will only ensure you remain alone.

The moment you invite and allow another person into your very private shadow side, that's where real connection and love can take root and grow. It's the exposing of the whole self that matters, the good and the bad. That's real love in my eyes. The infatuated *'everything she does is magic'* notion of love is all well and good, but the most courageous connection is where you 'see' and accept the person in front of you in their entirety. Romantic love is seeing the good, the bad and the ugly and consciously accepting and loving that person just the way they are – and letting them love you just the way you are. That's crucial, too.

If you take that pivotal, game-changing step in a relationship to trust someone and let them into your private self, that, in a nutshell, is true intimacy. Sexy? No. Exciting? Not so much. Risky? You bet it is, but falling in love doesn't include a safety net.

If you think back to the beginning of your relationship, ask yourself: When did it change? When did it deepen and go from dating and a bit of fun to feeling like a couple? Was it when you intimately shared those blush-inducing experiences that maybe even your best friend doesn't know about? Was it when you shared an emotion that scared you and made you feel exposed? It is quite likely it was, because it is there in that moment of vulnerability where connection happens. It is in that moment you move from being *me* to *we*.

COMMON ISSUES

Your self-worth plays a vital role in the health of your relationship. This sense of being (un)worthy of love, and its long, bumpy journey from birth (as outlined in chapters 1–3), can be deeply ingrained. That sense of being worthy is something only you can achieve, and it's up to you to take full responsibility for it. It is not your partner's job to 'complete you', no matter what Hollywood tells you. You are worth it, but you need to do the work to believe it.

Being intimate means sharing private feelings of fear, shame and personal insecurity. This raises the issue of feeling safe enough with your partner to allow them to see your deepest vulnerabilities. In today's society, this is a hard task for the 'selfie' generation when external appearance counts for so much. There is so much pressure to conform to how you *should* act that the gap between who you are perceived and how you are can be hard to manage.

Real love is understanding the frailty and vulnerability of handing over your heart and hoping that it will be cared for, minded, not rejected or lost through grief, divorce, affairs, physical and mental health or growing apart. This sounds very far from the wine-and-roses idea of love, but we do ourselves no favours if we persist in the simplistic belief that love will conquer all. The unhelpful myths of *'and they lived happily ever after'* have undoubtedly compounded and heightened unconscious expectations.

When you take the leap to fall in love, it is a risk. Fear blocks connection, broken hearts bear emotional scars that aren't forgotten. Fear closes people's desire to connect because they know the reality of the pain. It's far too easy to carry emotional baggage from one relationship to the next, which is why you need to work on yourself, asking the hard questions and finally changing old patterns that produce the same results. Maybe the old line *'it's not you, it's me'* is true.

The problem is that day-to-day life can really get in the way. Everyone is guilty at some point of neglecting their love and getting distracted by the to-do lists, chores and the *'I did more than you'* arguments, all of which are deeply unsexy and unromantic. Taking each other for granted and keeping score is toxic in a relationship.

In a 2011 episode of the *Graham Norton Show*, Norton asked if he could read the messages from two couple's phones. The first couple were two unmarried men and Norton shared their messages:

> *'we are leaving now pickle'*
> *'hurry hurry'*
> *'have a good day angel'*
> *'you too my darling angel'*

He then went to a married couple's messages and it just read like the weekly shopping list, *'get eggs, bread, milk'*. I laughed, but then remembered my last text to my husband was *'green bins tomorrow'*. You have to manage the day-to-day routine, but the trick is be mindful of how you are investing in your relationship and whether it is strengthening or weakening the bonds between you.

KEY THEORIES

Do you remember a quickly stated 'terms and conditions may apply' on your wedding day? No, because it's something no one asks us to consider before getting married. It should be a compulsory conversation. This chapter will allow you to explore and extricate the 'whys' behind the strong reactions you have (anger, frustration, meltdowns) and learn how to cultivate a strength-based relationship that is enjoyable to be in.

The marriage vows have some clearly stated T&Cs.

For richer or poorer: the likelihood of experiencing financial strain and/ or difficulties is a pretty sound bet for most people. Finances put strain on relationships because so much of your value, self-worth, identity and personal power are tied to money. This is often unconscious as you gleaned your money norms, habits and values from your parents. Ask yourself: what are the inherent beliefs you hold about money? If I asked you to write three words under the heading of 'money', what would they be? For some it is freedom, for others security. Figure out what money means to you and then find out what it means to your partner, and from that make a flexible plan that works for you both.

In sickness and in health: on your wedding day, in all your finery, you likely ignored the real meaning of 'in sickness and in health' and hoped that illness would never darken your door. The reality is that you will deal with sickness: yours, theirs, your children's and your parents'. Come back and tell me how much you're still besotted with your wife or husband after a vomiting bug … that's love in all its glory.

To love and cherish: this is perhaps the most overlooked and taken-for-granted vow, but it's also one of the most important aspects to having a fulfilling, connected and happy marriage. You can't stay in the gooey-eyed state of the halo effect indefinitely, nor is it a good idea. However, not only is it possible to love and cherish your partner but that love can be durable when you put the theory of love into action. One specific way to do this is to take the time to notice and tell your partner what they do well, or what you like about them. Often, one of the first things to go in marriages is politeness. Sometimes even basic manners go out the window. Many couples have described to me how badly they treat each other in little ways, such as not listening. It's like the opposite of 'saving the best till last' as you finish your day by reaching home and then lashing all your pent-up daily frustrations, from your boss, to the traffic, to that unmet deadline, at your nearest but perhaps not dearest. The way to combat this is to actively foster admiration and respect and active acts of kindness in words and deeds to keep your relationship growing. This can be in texts, in how you greet each other, to saying how grateful you are for all that they do.

We will bring Norm in here again. You'll remember him from Chapter 2, with his procedural memories and *'this is the right way to do it'*. You and your partner need to get to know each other's Norm very well. What was normal in your family most probably wasn't in your partner's. Norm is personal to every family. It is essential that you both understand where your strong triggers come from. Perhaps your blood starts to boil when he/she packs the dishwasher the 'wrong' way, which simply means in a way different from how it was done it your family. It's a superficial example, but this is where couples can argue very heatedly over seemingly silly things. Norm set up all your expectations, including those about love. When your internal expectations are not met, disappointment follows. Unless you know or tell your partner what your Norm is, conflict will continue.

Along with Norm, the other early experience that affects your romantic relationships is your attachment style. Your experience of getting your needs met as a child, whether through an emotionally responsive parent or not, built the foundations of what you believe about trust, empathy, connection and how you expect to be treated. As vital as they were to you as an infant, how do you go about getting your needs met now, in your adult romantic relationship?

It was from your parents that you learned the whole range of emotions of what was acceptable or not. Norm is behind all your hidden hopes and expectations of how you think relationships *should* be. Your early experiences set the framework for how you viewed the world, whether it was to explore and venture forth, or to pull back and proceed with great caution. These fundamental principles of childhood attachment were explored by two researchers, Cindy Hazan and Philip Shaver, to explore how they relate to adult romantic relationships.

First, in order to determine a person's attachment style, they created this questionnaire:

A. I find it relatively easy to get close to others and am comfortable depending on them and having them depend on me. I don't worry about being abandoned or about someone getting too close to me.

B. I am somewhat uncomfortable being close to others; I find it difficult to trust them completely, difficult to allow myself to depend on them. I am nervous when anyone gets too close, and often, others want me to be more intimate than I feel comfortable being.

C. I find that others are reluctant to get as close as I would like. I often worry that my partner doesn't really love me or won't want to stay with me. I want to get very close to my partner, and this sometimes scares people away.

(Source: Hazan and Shaver, 1990)

Which of the above do you feel best describes you? According to the findings of Shaver and Hazan:

* 60% of people choose option A, and have a secure attachment;
* 20% choose option B, and have an avoidant attachment;
* 20% choose option C, and have an anxious attachment;
* There is also a fourth attachment type, fearful-avoidant, which is experienced by perhaps 5% of people.

110

Also note that this isn't rigidly defined – you will have a dominant attachment style, but it is normal to have features from the other styles mixed in as well.

Let's look at the key features and reasons underlying each.

SECURE ATTACHMENT

A **secure attachment** involves:	sense of security, connection and love;
	high EQ – emotional intelligence;
	feel comfortable giving and receiving love;
	feel secure in yourself and with your partner;
	sense of personal autonomy, freedom and independence for both partners;
	mutual trust and intimacy;
	partners are equal;
	honest, no game-playing;
	good personal compassion and boundary-setting;
	positive self-esteem that influences your view of relationships and your interaction with the world;
	ability to seek comfort when upset or stressed, and able to give that support back;
	mature and resilient to setbacks.
You are securely attached because:	your parents were emotionally responsive to your physical and emotional needs, which established trust and a feeling of safety;
	a bond was created through touch, providing comfort and love;
	consistent parenting.
You can maintain that secure attachment by:	acknowledging that you will experience normal fears and insecurities within your secure attachment.
	working on good boundaries and open communication.

AVOIDANT ATTACHMENT

An **avoidant attachment** involves:	you might think and say you are independent, but it's a false-independence so as to avoid intimacy;
	keep people at emotional arm's length;
	will push partner away if you feel he/she is getting too close;
	fear intimacy and vulnerability;
	may come across as somewhat self-serving;
	may put hobbies, exercise, work, personal projects, fun first;
	emotionally closed off to themselves and others;
	may have difficulty committing, even within a relationship;
	don't seek comfort or give it.
You are avoidantly attached because:	you may have experienced abandonment, loss through grief and/or abuse;
	genuine sense of fear regarding close relationships – very conflicted as you want it and yet are terrified of the potential pain;
	feel fearful of other people, unable to trust them.
To address avoidant attachment, ask yourself:	What do you need to do for you to start healing any past issues?
	What is your worst fear of being close to someone?
	Have you ever spoken to a professional?
	What do you think when you hear the word 'relationships'?

ANXIOUS ATTACHMENT

An **anxious attachment** involves the following:	anxious to form a real bond, but the fear of intimacy leads to creating a fantasy bond;
	fantasy bond serves the anxious attachment as you 'feel' you are connected, but it's surface level only;
	an emotionally cut-off relationship: *'How was your day?'* *'Fine, dear';* leads to 'emotional hunger', which leads to clingy, possessive, jealous, demanding, chasing behaviour that you look for your partner to satisfy;
	if this is with a partner who has an avoidant style, there will be a constant battle of push and pull, pursuer and distancer, chaser and chased;
	mood swings and obsessive behaviour;
	self-fulfilling prophecy – if too many demands are placed on your partner to 'complete me', your partner will pull away;
	a 'rescue me' mentality;
	drama over real and perceived issues;
	may prefer a stormy relationship over a calm or 'boring' one;
	high insecurity requires a lot of reassurance and validation;
	suspicious of other people and filter information in a negative way: *'she must have meant …', 'why did he look at me like that, he doesn't like me';*
	pattern and history of turbulent relationships;
	do not like to be on your own.

ANXIOUS ATTACHMENT

You are anxiously attached because:	you received inconsistent parenting – the parent could be emotionally available or unavailable;
	this inconsistency led you to feel confused and distrust the parent, but simultaneously be clingy;
	it led to high rejection sensitivity, which continues to play out in an adult attachment if you feel your partner is backing away;
	it also led to high insecurity and need for reassurance, which no partner will ever be able to satisfy.
To address anxious attachment, ask yourself: Did Chapter 2 bring up anything about your primary attachment to your parents? What did you learn?	Do you recognise if you have a fantasy bond?
	Do you see the changes that you can make and how it would help you?
	Do you need a therapeutic space to work through this to heal old illusions of connection, possibly with your mother?
	In terms of feeling more secure and improving your self-esteem, what do you feel you could do to accomplish this?
	If you have feelings of not being good enough, what can you do to engage in self-care?

FEARFUL ATTACHMENT

A **fearful attachment** to your partner involves the following:	conflicted and ambivalent state;
	wavering from going towards feeling connected and then being afraid when you get too close;
	can experience frequent 'emotional storms': feeling overwhelmed by strong, conflicting emotions, being frustrated, sad, feeling out of control, worrying;
	high levels of anxiety and being overrun by feelings;
	when feeling rejected, you become clingy;
	if closeness occurs, the feeling of being trapped grips you;
	confused and fearful – you try to connect but fear it is not working out;
	an underlying belief that the relationship won't work;
	a lot of drama, with great highs and lows;
	there is a danger of confusing drama with excitement and chemistry with chaos;
	there is a danger of engaging in abusive relationships.
You have a fearful attachment because:	you may have experienced abandonment, loss through grief and/or abuse;
	genuine sense of fear of close relationships;
	feel fearful of other people and find it very difficult to trust others.
To address fearful attachment, ask yourself:	Can you acknowledge the reality and pain of your past? Honest acknowledgement is the first step towards change.
	Do you believe you can learn to connect in a safe and caring way?
	Would you be willing to seek professional help to work on your deep-rooted unconscious patterns and learn better ways of connecting?

The goal of understanding your attachment style is to work towards an 'earned secure attachment'. This is the goal of a lifetime. It will impact every aspect of your inner life, but none more so than your romantic relationship. This can be cultivated through gaining personal insight and catching yourself when you are triggered by your partner or by your own embedded belief system, rules or scripts. It takes a lot of hard work, but therapy can be very useful in this journey as the therapist's objectivity will help uncover major unconscious blind-spots that can transform not only the quality of your life but also that of your relationship.

It is so important to come at this with great compassion for yourself. People are incredibly multi-layered, with so many experiences and learnings. Just like our Russian doll, you are often focused on the visible part, which means you cannot see the true depths of how your attachment style influences your adult life. Often unbeknownst to you, your style plays out in so many ways on a daily basis. If you don't stop and look within, those patterns will remain on autopilot, as they have been for years. The start of change is to notice the patterns.

I want you to take a moment and remember the Russian doll analogy. We looked at you in Chapter 1, and then at your parental attachment in Chapter 2, and at your sibling attachment in Chapter 3, and now we are looking at you in your adult love relationship. Can you see the thread that weaves through it all and binds it together? Then you can also see how anything that snags on that thread, tugs at the whole doll, triggers a chain reaction.

Difficulties, conflict or stress can trigger your primary attachment style. When you know you are reacting rather than responding, your primary childhood attachment has been triggered and activated. The reaction takes over and emotional words fire rapidly out of your mouth: *'I can't believe you said that'*, *'How could you do this to me?'* This often leads your partner to get angry and defensive, and you may feel like you are emotionally overwhelmed or shut down. This is why changing your attachment is so difficult, because your brain goes straight back to a limbic reaction, which is emotional, and your brain disconnects from the cortex, which is the reasoning part of your brain. The solution is to become aware of what it feels like in your body, forcing a connection between the emotional and reasoning centres in your brain. It's as simple as pausing, stop talking and become aware of your heart and your breathing. Is it very fast? Even your brain knows relationships are all about connection.

Can you see other ways this may play out, for example when your partner wants to get close to you? It may be a very different experience for the person who has a secure, anxious, avoidant or fearful attachment, ranging from happy, excited, nervous, fearful to suffocated.

What belief systems do you hold about how relationships *should* be? Have you ever written them down? If you can't think of any, ask your partner what he/she thinks these might be.

Having picked your most likely attachment style, can you identify your partner's? Are you a good combination? If not, don't worry – you can both change. The purpose of knowing your attachment style is to help you learn how to get your needs met in a way that works for you and your partner.

However, there's a caveat here: not all relationships are healthy. Not all relationships will or should survive. Time to raise a warning flag! If your attachment style has had you gunning for the so-called bad boy/girl, repeating dysfunctional patterns and sometimes choosing abusive relationships that match your expectation of how a relationship is, it's time to question the impact the past is still having upon you today.

When two secure styles connect, the benefits of two mature, flexible people who know how to get their needs met as they did when they were a child can only bode well for their romantic relationship. Unfortunately, anxious and avoidant attachment styles are attracted to each other. This is because they meet each other's childhood expectations, or at least find within the other what is familiar to them. This often means both are in a double unconscious bind about how they are behaving and how to get their needs met through their partner, which is bad news. The adult relationship reignites historical attachment wounds that the other person can't fix, leading, sadly, to confirmation of the original bias. The underlying bias can be many different things, such as *'you can't trust anyone'*, or those insecure feelings of *'I was never good enough anyway'*.

In destructive relationships there are typically pursuers, who push, and distancers, who pull away. The anxious attachment style is not attracted to the secure attachment style, because it finds it hard to believe it to be true. For the anxious attachment person, the secure person does not match with their core beliefs about relationships as they feel *'no one can be that reliable or consistent'*. Instead, anxious attachment is attracted to avoidant attachment style, who will not meet their needs, thereby confirming their existing belief about relationships.

Why does a person become a pursuer?

- First, it is familiar: *'they are not giving me the love I need'*. While this is a source of pain, there is also comfort in that familiarity.
- It triggers a sense of possible connection because it is so familiar: *'we just got each other straightaway'*.
- You may confuse this with chemistry.
- You are unaware that this is not a good match for you.
- You may even feel excited and simultaneously nervous and anxious.
- The avoidant attachment style validates your fears and anxieties of abandonment.
- It confirms your faulty core belief that you are unlovable: *'I always knew they never really loved me'*.

If you recognise yourself in this, what can you do about it? In a nutshell, stop the chase. This may seem upsetting, but it is not going to get you the result you want, which is connection. This is something I would suggest doing for yourself and by yourself first. Work towards becoming more secure within yourself so that you are not looking for your partner to give you what only you can give yourself. Be kind, be compassionate and patient with yourself.

If you and/or your partner recognise yourselves in this description, that's a good start. Then you must be willing to engage in working together to heal old patterns about yourself, about the relationship and to work on cultivating a new model together. It requires hard work and effort, but you are not doomed to your primary attachment style.

Distancers, on the other hand, run away from attachment. The avoidant attachment style is attracted to the anxious attachment style because they need to be chased. Within the chase they can be defensive – *'it's all your fault, you want too much of me'* – with no accountability for their lack of emotional availability. They will either go straight for the jugular – *'you always …'* – or they withdraw. None of these strategies will allow connection, but this meets the avoidant attachment style's relationship bias: *'I knew it wouldn't work, relationships are such a waste of time, you always get hurt.'*

If you recognise yourself as a distancer, you need to kindly ask the pursuer to stop chasing you. Explain that it makes you retreat even more. If it's true, say you are committed to the relationship but uncomfortable with the idea of being vulnerable. If you want the relationship, or any relationship, to work, you'll have to set about making changes yourself, or with professional help.

THE PRACTICE

In Chapter 1, we learned that knowing yourself and feeling a sense of being connected to yourself requires you to be authentic, honest and genuinely self-aware. That is no easy feat. In Chapter 2, we learned that your sense of being lovable and worthy of love started with your experience of seeing, watching and learning from your parents as a couple, and also from how they connected and related to you as their child. Can you describe and understand your experiences in childhood? This is very important as it is your perception of that experience that sets up how you perceive your self-worth and lovability as an adult.

DIARY

◇ What aspects of your parents' relationship did you admire? _____

_____

_____

◇ What parts did you not like? _____

_____

_____

_____

◇ Have you over-compensated in any way to avoid these negative memories/experiences? _____

_____

_____

◇ Have you engaged in any polar behaviour to ensure you are the opposite, e.g. if your parent was very angry, you avoid conflict completely? _____

_____

_____

_____

◇ Any specific gender learnings that you have copied or gone polar on? __

_____

_____

_____

◇ What is your view of your parents' relationship? _____

_____

_____

_____

◇ What is your opinion of your partner's parents' relationship? _____

_____

_____

_____

◇ Have you discussed some of these issues together as a couple? _____

_____

_____

_____

◇ Have you discussed what type of relationship you would like to have together? _____

_____

_____

Once you have considered the above, discuss and agree your core values, beliefs, hopes and dreams. This will give you and your partner a blueprint for what constitutes a happy relationship for you both.

Your parents were your first image and impression of what love looked like. You saw and witnessed how they talked to each other, fought and made up. What you learned from nuanced whispers and looks between them told you how you should act within your gender roles. You saw open displays of affection, or the lack of them, and were home-schooled in how to express joy, sadness, anger or silence. This is where you learned, often unknowingly, the 'how' of their relationship, which became the basic code for your adult relationships. Marie's story provides a good example of this.

Marie was angry with Joe. Every year her birthday was a disappointment, even though he knew her birthday was a big deal to her. Joe was aware of Marie's anger, but he couldn't understand it. He had brought home flowers that evening and they had picked out the handbag she really wanted weeks before. But all he had received for his efforts was silence, although he could see she was seething inside.

He waited until the kids were in bed to broach the subject.

Joe: 'What's wrong, darling?'

Marie: bursts into tears – 'I can't believe you did it again.'

Joe: 'What did I do?'

Marie: 'You know how much I love birthdays …'

Joe, interrupting: 'Yes, I do. Didn't I bring home flowers, didn't I buy your present?'

Marie: 'Yes, but you didn't have a card this morning, and you didn't have a cake for me.'

Joe: 'Seriously, Marie, this is ridiculous, are you five years old?'

Marie left the room.

Marie and Joe had been through this scenario many times before. They had worked through it in couple's therapy and they knew they needed to put what they had learned into practice. Otherwise, this pattern would rear its head every single year.

If you experience a similar scenario:

- at this time, let the person walk away;
- take time out;
- it takes your brain 20 minutes to calm down;
- stop talking when your heart is pounding;
- when your body is flooding with emotion, i.e. feeling angry, sad or really mad, it's like pulling the visor of a helmet over the thinking part of your brain;
- when you are flooding, you cannot think straight.

....

Marie and Joe applied what they had learned in therapy about this trigger situation:

Marie: walks back into room – 'I need 20 minutes.'

Joe: 'OK, me too. Meet you in the kitchen in 20.'

Marie and Joe knew they needed to calm down. Joe was feeling quite deflated and fed-up. Marie knew she was flooding. If we checked her heart rate, it would be over 100 beats per minute. Marie didn't need a monitor as she could feel her heart pounding in her chest and a million thoughts were whirling around her head, all negative. This negative state was building momentum and gathering up past grievances in its whirlwind. She needed to stop and breathe.

Perpetual fights are exhausting and destructive. They both felt the slightest thing was setting them off recently. They knew in the calm-down period it would be a good idea to write out how they felt on their own. They had discussed doing this in therapy, where you write what comes into your mind, with no one looking at what you are writing. It is judgement-free, which allows you to really get at what has upset you.

Joe starting writing. At first it was hard, he really didn't know what to write as he felt he hadn't done anything wrong. He felt annoyed as it seemed that nothing he did seemed to make any difference. So he wrote that down.

Marie's words came fast, her pen scribbling furiously with strong feelings of upset, rejection and anger. She wrote and wrote and as she did, she felt better as she acknowledged why she felt so strongly about this.

In session they had explored different family values, beliefs and rules that were unwritten but deeply encoded into 'this is how we do it in my family'. She wrote 'Birthdays' and put a line under it. Birthdays have always been special to me and my family. It was at this point that Marie put the pen down and began to cry.

Marie went back to the kitchen. She saw that Joe also looked sad.

She looked at her husband and said: 'I understand why this means so much to me. I never really told you what birthdays mean to me or my family. There was always a bit of fanfare. The birthday person was put in the centre of my parents' bed. The feeling was one of being loved and really special. I now realise how these old 'rules' underpin special occasions for me. I also am aware that it was different in your house, so I suppose I have to remember we have different expectations based on different experiences. Thank you for the flowers today. I would love to start a new birthday experience in our house as it is a treasured memory for me. I was angry with you because I feel I make that fuss for the kids and for you, and I suppose I wanted to feel special just on one day.'

Joe came over and gave Marie a hug. 'You are a wonderful mum and a wife. I get it now, I was pretty pi**ed off earlier as I really thought I had got it right this time. I feel the last while that I just seem to be the bad guy. That is really tough on me as well.'

Joe and Marie were able to bring this experience, and their free association writing, to their next therapy session. It was an important example of how not clarifying your needs can lead to confusion and anger. But it's also an important example of how a simple act of communication can solve so many problems.

It is important to remember that your emotions serve a purpose. Physical pain in your body alerts you to take action. Emotions perform exactly the same function. Bring this next exercise into your relationship. If you feel hurt, or your partner is hurting, or you are hurting each other, stop immediately and practice Relationship First Aid.

- Step 1: Assess the emotional wound.
- Step 2: What caused/triggered the damage?
- Step 3: How can you stop the 'bleeding'/damage?
- Step 4: Is there any old emotional scar tissue, if so from what?
- Step 5: What can you do to help?
- Step 6: Do you need an expert opinion/guidance?

By engaging in this sort of relationship triage, you can assess the level of pain, urgency and decide what are the next best steps. Your relationship SOS could be: *stop, think and breathe.*

If we stay with the idea of the medical model, when you visit your GP, what conveys a sense of expertise is their calmness. This is an instant soother as you feel they know what they are doing. In a way, you are honouring and validating your own feelings first, and then you can do something about changing the pattern. A good question to ask yourself is: Where/when did I feel this before? Reflect on it for a moment. You will probably find that the feeling is very old.

There are sure-fire ways and behaviours to wreck your relationship, but less well known are the ways to nourish and strengthen it. It's easy to get mad and be bad, the trick is how to keep working on the good and ring-fencing and working effectively on the negative. In a world often driven by 'showing love' extrinsically, through gifts, holidays, picture-perfect social media images and public displays of affection, the heart of the matter is: how do you get on behind closed doors?

In an unhealthy relationship, it's often the case that the couple focuses only on the negatives. Sometimes this is a mechanism of self-protection, but it's not helpful. We know all the stand-up comedian's clichés about this – she nags, he won't commit – but they are really unhelpful. When trying to solve a problem, we need all the information we can get about that problem, so we can then identify the best solution. This is why I enjoy the idea of love and science joining forces. The science of psychology is a hugely useful tool when you are trying to identify your relationship problems and solve them. A primary aim of this book is to help you understand this and how to put it in action.

DIARY

Here's a good starting-point for information-gathering. Write out your answers to the following questions.

Mad

✧ What triggers you to feel mad with your partner? _____

_____

_____

_____

✧ How does your partner 'make' you feel angry and why? _____

_____

_____

_____

✧ Are there any patterns or particular areas this occurs within and why? ___

_____

_____

_____

✧ Have you ever seen this pattern anywhere else before? _____

_____

_____

_____

✧ How did your parents express anger towards each other? Take each parent separately: mum did x, dad did y. _____

_____

_____

_____

✧ How would your partner know you were angry? _____

_____

_____

_____

Bad

◇ What negative traits do you see in yourself that are destructive to your relationship? _____
_____
_____

◇ Is there any historical pattern of this from your parents? _____
_____
_____
_____

◇ Do you use personal insults against your partner? If so, what do you say or do? _____
_____
_____

◇ What one thing could you change about yourself that would benefit your romantic relationship? _____
_____
_____
_____

◇ Has your partner pointed out one of your negative traits? If so, what is it?
_____
_____

◇ How do you soothe your bad behaviour? _____
_____
_____
_____

◇ Do you numb the pain? If so, with what? _____
_____
_____
_____

◇ Do you have a negative pattern of reaction? _____
_____
_____
_____

◇ Is this something you have control over? If so, how could you change it? ____

_____

_____

_____

Sad

◇ What aspects of your relationship make you sad? _____

_____

_____

_____

◇ Why do you feel sad? _____

_____

_____

_____

◇ Has this been present in other relationships? _____

_____

_____

_____

◇ Where do you feel sadness in your body? _____

_____

_____

_____

◇ How do you express this sadness to your partner, or do you? _____

_____

_____

_____

Some of your answers to the above might bring in your sexual relationship. This is a key part, and sometimes a key trigger, in an adult relationship. Are you able to talk openly about sex in your relationship? You have all the adult responsibilities down, job, mortgage, etc., now please put some fun and pleasure back in for yourself and your partner. This intimate connection is primal and nurturing and it's essential to your sense of being a couple. That's why it's essential to talk about what sex means for the two of you. It can be a hard conversation to get going, so this exercise gives some helpful starting points.

DIARY

Do this exercise on your own first, and then have this conversation together and see how you get on.

✧ Do you share similar sex drives, desires, etc? _____
_____
_____
_____

✧ What type of sex life do you want? _____
_____
_____
_____

✧ What hasn't worked for you? _____
_____
_____
_____

✧ Make a list of all the good sexual experiences you have had and why. __
_____
_____
_____

✧ What was the best experience and why? _____
_____
_____
_____

✧ What was your worst experience and why? _____
_____
_____
_____

✧ Can you differentiate between casual sex and connected sex? _____

_____

_____

_____

✧ What turns you on? _____

_____

_____

_____

✧ What turns you off? _____

_____

_____

_____

✧ What is intimacy to you and why? _____

_____

_____

_____

✧ What would you like to change about the sexual aspect of your relationship? _____

_____

_____

✧ Does your body image interfere with how you feel about sex? _____

_____

_____

_____

✧ Are there any other sexual blockers, e.g. tiredness, physical sexual concerns, etc.? _____

_____

_____

✧ Do you feel confident or comfortable talking about your sexual needs? ___

_____

_____

_____

FIGHT CLUB

It may sound odd, but one of the features of a healthy relationship is the ability to fight well. This can be a challenge to achieve. We'll start by looking at the bad way to conduct a fight, stemming from his evidence-based research, John M. Gottman compiled the six signs of the bad fight, which I have adapted below.

1. The Harsh start-up

We all know how this goes – you head straight in, with a quick-fire of personal blows, followed by high-octane drama and accusations. There will be a lot of *'you never'* and *'you always'*. Gottman has shown that there is a 96% failure rate when this is your first line of defence.

2. The four horsemen of the apocalypse

These are Criticism, Contempt, Defensiveness and Stonewalling. Everyone will have done all four at some stage, so breathe, you are normal. What you need to look out for with the 'four horsemen' is not to have a pyrrhic victory. Don't win the fight and lose your relationship. This happens when you just have to get in the last word – that's the sword that plunges into the heart of your relationship. The four horsemen have been proven to wreck a relationship if they are pervasively present in how you communicate with each other. Take note which of them applies to you and take action on changing them.

You know when you feel *so* angry and that none of it is your fault, that you're definitely in the right this time, and you'd prefer to talk to the wall than your partner? Here comes the but … BUT, in a healthy relationship you have to do the harder thing of being emotionally mature and responsive to each other in the bad times. I know, it sucks, right?

Kids, especially teenagers, are told all the time to *'grow up and stop acting like a child'*, but do we ask the same of our own behaviour? How mature are you really? Maturity asks a lot, that you be level-headed, rational and reasonable. Three words that mix pretty poorly in the heat of conflict. Does your need to 'win' supersede your need to be in a healthy and happy adult relationship?

It's helpful to see your emotional triggers as a challenge to grow together, as two people. I know this is much easier to type than it is to practice, but with practice and will to succeed, you can master it. It's a great skill to be able to breathe and get past the anger that can blind you and your partner. It's about recognising that you are not in a ring together, and that you have the capacity to deal with it once and for all – until the next thing asks to be repaired. That is OK, though. Conflict shows that you care deeply about something and you are expressing those feelings, maybe loudly, but you are stating what is OK and what is not OK for you both.

Stop being scared of conflict. You just need to know how to fight well and not hurt each other. This is intimacy, engaging in the tough and often uncomfortable parts of being an adult. So drop your defences, be vulnerable and you will connect even deeper in the tough times. Get past the anger iceberg and connect with the pain below the surface. (There's more on the 'anger iceberg' below.) This requires hearing and verbally acknowledging what is being said, and validating each other's point of view.

The lesson here is to support rather than berate, and to soothe rather than stoke. Here's how you do that:

- If you are angry or upset, give yourself a twenty-minute time-out from each other. (This isn't an arbitrary figure. It takes twenty minutes to physically and neurologically calm down when your body is flooded with stress hormones.)
- Sit down, close your eyes and take a deep breath.
- Where in your body are you feeling tension?
- Breathe into that tension.
- If you feel tight, imagine softening that tension with your breath.
- If angry thoughts come into your mind, acknowledge them and let them float away.
- Bring your mind back to your calm place with your breath.
- Ask you partner to do the same.
- When you both feel physically calmer, ask each other what would help next? Would a walk or a hug help? How can you connect again?

- Make a list together of things you know would soothe in the aftermath of a fight. For one person it may be a walk on their own, for another a hug will settle them.

3. Flooding

People usually stonewall to avoid feeling 'flooded'. Stonewalling is easy to spot, as you would get more talk out of an actual wall! Flooding occurs when you are deeply shocked by what your partner has just said. It is felt very physically. You will then become hypervigilant to everything they say to avoid them 'attacking' you again. You interpret everything, even neutral statements, negatively. To protect yourself, you disengage emotionally from the relationship.

4. Your body speaking

Anyone who saw the relationship programme *Then Comes Marriage*, which I co-presented with Ray O'Neill, saw a lot of 'flooding' in action. This occurs when your heart rate goes up to 100 beats per minute. Participants in Gottman's 'Love Lab' showed elevated levels of adrenalin in blood tests taken after they had flooded. We were somewhat more easy-going and let our couples go and enjoy a lovely three-course meal.

What your body is telling you internally from heightened arousal (elevated heart rate and blood pressure, faster breathing and release of stress hormones like cortisone and adrenalin) is that you are not having a fun time. What your partner is reading from you externally can also exacerbate the conflict: tension in your face, posture and tone will impact how quickly the argument accelerates. Soften into your body, roll your shoulders, take a deep breath, stop yourself when you hear your tone becoming aggressive and argumentative.

5. Failed repair attempts

Repair attempts are essential to the health of your marriage. If the four horsemen have taken up residence in your relationship, there's an 82% chance that you and your partner will divorce, according to Gottman's findings. If you fail in your repair attempts, this figure rises above 90%.

If your heart rate doesn't go above 100 beats per minute, I would take this as a very good indicator of a good repair event. It means you were both able to cool the argument before it got to flooding, and this is an excellent indicator for the state of your marriage. Listen to your body: when your heart is pounding and you can't say what you want to say, take a break. Tell your partner how you're feeling and say you'll be back to continue the conversation in twenty minutes. Remember that humour, used well, can break tension and is an excellent repair attempt.

6. Bad memories

If a relationship gets stuck in a whirl of constant negativity, not only is the future and present in danger, so too are the couple's past memories. All couples naturally start marriage with high hopes and positive expectations, but if they get into a negativity loop, they can start to remember the past negatively. Their happy history gets rewritten as she remembers him '*getting drunk at the wedding*' and he remembers her '*being 45 minutes late to the church*'.

Common conflict management myths, such as active listening or not going to sleep on an argument, can do more harm than good. Research has shown different evidence-based results. For example, out of 650 couples Gottman observed who were in self-described happy marriages, they did nothing close to active listening when they were upset. It seems honesty is not always the best policy in marriage (not including important things like fidelity, finances, trust, etc.) The key finding is that no one way works for every couple. What is important is that the style works for both people in the couple. And as for sleeping on an argument, well, sometimes, you should sleep on it, because you may be calmer and clearer in the morning.

These 'bad fight' scenarios bring up the whole issue of anger. I felt I needed to invite anger into the relationships chapter and to give it the space it deserves as it has gotten a really bad rap for a long time because people are afraid of it, feel too much of it, or try too hard to suppress it. It is so important to remember that anger has a purpose. It motivates you to do something, when you feel something wrong, unfair or unjust has occurred.

I want to challenge your perception of and relationship with anger because it is such an important emotion and it will surely pay your relationship a visit. The question is: how do you handle it currently, and is there a better way?

Anger is a personal experience as it connects in with your moral code of what you think of as right and wrong. But it is the tip of the iceberg – the emotion you can see. Psychologists consider it a secondary emotion, meaning there is always another emotion that preceded it. It's just that the preceding emotion can't be seen and could be buried deep.

Tip of the iceberg/visible anger: Mary was furious, she couldn't believe Marcus had left all of his dirty football gear on the floor … again!

Below the surface/triggering emotion: Mary had felt lost since giving up work and she wasn't really sure who she was anymore. The only thing she was sure of was that she was turning into someone she didn't recognise, endlessly cleaning and feeling constantly tired, irritated and frustrated. Her personal sense of value as a wife and as a woman was plummeting fast; she felt like an unpaid cleaning lady.

Protected core feelings: self-worth, value, self-esteem, hurt, feeling invisible, gender roles, self-image, feeling 'not good enough'.

Anger is the swashbuckling protector of the vulnerable primary emotion, such as feelings of hurt, loss, worthlessness and shame. These are raw, painful emotions hidden deeply, and the anger acts as a surface emotion, papering over what lies beneath. The problem is, anger can be destructive and it prevents the couple from getting to the root of the emotion involved, or the root of the problem.

In the moment, it is so much easier to be angry because it surges quickly through your body, pumping norepinephrine to numb the pain. By being emotionally responsive to your partner's anger, not taking their anger personally and asking in a compassionate tone, *'What is really upsetting you?'* the anger may turn to tears very quickly and the real feelings can come to the surface.

Based on 30 years of research from the Gottman Institute, here are 6 steps to resolve your angry conflict.

1. **Soften start-up:** watch your tone. Don't lash out at your partner. Complain, don't blame.
2. **Accept influence:** let your partner influence you. Be aware if you are digging your heels in. Hear what they are trying to say. Neither of you is 100% right.
3. **Make effective repairs during conflict:** know what 'repair attempt' works for you as a couple.
4. **De-escalate:** know when you're getting too angry. Step away from your partner. Press the pause button.
5. **Take 20 minutes apart to cool down:** actively self-soothe.
6. **Compromise:** be generous with your partner. Recognise what you can do to make the situation better. Failing that, can you accept it if it can't change?

It's obvious by now that my own research interests in relationships are deeply influenced by the work of John Gottman at the Gottman Institute, a world expert in marriage, a mathematician and a psychologist. The Gottman 5:1 ratio has been called the 'magic relationship ratio' according to *Science* magazine. Why 5:1? It's back to evolution. We are primed to take note of the negative first, and it's good to know why it's so easy to do. Your survival depended upon reacting to the rustle in the leaves. In conflict situations, happy couples had five positive interactions for every one negative. They fought differently, there was a softened start-up, some humour and repair attempts. Whereas in couples who ended up divorcing, their anger was coupled with contempt, criticism and personal attacks: *'you're pathetic'*, *'you're so weak'*. Both couples fought, but differently, and with very different results.

When conflict hits your relationship, remember the 5:1 ratio. For every negative interaction, 5 positive interactions are needed to offset it. Happy couples have a variety of positive interactions regularly, such as hand-holding, focused conversation, apologising, joking and laughing together.

Their 'bank' of positives outweighs the moments of negativity. This is the secret to a happy relationship.

So, we've examined what 'bad' fighting looks like, time to look at what constitutes 'good' fighting.

Margaret rings up her husband, feeling very annoyed with him:

Ben: 'Hi Mags, how…'

Margaret: 'You took my bloody keys again.'

Ben, audible sigh: 'I didn't.'

Margaret: 'You did, oh, you always do this to me, I'm late, and you've actually locked me in the house.'

Ben, calmly: 'I'm telling you I didn't.'

Margaret: 'Check your pockets.'

Ben: 'Not there, I'm telling you …'

Margaret: 'Check your coat.'

Ben: 'Margaret, I'm at work.'

Margaret, shouting: 'Check your bloody coat!'

Ben returns a few seconds later and sheepishly replies: 'I'm really sorry.'

For the rest of the day, Margaret spiralled quickly into negative sentiment override. Every small and big grievance that Ben had done recently, and not so recently, was caught up into her negative whirlwind of thoughts. She finally managed to escape out the backdoor from her locked house, and Ben sent her apologetic text messages throughout the day, but she could still feel her anger increasing every time she thought of the keys jangling in his coat pocket.

Ben knew that Margaret would be furious that he had caused her to miss an important meeting that morning. He also knew that he could be absent-minded at the best of times. He knew his texts were likely being read through muttered angry expletives. Ben and Margaret shared a really good sense of humour, he knew how to go back and carry out a good 'repair attempt'. He sent a very self-deprecating gif to Mags and hoped that humour would save him one more time. He gave it three minutes and then called her, she answered.

'I still hate you.'

'Yes I know,' said Ben. 'I hate me too.'

They both laughed.

....

Thermostats are not just to measure temperature, the emotional thermostat can be reset in all your relationships, including your romantic relationship.

....

That evening, Ben brought home a small bunch of tulips, Margaret's favourite flower, cooked a lovely dinner, put the kids to bed and cleaned up. This 'repair attempt' showed how he could calm Margaret down by acknowledging her anger, and by agreeing and validating that he was, is and may always be absent-minded.

....

Use your partner's mood, sighs, silence or smile to be emotionally responsive to them. By tuning into what they are either blatantly telling you or subtly suggesting, you help to soothe them and yourself. This is a necessary skill and is called attunement. It is an integral part of a healthy long-term relationship.

Follow these steps to achieve attunement:

Step 1: Acknowledge and accept what you did.

Step 2: Validate your partner's feelings.

Step 3: Actively do five positives to reset the relationship's emotional thermostat.

Step 4: Know what soothes your partner. If that is letting them rant or be angry, then let them do that.

Step 5: When all is calm, reconnect and say sorry and that you will work to change this behaviour.

The key thing that Ben did well in this scenario was that he validated Margaret and her feelings. Validators soothe and calm rather than stoke the fires of anger and frustration. The validator does the complete opposite to the partner who goes on the defensive. The difference it makes to your relationship long-term is huge. The defensive partner, by contrast, will go on the attack and place all the blame back on you: *'well you never leave your keys in the place we have for the keys'*. The defensive partner never takes responsibility, so it's never their fault. If Ben had chosen this tack, he would have been angry too and the anger would have festered between him and Margaret, with neither backing down and admitting any fault.

What's interesting is to take one step back from this and ask: why be defensive, if it's so clearly unhelpful? This question underlies all dysfunctional and negative behaviours and emotions that people present. What is the function and purpose of being defensive? You defend when you feel you are being attacked.

Think of a physical attack, even the threat of it – if you think someone is coming at you to strike you, inevitably you will put your hands up to your face to protect yourself. In the absence of physical threat, the emotional impact of words cut just as deeply. Being defensive is your coping mechanism to ward off what feels to you an emotional attack. The problem is, it doesn't protect you because then your partner won't back down as you haven't taken any responsibility for your part.

I have counselled couples where one partner feels the other partner is the obvious *'baddie'*, for want of a better word. It can be incredibly upsetting to the partner who feels they have done nothing wrong to see the part they have played. In couples therapy, the intimate dance between what is done, said and not said and the roles we play, even being the *'good one'*, are at the core of psychodynamic therapy. If you are perpetually defensive, it will leave you stuck in an interminable roundabout, leaving everyone dissatisfied and going nowhere.

The vows ask you *'to love and to cherish'*, but the question is how you can actively do this in your relationship, and not just on Valentine's Day? You need to do frequent acts of kindness to strengthen and nourish your relationship.

Through your early attachment, you learned if the world was a safe place to explore and venture into or if it was a fearful place that produced in you conflicting feelings of pushing and pulling – *'I want to go'*, *'I don't want to go'*.

From my clinical perspective, when I see relationships in conflict, I imagine it as a door with each partner either side of it. The constant back and forth, pulling and pushing away from each other and not seeing it from each other's side leaves both parties exhausted – but they're still on opposite sides of the door! Nothing has been achieved.

My goal is to get you both on the same side of the door, to turn towards each other, rather than turning away.

You will find that turning towards each other is much more difficult than turning away. This is where the counterintuitive part of the science feels a lot trickier to apply in the heat of the moment, when you are so mad with your partner. It's incredibly easy to turn away because we have so many distractions we can throw ourselves into – numbing the feelings and pain with food, alcohol, other people and social media. It's a cinch to turn away.

The next time you are angry or sad or feeling like just giving up on your partner, please try and 'turn towards' them. Face them. Breathe. If you have nothing good to say, take 20 minutes to cool down. When you are ready, tell them how you are feeling, not how they 'made' you feel (there's a big difference). Watch your tone, and connect.

CONCLUSION

In his book *Intimacy*, Ziyad Marar uses the example of the film *Lost in Translation*, in which Bob (Bill Murray), a fading actor, and Charlotte (Scarlett Johansson), a young philosophy graduate from Yale, are both feeling somewhat depressed and enjoy a brief encounter. Free from any emotional baggage that a relationship carries and knowing they are not forging a future together, it allows an openness between them that is quite rare. A no-strings-attached vulnerability fest. Often it is in your most intimate relationships that you hold back on the truth, for fear of hurting your partner or your relationship, even if the truth would be beneficial. It's all too easy to deaden the connection needed to fuel an intimate relationship and slip into the 'shopping list' mode of love. This kind of 'love' is like eating scraps from the bin when there's a feast laid out on the table right in front of you. It brings no satisfaction or joy.

True intimacy, Marar says, is 'reciprocal, conspiratorial, emotional and kind' – that sense of *'I know you and you know me'*. For connection, the prerequisite is allowing another person into your vulnerability. As Marar sees it, the conspiracy comes from the power that person has to hurt you because they know you.

I'm asking you to let your loved one see the real you. This is the key for true love. The risk is always worth it. Be kind and gentle, but also be courageous and daring. Love deeply. Pay attention and be emotionally responsive to your partner. Nurture each other and remember love is not just for the young, your heart desires and needs a deeply fulfilling expression of love.

Bowlby, the father of attachment, was talking with his wife and she asked: 'Why don't you call it the theory of love?' 'Because,' he said, 'I'd be laughed out of science.' However, there is a new revolution of understanding what love means and how we are wired to connect. I feel there is a marriage between love and science and we can all benefit from understanding ourselves and what love means in our most important relationship.

For all the bad stories about marriages and relationships, I want to finish on the good. Build up your emotional bank account with each other. Purposefully remembering the good and what you like about each other is an exercise that will bring you both a lot of joy.

DIARY

✧ *'I really love my partner.'* Write down three things you like about them and why, and then tell them. _____

_____

_____

_____

✧ When did you realise you had fallen in love? Write them a card with where it was, what happened and how you felt. _____

_____

_____

_____

Parenthood

Common sense is genius dressed in its working clothes.

Ralph Waldo Emerson

INTRODUCTION

This chapter looks at the relationship you have with yourself as a parent. It's a personal explorative guide as to what parenthood means and feels like to you. If you have children, you are already aware that nothing can prepare you for the effect being a parent has on you and your partner or spouse. Being a parent is both amazing and amazingly challenging.

But modern parenting seems to have become very complicated. There are so many facets to it, from birth choices to social media. We are inundated with parenting advice, but we are also inundated with bad news that creates a constant and immediate sense of threat and danger. Add to this the fact that completing daily superhuman tasks is the job description of every parent. Quite frankly, it can be head-melting.

Parenthood is a battleground of opposing forces, both internal and external. It's a rollercoaster of the strongest emotions – from feeling overwhelmed and overwrought to the highest peaks of joy. All of these are bound by the common thread of love. Then there are the inner worries – *'Am I doing a good enough job?'* – and feelings of guilt stemming from the conflict between home and work life. I feel many have lost confidence in their natural parenting instinct due to information/advice overload.

Parents need to trust themselves again. Parents know their children.

I want you to leave this chapter knowing that, in terms of your children, you are the expert, and having a renewed sense of confidence in yourself as a parent. This chapter asks you to stand back and see all the parenting notions that bombard you with their opinions of how you should parent, and also to look at which elements you've inherited from your own parents. What you've brought with you from your own childhood is the origin of your belief systems, values, rules and roles as a parent. Here you'll find the blueprint of your beliefs and behaviours about how children *should* behave and how you *should* parent. The *shoulds* always carry guilt, so becoming aware of these is a huge first step in understanding yourself as a parent and assessing if any changes are required to improve the experience for you and your child(ren).

COMMON ISSUES

One of the toughest things about being a parent is the dizzying number of roles and expectations it encompasses. On any given day you will be a chauffeur, cook, teacher, slave (I jest, sort of), carer, nurturer, 'doctor', problem-solver, parent, partner, cleaner, guardian of right and wrong, organiser. Parents are a walking memory bank of a million bits of flittering information, from birthday parties, to bringing in the euro to school, to one sandwich with butter and the other without, WhatsApp activities scheduling director, worker/boss or stay-at-home parent. It's a full-time juggle. It's no surprise, then, that over time many lose themselves to the needs of parenthood.

Parents have stepped up their game so much for their children in terms of their physical, emotional and psychological development, but I ask you: what have you done for yourself lately? I will come back for the answer at the end of this chapter where we will look at how to make it happen.

It is so easy to lose yourself to parenthood. The constant demand, and being on the clock, or more specifically on the kids' clock, with demands coming at you from every angle. If we take each of your inner lives as parent, partner, daughter/son, worker and friend (when you can manage to arrange a night out!), there isn't much space left for you, or is there any at all? That space seems to be getting smaller and smaller. My concern is that the joy is being eroded by an unending to-do list, never fully finishing anything and scrambling to get that work email back at 10.00 pm. All this leaves parents feeling exhausted and like they are not pleasing anyone. Guilt, loneliness and increased stress are becoming all too common. Comparing themselves to other parents and the deluge of opinion via the media can leave parents feeling sorely lacking.

I want you to get your sense of self back. This will require bucking the guilt trend and doing things that you like. Here's the thing: parents are highly appreciative creatures, small amounts of time to themselves to pursue a hobby or hit the gym, meet a friend for coffee or just sit and chill in silence with a book are golden tickets to worn-out parents.

Let these ideas sit with you for a while.

Your past family dynamics govern how you react to your own children today. Your children set off old emotional feelings that make you sensitive to certain words, tones or situations. These triggers are made up of your inner child's unmet emotional needs, and the voice of a harsh, critical, angry or emotionally distant parent. These parenting buttons are freshly triggered by your children and/or by how your partner parents, which can directly impact the connection and relationship you have with your children. Your primary attachment style will be activated, often unconsciously. This is when the implicit *shoulds* come into play and why you feel such strong reactions when your children do something you think they *shouldn't*.The aim of the discussion and exercises here is to illuminate and help you notice what is not working for you, but with no judgement or guilt. That way, you can change patterns of behaviour that seem like split-second reflexes into something more helpful for you, for your children and your relationship. The trick is to bring some mindful awareness into your day and really notice the small joys that happen amidst the chaos. To notice that funny little smile, to luxuriate in the morning snuggle or that lovely leg hug as they look up at you and beam. One of the issues common to all parents that can become an obstacle is procedural memory. We met this in Chapter 2, but it is central to how we parent. It comes out particularly in the 'mummy wars', where judging, being judged and feeling judged take up a lot of headspace. There is a reason for all the judging, as child psychiatrist Dr Kaylene Henderson explains, and it's all down to procedural memory, which is the voice in your head insisting, *'this is the right way to do it'*. So when the words *'I'm turning into my mother'* tumble out of your mouth, they reflect the truth – you have been learning how to parent from day one, from how your parents parented you.

Procedural memories are memories of how you do things, from getting dressed to riding a bike to driving a car. Without them, everything would take a long time to do, so this type of autopilot gets the job done. Consciously, people balk at the idea and think, *'I'll never do/say that to my kids'*, and yet, much to your horror, you find yourself doing exactly that. This is not your fault, it's just a case of unconscious hardwiring.Parenting feels so personal, that's why comments or unsolicited advice about your parenting can feel like a personal attack because it relates directly back to your understanding of *'how'* to parent. So, they are not just saying it to you, they are saying it to your mother as well! Dr Henderson shows that judgement and defensiveness from other parents directed towards you stems from their deep-seated belief that the way you are doing it is wrong, merely because that's not how they do it. They *feel* this at that deep *I* level, which is very hard for them to counteract.

When this happens, it's down to their procedural memories being different from yours. It's like seeing a person trying to drive from the passenger seat. The familiarity of how you should drive coming up against the ineffective and plainly wrong way you are doing it sits really uncomfortably in the brain. It looks and feels wrong and judgement jumps in.

We are assigning this opposing procedural memory to 'other people', but a common problem is when the two memory types are residing in the one house. It becomes even more complicated when you have your own dyad with your parents, and then you add to the mix your partner's dyad with their parents. As you discover and unveil each inner self in your Russian doll, you can see the thread from understanding yourself, the influences of your siblings and your romantic attachment, to the triggers of unmet emotional needs stemming from your attachment style with your parents. The thread continues and intensifies as we bring all these layers, belief systems and values to parenting, all of which are unconscious and stored in great detail in your procedural memories. No wonder parenting is tough! The truth is that if you want to consciously parent, rather than revert to the autopilot version, which of course is much easier to do, you need to put the work in. You have to notice and be aware of what you're doing. Standing on the side of the parenting 'pitch', watch how you parent play out, look at how you react to your child when they throw a temper tantrum, at any age. What is your immediate reaction – are you calm, or do you feel irritated and/or annoyed by them? Now, close your eyes and remember how your parent reacted to you in that situation. Your child has now learned how to react to their future child.

It is so easy to react in the moment, and miss what need the child is expressing. It is this connection that we are wired for and it's when a child's behaviour seems frustrating or bad that you need to pause and think: what is this really about? This is emotionally responsive parenting in action.

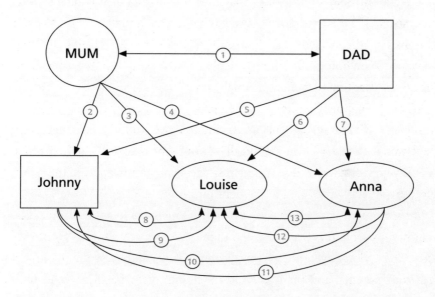

I'm showing you the family dyad again to illustrate the complexity of all the separate dyads, or pairings, between each person in a family and how it is also intergenerational, with beliefs and norms carried from one generation and family to the next. The point of showing you the relationship dyads is to clearly show the behind-the-scenes unconscious threads that we often have no awareness of and yet, like puppets on a string, our behaviour is influenced and directed by the procedural memories of:

- *'This is how it is done';*
- *'This is the right way';*
- *'This is how I parent'.*

DIARY

1. Think back to any major arguments you've had with your partner about parenting. What were they about? Is there a common pattern? _____
   _____
   _____
   _____

2. Did you feel very strongly, even to the point where you didn't know why you felt so strongly? _____
   _____
   _____
   _____

3. Did you have a strong sense that what you were feeling was right? ____
   _____
   _____
   _____

4. What were you defending? _____
   _____
   _____
   _____

5. Are you abdicating any responsibility for your part in the argument? ___
   _____
   _____
   _____

6. Why is this? Is it because you feel your partner is just not doing it right?
   _____
   _____
   _____

Here's a tip on how to recognise when you, or your partner, hits upon one of these procedural memories and a *'this is how you parent'* rule.

1. The feeling will come very fast.
2. You will feel highly reactive.
3. You will probably utter not-very-mature things in rapid-fire mode, such as *'I can't believe you said that to him'* or *'You did what? That's not how it is done'*.

When this happens, it will quickly trigger unresolved emotional hurts from childhood, and you will project these onto your partner.

The question to ask when this happens is: Who are you really angry with?

Anger is the usual emotion in this line-up as the over-riding feeling is, '*this is not the right way to do it*'. First, try to acknowledge why you feel the way you do. How do you 'know' that this is the right way to do it? Where did you see this done first? Stay with the feeling – if possible, take a few minutes by yourself and connect to what you are feeling. Breathe in and out and ask yourself: What am I really angry about? At first, you may find that the surface anger is still towards your partner, but when you sit with it for a bit you may see that they have inadvertently activated your attachment and internal working model of '*this is how it is done*'. These procedural memories can trigger a strong response. So much of this is happening below the surface of consciousness, which is why the partner usually bears the brunt of it, even though it has nothing to do with them really.

Stand back, explain to your partner what this means to you. It can be really helpful to have a discussion afterwards where you both come up with a new way of doing it. This can create your own unique parenting style that both parents find helpful. You could even come up with a humorous way of saying '*you're triggering me*' to break the tension. These implicit, hardwired ways of behaving get triggered very specifically in parenthood. The key is to know when you are being triggered and to decide that you want to choose how to respond, rather than blindly react.

If you come from a difficult or dysfunctional family, you might find your procedural memory buttons are highly receptive to being set off. Your primary attachment is activated when you feel threatened. These buttons are highly sensitive because of past hurts, unmet emotional needs and fear. Often children from families where there were a lot of issues will have been in a state of hyper-arousal and hypervigilance. When they felt threatened, they needed to know how to react, for example to escape to their room or stay quiet to avoid the consequences. Their pattern of avoidance, anxiety or confusion in these untenable circumstances made it impossible to use a healthy strategy to work things through. This can be seen in children with a parent who had addiction problems, as this hypervigilance carries into adulthood. This dynamic can create hot spots of reactivity between parents. If one parent has a secure attachment style, they can facilitate growth in their partner by showing it's possible to have an argument without serious consequences.

Parents may say things like *'they are my children'* in a heated argument as a counter-threat to tell a partner to back off when a perceived threat has been activated. Mary's story provides a good example.

Mary's whole body seemed to be beating. Her head felt like it might explode. She couldn't believe John had been so harsh to Anna. It was nothing, she just spilt her water. Yes, it went everywhere, but it was easily mopped up. Dinnertimes of late had felt anything but 'happy families', more like 'stressed family'. She hated seeing Anna's frightened little face when he shouted at her. Her little eyes welled up with tears as she looked at her daddy in disbelief.

Dinnertime was a value that Mary held close to her heart. She wanted so badly to create a 'normal' family for her children, like the ones she had seen on TV as a child. The reality for Mary was that she had a father who drank too much and until the door opened each evening, she didn't know if 'nice daddy' or 'angry mean daddy' was coming home. Drunk daddy's anger filled up the whole house, even when he said nothing. She could tell from how he breathed what mood he was in. It filled Mary's body with fear.

Mary stood up from the table and quickly excused herself, as she knew the tears were coming, and fast. John followed her up the stairs.

'I'm sorry, Mary, but come on, I never get cross with Anna. I think this is a complete overreaction.'

The normally quiet and reserved Mary unleashed a torrent of anger on John. He stood there, shocked, as she personally annihilated him.

John was really thrown by the whole episode and Mary couldn't seem to get past it. She was so angry, and no matter how much he apologised, it seemed to make no difference. They decided to go for therapy. When both parents gave their account of what had happened, Mary became very upset again. John was really uncomfortable as he felt like she was making him out to be a monster and he knew he was a really good dad, not perfect, but a really good dad.

Becoming a parent brought up many issues that Mary had about her childhood. She had an issue with anger, she hadn't realised she was terrified of it. When she looked closer, she saw the pattern had always been there. But it really came to the fore when she became a mother. She fiercely protected the kids. It upset her to the core if they were upset, even more so if someone else had upset them. As they worked through timelines and the psychodynamic patterns from Mary's childhood, she knew what she didn't want to do as a parent.

She began to realise that she hadn't left any room for John to make any mistakes. She had unconsciously created an impossible expectation for him to be a 'perfect parent'. Any mistake he made received such a huge outburst, it left John feeling somewhat defeated and worried for the future of their relationship. She apologised for the personal attack on him as a father, and recognised that her anger was misplaced.

She began to write out and acknowledge what her experiences were as a child. It brought up a lot of pain, sadness and fear, but in doing so, it also validated many important sad and difficult times that had been sitting so close to the surface in her for years. The weight of this had made Mary feel very vulnerable.

She began to create healthy boundaries. She shared with John how she hoped they could parent, and he began to understand that if her reaction was very strong, perhaps it was an older wound being retriggered. As a result, rather than be defensive, he would come at the issue with compassion and kindness, and would ask her, 'Was it really about split water ?'

It's worth noting, though, that without that insight, which is so hard to identify yourself, the cycle of unmet needs from Mary's childhood would have been projected into their relationship, and to their watching child. This would have kept the cycle of intergenerational hurts going.

Framing your feelings and response from a place of kindness, with a sense of compassion for your inner child and their unmet needs, can release you from these emotions by clearing and processing them. The key is to notice them, name them and realise what they are telling you. When you do this, you can own the emotions rather than the emotions owning you. Parents can engage in being emotionally responsive to each other's needs, which can be a major salve to old wounds.

Parenting isn't easy, and it can bring up all sorts of emotions you may have thought were long buried. I commend you on your desire to understand yourself better, the consequences and benefits of which will positively affect you, and everyone in your life.

KEY THEORIES

It's a fairly safe assumption to make that all parents really want the best for their children. Parenting is noisy and busy. A lot of the noise comes from within your home, but much of it also comes from outside your home, in the form of ideas on *'how'* you should parent. This overload of opinions is a key issue for parents. It's a mixed bag – from some expert and evidence-based theories that are really helpful to opinions that can be conflicting, confusing and unhelpful. This chapter is about you and supporting you as a parent. I have always championed the importance of minding parents' mental and emotional health. Within all the noise of advice, I am asking for you to know yourself, to find your parenting voice, to get back to trusting your own parenting instinct. To that end, I'm going to zone in on one theory that I feel cuts through the noise and gets to the heart of being a parent, linking straight back to the fundamental principles of attachment in terms of the quality of the parent-child relationship.

Professor Alison Gopnik, author of *The Gardener and the Carpenter*, gives the view that as opposed to 'parenting', we need to think about what it means to be a parent. This is an important distinction. Parenting is about 'doing' and creating your idea of the best future for your child. Being a parent is about the primal job of connection and nurturing, it's about creating that future now, with the strong bonds of love and parental connection. I like Gopnik's 'manifesto against parenting', in which she argues that parent is not a verb.

Gopnik describes the 'carpenter' approach as the modern parenting blueprint, which sees 'parenting' as the job of turning your child into its most 'successful' adult self. This works off a predetermined, fixed idea of how you want your child to turn out. A carpenter sets out to make a chair, even though the 'chair' might want to be something else. How many parents have tried to make their child 'be a chair' because that's what they did and what their grandparents did before them?

The side-effect of this approach is that children are afraid to try and fail. This type of parenting robs children of the chance to learn, grow, fall and then stand back up again. The consequences of this over-handling can be seen in rising levels of child and adolescent anxiety. Skills such as autonomy and resilience and day-to-day coping seem to be dipping, directly affecting the quality and wellbeing of young people's lives.

The 'gardener' approach, on the other hand, provides a child with a safe space where they can grow and thrive. This is what Gopnik describes as 'being a parent'. You give your child space to face and manage adversities, and you give them space to try and fail. Failure is a wise teacher. It allows the child to feel, acknowledge and learn. It is a real growth mindset in action.

The 'growth mindset', coined by Stanford psychologist Carol Dweck, states that people who have a fixed mindset believe their intelligence or talent is fixed. Whereas, people with a growth mindset see that hard work, resilience and a love of learning are the starting point to their basic qualities, like intelligence.

The carpenter-parent carves out a person in terms of their idea of success; the gardener-parent plants seeds and watches how they choose to grow – they might fall on barren ground, learn and regrow, or they might fall on good soil and bloom. It's an interesting dual image to consider, and it can help you decide what kind of parent you want to be.

If you question if you're doing a good job as a parent – and, let's face it, we all go through times like that – one good way back to yourself is to ask: Why did I become a parent? What does being a parent mean to you? In my work, universal themes show up time and time again. Meaning is one of them, through the idea of living a meaningful life. This is intimately connected to a sense of purpose. One positive aspect of being a parent is that it gives your life deep meaning, and you'll rarely find yourself without a purpose! This is a very comforting thought when times are tough.

Ultimately, being a parent – as Gopnik sets out – means to care and to love, to nurture and to foster a relationship with your child within an emotionally responsive, open and kind family. 'It is to love, connect, bond, share, cry, laugh and to give and take.' You don't see gardeners hovering around their flowers and shouting, *'Grow, will you! Not like that!'* Flowers know what to do, the gardener just has to provide good conditions for growth.

If you find it difficult to be hands-off, ask yourself why this is. Is it because you don't trust your child? Do you fear their mistakes? Or are you afraid that you're not good enough as a parent and this is your way of trying to control your own fears of their failure? I ask you to step away from judging yourself, it's quite possible your child/adolescent has made a mistake and it was very hard to watch this happen. Having said that, if you pick up and fix every problem, they won't be able to have or develop the skillset to problem-solve, and ultimately the message is that you don't think they can do it, which impacts their self-efficacy and confidence. It seems counterintuitive, but failure will help them grow and they will grow in confidence and self-esteem because they did survive or get through it and it was hard.

The ever-increasing figures for numbers of people, of all ages, suffering from anxiety tell their own story. A carpenter-parent is going to be anxious, as is their child. It is very helpful to review your idea of what being a parent means, and what your job is. Try to see yourself as a conduit, creating a reliable, loving and supportive home environment in which your children can grow to become independent adults who are true to themselves.

The gardener-parent knows that:

- your child knows how to grow;
- you can nurture and clear the weeds;
- ultimately, your child is an individual and inherently knows what's right for them;

- real independence is the goal, which is a healthy mix of them knowing they can depend on you emotionally, that you are their safe haven and base from which to explore and venture forth on their own;
- there will be mistakes, but also that failure should be viewed as learning. Your job is to be there to see, hear and validate the wounds.

The tools a lot of children and adolescents are missing are life skills. Children need room to grow, so guide rather than direct them, let them learn to grow through and within adversity. You did, and it served you well. Your parents did, and it served them well. Let your children do the same. At the root, you are their stable place that they return to be heard and seen. Within that relationship of emotional responsiveness, you are their home.

If we look to the 'baby', the last piece in the Russian nesting doll, it is the only one that is an undecorated and unpainted piece of wood. What shapes that baby is 50% the combined genes and temperament of you and your partner, and 50% the child's own nature and their response to your nurture. Without going into the nature/nurture debate, suffice to say as a parent, you can lead, direct and inspire, you can love and learn together, but you cannot control.

As we have already seen, the 'golden ticket' in parenting is to develop a secure attachment style with and for your child. You may or may not have this attachment style yourself, but that doesn't matter, because you can create it for your child. It requires you to be an emotionally responsive parent, and do be this consistently. These are the key things an emotionally responsive parent does in any situation:

- kneel down, with open arms and heart, meet your child eye to eye;
- heal through your touch and voice;
- comfort, soothe and be there when they need their needs met;
- let them find in you a safe haven when they are scared or worried;
- listen.

The theory of this is clear, but the practical side of doing this when you are bleary-eyed with sleep deprivation is another thing. That is why as a parent you need to practice self-care and compassion for yourself, which we will look at in the next section.

THE PRACTICE

Parenting is not about perfection. You need to repeat that last sentence and remember it like a mantra.

Parenting is not about perfection.

If you keep the core tenets of love at the centre of your parenting, you will have a guide and this will help you identify when you have gone slightly, or completely, off-track. There is no shame in making mistakes, but it is a shame when you don't learn from and correct your mistakes. For a happy and emotionally healthy home, let love guide your parenting. Prioritise and incorporate love, as you would the other four prerequisites of daily parenting: feeding, washing, dressing and bedtime.

DIARY

Let's go back to that key question: how do you want to parent? In order to get at a comprehensive answer, answer these questions:

◇ What does it mean to you to be a parent? _____

_____

_____

◇ What are your hopes and dreams for you, your children and your partner?

_____

_____

_____

◇ Do you have any unrealistic expectations of yourself, your partner or your children? _____

_____

_____

_____

✧ Are you/would you be disappointed when/if these expectations don't/ didn't happen? _____

_____

_____

_____

✧ What has surprised you in reality about being a parent? _____

_____

_____

_____

✧ What have you found most challenging? _____

_____

_____

_____

✧ What has exceeded your expectations? _____

_____

_____

_____

✧ What brings joy to your heart as a parent? _____

_____

_____

_____

✧ Do you think your inner child or any old wounds have been triggered by yourself, your children or partner? If so, how? _____

_____

_____

_____

✧ How has becoming parents changed your relationship with your partner? List how it has changed it 'for the better' and 'for the worse'. _____

_____

_____

_____

_____

You now have a better idea of what kind of parent you are, and what kind of parent you would like to be. What are the obstacles to fully becoming the kind of parent you want to be? One of the main obstacles will be your triggers – those buttons your kids instinctively know how to push that cause an automatic reaction, from anger, to frustration, to envy. You may feel a sense of loss when you see your child doing something that you would like to have done as a child. The core principle is evident in this case: it is about you and not them. In the heat of the moment, that can be a very tough thing to see or feel clearly. Again, it might be useful to say, *'this isn't Mark trying to make me late on purpose, my old trigger is what lateness meant in my family'*. The key words are *'my trigger'*. The child's behaviour may seem to be triggering this automatic response in you, but it is really *your reaction* to what the behaviour means to you, and that has been triggered by your past. You need to sit with the *I* of your hidden belief systems and ask yourself: why am I experiencing these strong emotions?

You will be in no doubt when you have been triggered: it is a strong, immediate reaction to your child and often you will feel they *'are doing this just to annoy or upset me'*. You may find yourself shouting, becoming upset, angry or all three. Watch your reaction to them, are you angry? Do you want to punish or shame the child? How did you parents react to you when you were loud, noisy, messy, rude, silly?

Common triggers can be when your child is:

* being noisy;
* arguing back at you;
* ignoring you;
* not eating their food;
* eating too much food;
* being able to be themselves;
* doing risky things;
* fighting with their sibling;
* not sharing;
* being unkind;

* being rude;
* being angry;
* moving too slowly;
* being bossy;
* lying;
* being messy;
* crying;
* being silly.

Can you add to that list any triggers that are specific to you? Being aware of your triggers can really help you. Another common one is when the parent doesn't actually know how to respond to the situation. This can make you feel frustrated, helpless and the *'not good enough'* fear raises its ugly head.

In that temporary feeling of irritation to anger, parents can feel impulsive, words coming out of their mouths that they later regret when lying in bed awake. It is your discomfort, fears and past experiences that can lead you to become over-protective and deeply upset when you see your child in pain and you want to protect them at all costs. Triggers are not straightforward, they may feel like your child is pushing all your buttons just to get a rise out of you, or to drive you mad. But in fact, the triggers belong to you.

This is where you have to look back within your Russian doll of you, the many layers and roles you carry. How were you reprimanded – was it through guilt, shame, ridicule, anger, fear or respect and kindness? You can change this to being an emotionally responsive parent to the child in front of you, and not your inner child, in that moment.

The easy part is being triggered, but what can you do to change your reaction to a response that helps you sleep better at night? First, identify your triggers, then ask: why? The example below of Melissa shows how lying proved to be one such trigger for her. Why does lying trigger such a strong response in you? What does that behaviour mean to you? How were you reprimanded as a child in that specific situation?

THE SECRET LIVES OF ADULTS

Melissa was about to lose her head, she could feel it, the anger was coursing through her body and her biggest fear was it was about to burst out of her mouth and be launched on her daughter. 'Why am I so angry right now', Melissa thought to herself. Yes, Lisa was lying to her face, she could see that, but she was only a child. 'Lisa, I'm going to ask you to think about what happened again and we'll chat together later.'

Melissa couldn't believe that she was crying, what was wrong with her? Who was the child here? But the tears fell down her face as she locked the bathroom door and to her utter dismay, the tears kept coming and she sobbed. She sat with how difficult this felt for her, and decided she needed to get to the bottom of it. In sessions they had talked about her inner child, she thought about when she had lied as a child. This was fairly easy, as she lied a lot as a child. In her mind it was a fairly good strategy as her mother would lambast her verbally when she forced her to tell the truth. It became a major power struggle between them, but her fear stopped her from being able to speak. Her mother took this as extra insolence and would lash at her personally: 'you are nothing but a horrible little liar. Look at you, look at you, what is wrong with you?'

Can you see the origin of the triggered feeling? Can you list these, e.g. feeling ignored, unheard or pushed around (when your child triggers this from not listening to you or being bossy). Bring it back to your inner child's unmet needs. How did you get your parents' attention, did they listen or were your bids for attention ignored?

Even though the tears kept coming, Melissa felt a sort of relief. Lisa was only a child, and a scared one at that. She thought back to Lisa's big eyes looking up at her a moment before, and she recognised the fear. Her mother's harshness and absolutes created a very black and white, right or wrong framework that Melissa wanted to change. She went back to Lisa. She knelt down and looked her daughter in the eye and spoke softly: 'None of us is perfect, if you did lie, that's OK, what I'd hope is that you can be honest with me. I may not like what I am hearing, but we all make mistakes and I will still like you. I want you to be able to tell me.'

Not only does changing your triggers improve the relationship with your child, it will directly help you as well. It frees you from years of being triggered. Being able to identify and spot them is a wonderful tool to have in your parenting toolbox.

So think to times when you have been triggered and see if you can discern a pattern specific to your reactions.

- Is it when you have too little time, are hungry or tired?
- Is it when you have too much to do and feel stressed or overwhelmed?
- Are you less patient if you're hungover?

These relate back to you, the initial trigger starts with how *you* have been triggered by your child and how it relates back to what it means to *you*. Added to that are your own human feelings of being hungry or tired. Keep breathing, acknowledge how you feel – *'right now I am feeling unhappy, stressed, too rushed'* – as this can bring the frustration down and even though it doesn't change the fact that you are late or stressed, validating that feeling is deeply supportive to yourself as you are recognising how hard it is for you in that moment.

What can you do to change your reaction next time?

- Identify the root of the trigger.
- It is not the child, it is your automatic reaction and what this behaviour means to you.
- To reduce parental regret, take a break, pause and reflect on what you need.
- Self-soothe – what unmet need in you is being brought to the fore? Write this down.
- How can you meet those needs in yourself now, e.g. if you feel unheard, can you learn and try to bring in more assertive behaviour?
- Say sorry to your child – *'I'm sorry I shouted at you, I can get angry sometimes as well, I wasn't sure of what to do either'* – and ask can you give a big hug. Not only will this repair attempt strengthen your

connection, it models healthy behaviours and emotions for your child as well.

- Actively engage in self-compassion and self-empathy. Listen to your inner voice, ask for it to be kind and not rude!
- Notice who sets your triggers off. If it is your child, did your parent(s) react in the same to you? Take a moment to reflect on this.
- How did it feel when your parent(s) was irritated or cross with you as a child?
- Do you still have an inner critic?
- Did you ever wonder where that parental inner voice came from? How did your parent(s) talk to you?

While it might be difficult to acknowledge, it is important to remember that your voice may become your children's inner voice, narrating how they react to their successes and failures and how they decipher the cues given by people and situations across their lives. Speak to your child as you want them to speak to themselves.

Learning how to pause before reacting is a very powerful tool. When you feel yourself reacting strongly to a situation, ask yourself: Is my reaction really just about this? You'll often find that your surface reaction relates to a hidden trigger, or past wound.

1. When strong feelings start, press your *pause* button.
2. Breathe and then breathe again.
3. Remember to 'mind the gap' between the stimulus (child is cheeky to you) and your response (immediate anger).

The key action after you have hit your 'pause' button is to 'mind the gap'. When automatic triggers are hit, it can feel like you have no control and impulsive words and actions spill out – *'you are so messy'*, *'you rude child'* – and on they go. By being aware that these old feelings are being quickly triggered, you can choose to see that there is a gap between what has occurred and your response, in other words, that your reaction is greater than the incident warrants. If you can see the gap, you become in control again. This is not to say it is easy, your body knows how to react without a second thought, so it takes patience, skill and a lot of breathing to change to how you want to be.

How to change your response:

- Ask where and when did you feel this feeling first?
- Write out and acknowledge how you feel – do this on your own.
- Notice other times this pattern has been triggered, and why?
- Reconnect – talk to and include your partner.
- Make a plan together of shared parenting values.

DIARY

More work for you now – let's look at your embedded ideas and values around parental roles.

✧ What do you feel your role is as a mother or father? _____
_____
_____
_____

What did you learn about your role as a parent from:
✧ Your mother? _____
_____
_____

✧ Your father? _____
_____
_____

✧ Your grandmother? _____
_____
_____

✧ Your grandfather? _____
_____
_____

◇ Your siblings? _____
_____
_____

◇ Your extended family? _____
_____
_____

◇ Your friends? _____
_____
_____

◇ Other mothers? _____
_____
_____

◇ Other fathers? _____
_____
_____

◇ Work? _____
_____
_____

◇ Society? _____
_____
_____

◇ Books? _____
_____
_____

◇ Media? _____
_____
_____

We've established that you've taken in information from many different sources, and added your own experiences. Drawing on all that, what are the key psychological bases of parenting? In my opinion, there are five prerequisites to consider.

1. Love.
2. Being emotionally responsive.
3. Boundaries.
4. Fostering failure.
5. Parental self-care.

These prerequisites are the foundations upon which families flourish. They are basic, but nonetheless fundamental to establishing a connected and quality parent-child attachment. In the rush of highly scheduled lives, theirs and yours, it is easy to lose that connection. Keeping these as your family staples will guide you and nurture their sense of security, of being a valuable person in their own right and within the family, and increase the sense of joy of belonging in your family.

1. Love

The overarching theme through this book is love. That sense and inner knowledge of feeling that you belong and are safe are the basis of adult happiness. Love brings a whole host of good feelings, while an absence of love has the opposite effect. If your parents gave you a secure sense of attachment, you will have felt loved. This sets you up for adulthood. If, however, your parental attachment was insecure or ambivalent, you will have to deal with a difficult legacy. But as we noted in Chapter 1, that legacy does not define you. If you are willing to work on yourself, you can change and grow.

Components of love	Feelings associated with love	Feelings associated with absence of love
Acceptance	An acceptance of you, warts and all	Feeling unaccepted
Security	A sense of safety that comes from the bond between a parent and child	Insecurity, doubt, caution, fear
Belonging	Feeling a part of the family unit	Distant, no sense of belonging or connectedness
Warmth	Warm-heartedness from your parents makes you feel whole	Feeling of emptiness or a void
Respect	Having a connected relationship built on mutual respect and admiration	Lack of respect, feeling you are unimportant
Admiration	Fostering a sense of self-worth and value	Lack of self-worth

We'll examine each of those components of love in turn. This can help you identify the 'how', which is often the missing link.

Acceptance: Acceptance is a word often used, but often misunderstood. It does not mean you like or agree with something, it means you have accepted the situation as it is. The practice of this can be tough when family culture, history and pride are at play.

Sean had always dreamed of being on the stage. He was thrilled to get accepted as the lead in To Kill a Mockingbird. *But with the high came a quick sinking feeling. He knew his dad, John wanted him to play rugby, and the times clashed. Sean hated rugby with the same passion as his dad loved it.*

Sean: 'Dad, I've something I need to talk to you about. I know how important rugby is to you, but I really don't like it.'

Dad: 'Sean, you have to give it a chance, you've only been playing a few years.'

Sean: 'I'm quitting rubgy because I got the main part in a play and ...'

Dad: 'You are not! No son of mine is a quitter.'

Sean: 'I am and you can't stop me. I'm not you!'

The two walked away from each other and John spoke with his wife, Susie. It was a hard conversation, and one that took over a week to really sink in. John's choice was to accept Sean as he was, or risk losing the relationship they had, which was usually good. For John, rugby was important to his whole family and it was the bond between his father and himself, so it was difficult to let it go.

Sean asked his dad to come to the play. He did, and John felt so proud of his son. Sean was superb in the role and it was obvious acting was his talent. John felt a whole new level of respect for his son's commitment and courage.

Acceptance of people, especially your own children, can prove tricky when your own past, feelings, hopes and dreams may be projected onto your child. Parents can feel disappointment when their hopes don't come to fruition. Accepting your child as they are is a beautiful but sometimes painful process. But accepting them, their choices and their individual identity as separate to yours can create a deep interconnectedness through lovingly accepting them as they are.

Security: Security isn't just the roof over their head, your children's emotional security is where they know they can trust you and they feel safe. To promote a sense of security, it is essential to keep the dialogue open and authentic – at every age. You need to be their go-to person, especially when they need to tell you about something that made them feel bad or sad. Shaming is a silencer and a conversation-killer. You need to listen and not judge. If you don't listen, or if you knock the small daily worries down, they won't come to you with the big one that you will want to be part of.

Parent: 'What's going on, Ben? You seem very quiet? Can I help with anything?'

Ben (age 10): 'No.'

Parent: 'Is there anything bothering you? I can see that you look worried.'

Ben: 'I said nothing was wrong.'

Parent: 'OK, I'm here if you'd like to talk.'

Parent goes off and comes back fifteen minutes later and joins Ben on the floor, where he is building Lego.

Parent: 'What are you building?'

Ben: 'A fort.'

Parent: 'That's cool, I like forts.'

Ben: 'Yeah, me too.'

Parent: 'A fort is strong and can keep people out.'

Ben: 'Yeah.'

Parent: 'Would you like to keep anyone out?'

Ben: 'Yeah. Mark.'

Parent: 'Mark, from school?'

Ben: 'Yeah.'

Parent: 'What happened?'

Ben: 'Nothing.'

Parent: 'I can see you are not happy, you can tell me.'

Ben: 'He called me an idiot today in front of all the other guys in yard.'

Parent: 'Has this ever happened before?'

Ben: 'Um ...'

Parent, gently: 'Ben?'

Ben, crying: 'Every day he picks on me.'

Parent: 'I'm so sorry to hear that. Right, I'm going in to beat up Mark tomorrow.'

Ben: 'What?!'

Parent, laughs: 'I'm only joking, ok, what would you like to do about this? Let's make a plan.'

Belonging: Many children have a special teddy or blanket that is their security comfort. A certainty to their day and world. It's the one that's taken to bed and looks 'loved'. It makes them feel that they belong in that bed, in that home. The teddy is merely a childhood symbol of that sense of belonging. As much as hunger is a real need, so too is the emotional need to belong. That sense of belonging, or lack of it, has far-reaching life and relationship implications.

What does belonging feel like? It's that sense of being part of a family that is truly yours. The sense that you are accepted, and that acceptance is validated by everyone's actions and reactions. Your family is your tribe, and you have a natural and unassailable place within it.

Joan has just received a phone call from another parent to say that a photo of her daughter, Julie, in a compromising position is doing the rounds on Snapchat. The immediate feeling for Joan is utter humiliation, then anger, then embarrassment and back to being furious. Joan calls her husband and breathlessly tells him about it. Her normally calm husband is horrified and equally furious. 'I can't believe this, not my Julie. Oh God.'

Joan knew that she needed to process the feelings that were coming up for her. She was fighting back the tears, but she took out her journal and began to do free association, the words splashed on the page with the same speed as her tears: What was Julie thinking? How could she have let something so stupid happen? Did she have no respect for herself? Did she have no respect for us? I have utterly failed her. This will be out there forever. I am so humiliated. How will I face the other parents tomorrow at the school?

Joan took a deep breath and tried to identify the primary cause of her feelings. She began to write again: 'Apart from feeling sick, I know that this is my own shame. I got pregnant at 19 and my mother kicked me out of home. I felt so bad, and I knew she was disgusted by me. I never told her anything again and our relationship ended that day. She seemed to care more about what she thought the neighbours, the priest or her family would think.'

Joan stopped writing and broke down in tears. That was the ultimate rejection, and it had affected her sex life as she ended up feeling that sex was dirty and wrong. The only difference between her situation and her daughter's was that one involved a smartphone. A huge weight lifted off Joan's shoulders. She would not make the same mistake with her daughter. She knew what she had to do – dig deep, put aside her own feelings and focus on listening to and helping her daughter through this difficult time.

When Joan's daughter crept cautiously into the house some time later, Joan gathered her up in her arms. The hug said: you still belong in our family.

Warmth: The feeling of love, belonging and being connected have one thing in common: warmth. There is something so soothing about warmth that changes how you feel, when you know that the people around you accept you for who you are and love to be in your company.

I like the daily inclusion of *hygge*, however it's pronounced! It's the Danish concept of the warm intimacy that arises from eating together and sitting together in a warm, candlelit room. If you and your family walk in your front door with a happy sigh to be 'home', you are doing a lot right. Research backs up the importance of warmth in your daily rituals, such as kissing each other goodbye and again on return. Sounds corny, but I don't think so, it is a physical acknowledgement of you as a person, that you are liked. The intimacy of a kiss, be it on the lips or cheek, says, '*Hi, I really like you and I'm so glad we are together again.*'

In a frantically busy world, these small but important rituals are the backbone of a family. It literally physically connects you to each other. With so much of connection now occurring with our heads bent low, staring at a screen, it's one that I recommend you incorporate into your family life. Here are some ideas for how to do that.

- Watch a film together under a blanket.
- Eat together at a table as often as you can.

- Ask how everyone's day is while looking at them and listening to the answer.
- Look at and listen to whomever is talking to you. If you have smallies, get down to their level and make eye contact. The neurological implications of those eye-to-eye connections create neural pathways for life. Answering half-heartedly while looking at your phone is not the same as making eye contact.
- Have warmth in your tone; warmth in your words; warmth in your hugs.
- Hold hands.

Respect: This is a big one. For parents, disrespect can come in the form of opposition, defiance, not doing what you tell them to do, even if *'because I told you to'* hasn't worked. Parents can feel disrespected when their child doesn't do what they've been asked/told to do. Often, it seems there are only two options: the 'authoritarian' approach, which is not going to cut it; and being 'permissive', but this does neither yourself nor your child any favours.

So, how can you get respect from your kids? Well … give it.

Sometimes I see double standards, and they bother me. We cannot expect to receive what is not given. This is an important question: are you respectful to your children? The old adage of 'respect your elders' is a good one, I think we just need to add 'and respect your youngers'. This way, we create a circle of respect. It's the old 'monkey see, monkey do'. Respect must be mutual.

Tony went out to bring Matthew in. As he approached the group of friends, Matthew rolled his eyes and said 'I'm not coming in yet' and turned away from him. This was like a red flag to Tony as he was truly sick of Matthew's current attitude and disrespect towards him.

'Matthew, you are coming in now. I have given you 20 minutes more than usual.'

'I said I am not coming in. Go home will you, you can't make me.'

Tony knew he was being triggered now, he would never had dreamed of speaking to his parents like this. He also knew this power-play wasn't going to end well for anyone.

'That's OK, Matthew, but I'm plugging you out tomorrow from your game.'

Matthew looked up in horror. 'I actually hate you,' he said as he walked behind his dad.

Matthew went straight online and his dad turned off the Wi-Fi.

'What are you doing? You are trying to ruin my life. I came in, didn't I? Everyone else is still out there.'

'Enough, Matthew, go to bed. We can talk about this tomorrow.'

Tony really wanted to deal with it, but he knew that neither of them would be able to listen to each other as they were both so fired up.

The next day, Tony knocked on Matthew's bedroom door. He sat down on his bed and said, 'I'm sure you were embarrassed with me coming over to your friends, and I understand that, I don't want to embarrass you again but it was not OK to be disrespectful to me, so we need to change this now.'

I am going to trust you to come in at the time that we set. If you break your curfew, then I will not let you out the next night, do it again and it will be for a week. Respect between us is so important, but it's a two-way street. I understand that you want more freedom, but you are only 14, it's my job to be your dad, and you will not like some of my rules but I am going to apply them. You know how exhausted you are in the morning, of course you want to stay out later, I get that, but then I can't wake you up in the morning for school. Do you want to say anything?'

'No.'

'OK, if you change your mind, you know where I am.'

Even though basically no dialogue happened, Matthew could hear what his dad said when he was calm and he knew that he had stepped over the line. He also felt understood in terms of how embarrassing it was for him as his dad was the only dad who came out to bring him in, so he was relieved that wouldn't happen again if he played ball.

Admiration: Admiration is a very strong reward, and it makes us feel good. You only have to look at the online 'like' culture to see our inherent desire to be liked and accepted by those who mean the most to us. The key with children is to foster admiration without giving worthless praise. Foster pride in effort, tenacity and persistence and reward resilience, courage, strength of character and kindness. Catch your kids when they are being kind and acknowledge that. Whatever you focus attention on will grow. You choose if you want that to be negative or positive. Showing your interest and admiration in your children builds their intrinsic and extrinsic self, their sense of personal worth and value as a person in their own right.

Jennifer woke up late, did she actually sleep through her alarm clock? Either way, they were already behind schedule. She woke up Mark, he told her where to go. She tried to wake up the other kids, but no one was budging. She could feel her irritation building and tolerance levels were quickly going down. 'Get downstairs, now!'

The final straw came when she couldn't find Emily's other shoe. She shouted at her and Emily's lip trembled and then the tears came. Even though Jennifer felt so bad, the anger had taken over.

'Where is your shoe?'

'I don't know', said Emily, who just stood there.

By 9.15am Jennifer felt exhausted and defeated. The house was a shambles and she felt everything, from the washing to her mood, was out of control.

She sat down in her messy kitchen, made a cup of coffee and started reading a book her therapist recommended to her, The Everyday Parenting Toolkit *by Alan Kazdin. It all made so much sense. Every word made sense to what was going on in her kitchen that morning.*

The decision was made and she had a plan, she would start pointing out the good to increase this behaviour, such as the kids tidying up and getting ready the night before. She would point out when Mark was kind to Emily. She would point out when Emily was forgiving. She would let the negatives go, or at least she wouldn't give them any attention. She felt empowered and like she had a new language that would work for them all. She started with herself. She gave herself credit for taking the time to read the book while the house was a mess. She knew in that moment she needed to ignore the housework to learn a new language where she fostered admiration towards herself and the family.

....

2. Being emotionally responsive

The key take-away from this chapter is how to be an emotionally responsive parent. For all the components wrapped up in love, it is the practice of being emotionally responsive to your children, your partner and your needs that makes for a happy, contented home.

The three core principles of being an emotionally responsive parent are that you behave in a manner that is:

* sensitive;
* appropriate;
* consistent.

It's about being in tune with your children, recognising and allowing space for individual differences and preferences – *'Jake needs a lead time into what the plan is for the day, whereas John goes along with the plan as the day rolls out'* – and responding in a sensitive, appropriate and consistent way. To ward off any fears of this being unachievable, there will be days when this doesn't go to plan. Just refer back to your mantra: *you don't need to be a perfect parent.* But taking ownership of your own humanness will only add to the connection between you and your children.

There was an interesting study in *Health Psychology* that followed 163 individuals from birth through to age 32, and whose lives had stress present. Predictions of negative long-term impact showed that 'higher maternal sensitivity, however, buffered these deleterious effects'. This is integral to the core of parenting. Regardless of the stress or difficulties faced, if a secure attachment is in place, even with one primary caregiver, it protects and buffers. This is something I have seen in practice from years of working with clients, and it is very heartening and full of hope.

3. Boundaries

One of the best gifts you can give your children are boundaries. They won't thank you for them at the time, but they will stand by them throughout life. The boundaries you set are your family rules. They need to adhere to the 3 Cs:

- ✪ clear;
- ✪ clean; and have
- ✪ consequences.

If you child wants to argue against a boundary you've set, listen before responding. Understand it from their point of view. Explain to them what you have heard: '*this is what I understand …*'. Empathise with them: '*that must be hard for you*'. If necessary, offer a modified alternative, but maintain the set family boundary. Of course, this can be very hard to do in practice, when you have a real, live child complaining bitterly and acting up. The key is to stay calm and not lose your temper.

- Your role is to make the boundaries clear: **these are the rules**.
- Your job is to be the **parent**.
- You will be **un-liked.**
- You will have to **say no.**
- You will **not be their friend**. They have friends, their friends have equal power, you need the power to be unequal as a parent until your child is an adult.
- When limits are transgressed, you have to consistently and firmly stick to the promised consequences.
- Don't make consequences that you won't or can't follow through on as the child will know they have the power and that you're all talk and no action.
- Limits help children make better decisions and engage in less risky activities.

Daughter, heading to local youth disco, comes down wearing very short skirt: 'What? But everyone is wearing ones much shorter than this!'

Parent: 'I hear what you are saying, I can see that you are upset and frustrated as all your friends will be wearing short dresses and skirts, so you want to be the same as them. I understand why you are upset and angry.'

Daughter, breathes, hopeful as she thinks she'll be allowed to wear it.

Parent: 'I remember what it felt like when I was your age, and I thought my parents hadn't a clue. It's weird because actually they did. But trust me, at the time I really, really didn't think they did, and I can imagine you feel the same way now. As your parent and not your friend, I am asking you to choose a dress that is a little longer and I'm offering you the choice to completely blame me to your friends.'

Daughter: 'This is ridiculous, you can't control me. If I can't wear this, I'm not going.'

Parent: 'That's your choice.'

Daughter in disbelief: 'I hate you.'

Parent: 'OK, let me know if you want me to take you. I'll see you in 15 minutes when you have changed.'

4. Fostering failure

Bruce Wayne: *'I wanted to save Gotham. I failed.'*
Alfred: *'Why do we fall, Sir? So that we can learn to pick ourselves up.'*
(*Batman Returns*)

The cult of overnight 'celebrity' has a lot to answer for. It has robbed many young people of understanding that tenacity, hard work and persistence, especially in the face of adversity, are how you succeed. Instead they are presented with the idea that with a cute haircut and a splash of good luck, they can succeed effortlessly. This delusion has created a negative psychological paradigm shift that can be seen within the ethic of school work, and in a fragile, over-inflated self-esteem that can be flattened by normal feedback.

Failure is inevitable, and a great source of growth, it just doesn't feel that way at the time. Life is tough, life is not fair, so it's essential to cultivate the skills you'll need to get back up from it. Life requires mental toughness, and you won't get that from being shielded. This is why I'm an advocate for failure. Children should be given the freedom to try and to fail and they should be allowed the space to stand up and learn from their failure.

I admire babies and toddlers, because they have this gumption to keep getting up when they are literally knocked over. The motivation and desire to move ahead is so powerful because it is without self-consciousness. They aren't thinking, '*What if mum and dad think I'm silly?*' They are completely unencumbered by such thoughts, which means they have the freedom to learn.

As a family, make a point of celebrating effort, as this will count far more than any measure of your child's intelligence or natural ability.

- Be inspired by people and their stories of overcoming adversity and share these stories with your children.
- Talk about what your strengths are and ask what you think their character strengths are. They can try the Values in Action (VIA) youth survey for ages 10–17 (www.viacharacter.org).
- Create a family motto of learning through failure, or get the kids involved in making their own motto about effort, hard work, challenges and how they would handle them.

The key benefit of failure is that you learn how to be resilient, and that in itself is a huge reward. It is a skill, one you have to earn and learn. If we can fall back on ourselves when things go wrong, we'll always have the right support. When your children are young, this is your job: to support them so they can learn how to get back up again. Think about the trampoline you probably have in the back garden. Your children can jump high because the strong springs make sure that when they come down, they bounce right back up again. As a parent, you are their springs.

When a child has this support, they can go forth and try. To try is to learn, but it's also risky and uncertain. It can be attended by fear and feelings of dread as the child drowns in a sea of *what ifs*: what if I do it wrong? What if I am the worst? What if everyone laughs at me?

Remember: to future-proof your child's life, you can't failure-proof it.

5. Parental self-care

So, that covers the key ways to nurture your child, but what about nurturing yourself? This is a crucial part of being a good parent too. For all the giving you do in parenthood, no matter who you are, you have to recharge. I bet you charged your phone today. Why? Because if you don't charge it, it will lose its power and die. Well, the same goes for you. If you don't practice self-care, you may become grumpy, worn out, exhausted, irritable, less effective and not much fun to be around. This can add to your parental guilt if it makes you less tolerant with the kids because your needs haven't been met or are being utterly ignored. You wouldn't ignore your kids like that, they wouldn't let you, so you need to stop ignoring what you need.

Self-care is a huge area – it requires its own book really. That means, much as I'd love to write pages and pages about it, we can only cover a few key points. So I'll break self-care down into its six basic elements.

Sleep: The psychological, emotional and physical importance of sleep is well documented. Putting it into practice can be the hard part. Commit to it for your health and to improve the health of your relationships. Create a healthy bedtime routine that promotes sleep and stick to it for optimum results.

Food: We all know what we ought to do, but it's so easy to take the easy and convenient option when we're busy, stressed and feeling overwhelmed. You need to plan for the week ahead so that you eat three decent meals every day, with three snacks. It doesn't have to be cordon bleu cooking, just simple home-cooked food that your family can enjoy together. Put a few ingrediaents into Google and add 'Jamie Oliver' for some inspiration.

Exercise: Again, hectic schedules can work against us, but once you make a conscious effort to include exercise in your day, you'll soon have created a habit you don't want to drop. Exercise is as much about mental fitness as physical fitness, and it will help you cope with the demands of your life.

Stress: There is so much talk about being happy and about how stressed and overwhelmed people are feeling. If you want to change, you have to make and maintain change. In a society that values busyness as a status symbol, I see our nation heading towards burnout. We are told stress isn't bad for us, but like all things, it needs to be in moderation, and this is the problem in our 'always on' society.

Ask yourself: When was the last time you felt energised or refreshed? Can you identify your stress triggers? Are they people or situations or both?

In order to make the necessary changes, it helps to see yourself as a 'project' and you are the project manager. I see clients who are competent and confident in their work abilities, but then they come home burnt out, exhausted and empty, with nothing left to meet their desire to change things for themselves. Add your needs to the calendar. By breaking each thing down piece by piece, you will do it.

Alcohol/drug intake: Often clients look surprised when I ask if they had been drinking or taken any substance the night before their anxiety or panic attack happened. The only reason I ask is because alcohol and drugs are guaranteed triggers. Your relationship with anything addictive is not a relationship to foster mental wellbeing. It is recommended by health professionals to have non-alcohol days in your week. Is this something you do? Is this something you think you should do? In your Diary, keep tabs on drinking – honestly! – for one week and see for yourself exactly how much you are consuming. If you want to change this, how can you do it? Perhaps make a contract for yourself for the nights you will and will not drink alcohol.

Parental pause: Be actively kind to yourself. Flip the guilt to see all you did well today. Give yourself credit, thanks, encouragement and well-deserved praise. Mind your physical, emotional and mental health. Pause to see the small moments of joy.

And now for the safety warning:

- You can choose not to pay attention to the emergency information on the 'parental' plane.
- Your body will give up before your brain does.
- Don't wait for a health or mental health crisis before you take action.
- You are not a robot.

CONCLUSION

This chapter is merely a snapshot on parenting. I think parents try so hard, and modern parenting seems to have become harder with so many demands and so much advice and such high expectations. The demands on mothers and fathers often seem excessive, and yet parents plough on. The joy of parenting can get lost into busyness and routines, but it needs to be given space to grow. The commodity of time seems to be the missing ingredient.

There is so much information and I could only provide a preliminary glimpse inside the parenting home, mind and self. I am fully aware that there are many other elements in our lives outside of our control that influence our abilities to be the parents we would like to be, such as ongoing or emerging health issues, and many more issues ranging from debilitating doubt to insecurity. My answer is to seek support from your partner, from friends, from professionals. By asking questions and understanding why you feel and think the way you do, you will help yourself in your journey to grow, develop and learn as a parent. Please drop the judgement and engage daily in the practice of self-compassion.

Be that emotionally responsive parent, be sensitive and tune into your needs and be consistent and appropriate when answering yourself. Move from accusation – 'I knew you would do a dreadful job' – to a self-supportive role – 'Wow, this is really bringing up a lot for me, this is very hard' – with empathy and self-kindness. Let this be the cornerstone of your parenting.

Stop fearing getting it wrong. When you make a mistake or the connection breaks, pause, see what is coming up for you. Take a break, if you need to, and then come back to it. Be honest and human with your kids. As you model the breadth of emotions, they come to see how to experience the highs and lows and how to form a healthy response to uncomfortable and difficult emotions and life events.

Connect to you, connect to your parents, connect to your children. Notice what you do well and foster that admiration for yourself and your family. Notice what triggers you and work on these as one learning opportunity at a time. Fear, doubt and judgement are normal but not useful strategies. Give time to notice the good and give yourself the credit you deserve.

Be aware of your own past, and decide how you want to live in the present. See the choices and embrace them. What do you want the story of your family to be? See your key role in this and release old attachment wounds: they do not define you.

Children thrive on certainty, routine and clear boundaries. Many of these parental lines are becoming blurred as parents wish to be their children's friend. Also, the influential impact of social media and technology is diminishing communication skills. In a relatively short space of time there has been a dramatic cultural change in parenting as, thankfully, corporal punishment became taboo at home and in schools. We left behind the old mantra of *children should be seen and not heard*. The constructs of parenting are complex and have changed. This chapter is for you, the parent, to find your voice, guided by evidence-based theory.

DIARY

This is an exercise to focus on the positives and encourage your mind to see possibilities and paths forward.

✧ What are your hopes and dreams for you and your family? _____

_____

_____

_____

✧ Think about this and write your own parenting manifesto. _____

_____

_____

_____

CHAPTER 6

Friends

A friend is one that knows you as you are,
understands where you have been, accepts what
you have become, and still, gently allows you to grow.

William Shakespeare

INTRODUCTION

Robin Dunbar, a professor of evolutionary anthropology at Oxford, has argued that friendship is the single most important factor influencing our health, wellbeing and happiness. This is why learning how to make and keep friends is so important. It's not a given that we'll be able to do this. It takes time and effort to find a friend and to be a friend. Dunbar described how this is 'extremely costly' in terms of the time that has to be put in and the 'cognitive mechanisms that underpin them'. There's a science to friendship and, like each relationship, it is a matter of pulling out the evidence-based information and applying it to our lives in order to garner some serious benefits.

From a psychological perspective, a 2017 study by Chopik of 271,053 adults found that having 'supportive friendships in old age was ... a stronger predictor of wellbeing than having strong family connections'. Why is this? A sense of 'duty' may have impacted family relationships, even if they were good, as opposed to the unencumbered merits of friendship with peers. Friendships enrich our lives in so many ways. Support, kindness, fun, laughter and sharing each other's tears can provide a mutual depth of meaning as you share the highs and lows in each other's lives.

This chapter explains the mechanics and foundations of adult friendships and shows how you can leverage this to help you in every aspect of your personal and working life. The goal is to show you that every single new interaction is an opportunity to build new connections and friendships. Friendship requires effort, of course, and this can pose a problem. A Finnish study found that we continue to make friends until the age of 25, at which point it starts declining. A study from Oxford found you lose two close friends when you fall in love or move house, which are two major adult aspirations. So we shed friends as we go through life, and if we don't replace them, we lose out in a huge way.

'*I made a friend!*' Can you remember the first time you said those joyous words? Most likely, this happened at primary school, when you met that special person who would be with you through your school years. That special person or partner-in-crime who made you laugh until you couldn't breathe. Close your eyes and remember. What was your first friend's name? Where did you meet? What 'thing' or moment turned you into being friends?

It was in the classroom that the fundamentals of the friendship network first became apparent to you. Can you remember the name of the popular kid(s)? Can you name the kid who was left out or rejected? Or the 'controversial' kid who everyone laughed with in class but you weren't friends with outside of class? Or the one who no one noticed, who got casually ignored? The hierarchy was clear, even at that early age. Have you ever wondered how your popularity, or lack of it, has impacted your friendships or, indeed, your life?

It seems that your popularity level at school is well established by the age of sixteen. The interesting part is how influential its impact is upon each new social experience you have as an adult, at work, with friends, making new friends. It seems those teenage experiences act as a positive or a negative interpreting filter that you use to pick up on social cues and make sense of them. If your experiences resulted in a high rejection sensitivity, you will be acutely aware of negative social cues – '*he did that because he doesn't really like me*'. On the other hand, if you have enjoyed being liked and popular from a young age, it does the opposite and you either don't see negative social cues or you interpret them differently – '*maybe he's having a bad day*'. In other words, you experience what you expect to experience. This is why the goal is to change, and to see each new social experience as a chance to start afresh.

The lifelong impact of that social capital of being popular in secondary school may surprise you. If we break down what being 'popular' means, it is divided into status and being liked. Status is about being visible, influential and everyone knowing your name – in a way it's 'celebrity', or infamy, at a minor level. This was what mattered in school. Being liked means you are likeable and Prinstein's research in *Popular: The power of likeability in a status obsessed world* shows that in adulthood, this is what will bring you happiness and success.

The general traits of likeability are fairly straightforward but work together really well. Likeable people are often well-adjusted, have a good sense of humour, are good conversationalists who give others their turn to talk as they listen, are good problem-solvers specifically in awkward and difficult social situations, don't dominate or disrupt the group and are smart but not too smart.

In psychological terms, your ability to make friends is laid down by many factors, such as your biological predispositions, personality and preferences (shy, introverted, extroverted or ambivert, a mixture of the two) and your attachment style. Someone with a secure attachment style, who is open to talking with people, may just show up more (parties, coffee break, engaging in small-talk) and this will give them a chance to get to know people better, coupled with feeling more comfortable within themselves (Schneider et al. 2012). Proximity and familiarity are two psychological factors that can increase the likelihood of a friendship developing.

Can you see how 'accepted' people continue with this status, shrugging it off easily with, '*I guess I'm lucky I make friends easily*'. On the other hand, children who have experienced rejection or being ejected from the group may struggle to make or maintain friendships thus adding to their sense of isolation, high rejection sensitivity and sense of not belonging as you missed out on building key social skills that came from that party invite or playdate. Or were you controversial, vying for popularity over 'likeability', which continued into adulthood and means you are still looking to take that risk or be impulsive? Whatever category you fall into, you are not stuck there.

It's not like your eye colour, you have the ability to change. You can do so by challenging your own status quo. You can learn these skills. One sure-fire way of doing this is to apply the golden rule of friendship, which is to make people feel good about themselves.

Friendship may have seemed at its utmost importance to you as a teenager, and you were right to think that. In the black-and-white world of the teenage brain, you were either in and cool, or out and not cool. The importance, drive and need to fit in was due in part to the activation of your ventral striatum, which kicks off at age 10–13 years (Haber, 2011). The ventral striatum is the neuroanatomy of reward and is involved in how you process and seek reward. Think of it as a pinball machine. Each time you had a great social experience, the ball got fired up and you were rewarded with a potent mixture of oxytocin and dopamine, *bing, bing, bing,* and you felt like a winner.

Oxytocin makes you feel connected to your peers, and dopamine just feels good. This stage of life, which involves a natural pulling away from your parents while simultaneously seeking approval, acceptance and admiration from your peers, isn't just a teenage fad, it's a neurological drive. In terms of social media, this neurological drive is why the teenage brain is so sensitive to the addictive motivational drive to get more 'likes' or followers. They are conditioned to seek a high through friendship groups.

The research into friendship suggests that whether you were accepted or rejected by your peers in childhood impacts your adult life. It can set up a popular or unpopular loop that is sustained in adulthood, unless changes are made. This might sound drastic, but studies have shown that popular kids were more inclined to make and repair friendships. When faced with a row or a friendship problem, children who had experienced negative or higher social rejection were more likely to walk away, respond aggressively or avoid the confrontation. Rejection is a very painful feeling, and for the teenager it can be overwhelming. It can have far-reaching effects on the rejected person.

In one study by Lemerise et al. (2006), 400 youths were shown videos of bullying scenarios. They were asked to imagine they were the victim of the bullying and were asked how they would respond to each scenario, such as being made dirty on purpose, being called names, having water spilled on them or their toys broken. They discussed what they had seen with the psychologist researchers, and the findings showed that those who were used to being accepted and popular tried to fix the situation, and even befriend the bully. Those who had experienced rejection or being unpopular wanted to seek revenge, and their behavioural response was to be aggressive, defensive or to avoid the offending person. When you think about it, it makes a lot of sense as avoiding the bullying is an adaptive and self-protecting mechanism. However, the aggression and defensiveness will only propagate future unpopularity.

A teacher came up with this fascinating exercise (Melton, 2018). Every Friday, she asked her students to write on a piece of paper the names of four children they would like to sit with the following week. They knew that this wasn't a given and might not happen. They were then asked to name the student they felt had been the 'exceptional classroom citizen' of the week. All the lists were anonymous. The teacher would then study the names and look for patterns.

She was looking to see who was not getting picked by anyone (The Rejecteds). She was looking for who couldn't think who to pick (The Neglecteds), who had a popular week last week (The Accepteds) and who was really unpopular that week (The Controversials). Through identifying these patterns, she sought to identify:

- the lonely kid;
- the kid who couldn't seem to fit in with the others;
- the kid who was falling through the cracks of the class's social system;
- the kid being bullied;
- the bully.

This teacher was prompted into doing this by the Columbine massacre. She knew that mass shooters were often the neglected and rejected of the classroom, and that at the heart of their social disconnect was loneliness and isolation. This is a stark finding, and it emphasises the importance of friendship. Connection and inclusion change people. Lack of connection and exclusion also change people. As we've seen before, a sense of belonging is a key indicator of psychological wellbeing. Kindness matters.

Can you see how the past experiences of being accepted, rejected, neglected or controversial have followed you into your adult friend space? Is your adult brain still working off your adolescent experiences? It's not surprising if it is, because these far-reaching emotional experiences form a deep layer in our concept of our inner selves, leaving a strong imprint of these emotionally charged experiences. They say love hurts, but so too does social pain.

COMMON ISSUES

One of the most debilitating common issues related to friendship is not having any friends. When we lack friends, we lack a sense of belonging, and that's where loneliness flows in. From a clinical perspective, I know very well the impact of loneliness on a person's wellbeing. I encounter loneliness on a daily basis among my clients, and in so many guises. For some it's that there is no support, or they don't know how to reach out to others, or when they do it confirms what they were already primed to expect by their high rejection sensitivity bias.

Downey and Feldman (1996) say that a high rejection sensitivity bias makes you 'anxiously expect, readily perceive, and overreact' to social rejection. Where each social experience is interpreted as a potential threat – *'why did they say that?'* or *'what exactly did they mean by that?'* – it leads to a vicious cycle of unpopularity and loneliness. This results in a deep yearning to be popular, painfully coupled with an underlying assumption that you are not, and round and round the thoughts, feelings and behaviours go. This can have lifelong negative outcomes, such as burnout at work, body dissatisfaction, depression and loneliness.

Loneliness has such an impact on physical and mental health that in 2018 the UK appointed Tracey Crouch as its first Minister for Loneliness. This is in response to the finding that nine million adults in the UK reported feeling lonely often or always, and that loneliness brings a 26% increase in mortality. It is a serious social issue, as well as a personal issue. It's important to add that your status – accepted, rejected, dejected or controversial – and negative social biases can alter how your brain is wired. The salient point is, you can change, but it will require a lot of work. Neural plasticity is the goal, but you and you alone are the driver of this. I would encourage you to take the social risk, to engage in those difficult or awkward situations and to allow yourself room to learn, grow, fail and pick yourself back up. I would encourage you to be your own social mentor, guiding and encouraging each and every conversation. Behavioural change is slow, but slow and steady is the way to go as you nudge your way towards creating new ways to respond to yourself and other people.

Men and women tend to conduct their friendships differently. I often encourage male clients to rob some female friendship traits, and vice versa.

For the men, I recommend they borrow the female traits of being more open and honest, and also being serious about the serious things. This allows real conversations to happen, where friends feel they can be honest with each other. Culturally, I think there has been a positive shift in this direction. Today's men are more physically affectionate with each other and we're seeing a slow change in ideas of masculinity, encouraging men to be so much more than the cardboard cut-out 2D 'manliness' they used to have forced on them.

One aspect to male friendships that men need to be aware of is slagging. It is often just brutal and straight out shockingly mean, but played off as nothing. Men assure me they are used to this and its water off a duck's back, but I know clinically this doesn't apply to every man – and how could it? It's important that men use their powerful trait of directness to challenge 'banter' when it gets out of hand and turns harmful and hurtful.

As for women, they could learn a lot from men's directness. For all the talking that is done with friends, women often don't say what they need to say. Don't tell Mary, Ellen and Joan if the person you actually need to talk to is Melissa. Be brave, have courage and be direct.

For all the openness women have, the power structure and complexity within female friendships and groups can be immensely dynamic and sometimes toxic. Perhaps a bigger conversation about the cultural acceptance of the 'mean girls' phenomenon needs a challenge and shake-up. This is where the status level of teenage popularity is still being played out. It may now be wearing more sophisticated clothes and have a better handbag, but the old power pattern of knowing who's the alpha female is still there. That's when mean girls become mean women. If you find yourself part of a group with this dynamic, there are a few things everyone can do. First, do not be a social bystander. Instead, I ask you to be an upstander, by calling out the one in the group who is belittling or shaming another, often polished off with an offensively charming smile that dares anyone to rebuke her. Literally stand by the person who is being 'meaned on' and show your support in word and in deed. Stand up to it and you will feel great afterwards. You will feel dreadful for letting it happen again if you don't.

Three words to change this for you forever: inoculate, inoculate, inoculate. Because the alpha female will challenge you. *'Sorry, what did you just say?'* will be said with accusation. *'You heard me, I said, wow, that was incredibly rude.'* Another tack can be to say something positive, not only will this inoculate but the offender won't have anything to push back on and they will be so surprised, they might be stuck for words – *'you are so impatient'*, to which you reply: *'yes, you're right and you are very quick to notice that'*.

Regardless of gender, what's most important for friendships is to share quality time together. Frequent interactions and seeing and talking with each other is a necessity that many friendships wither upon. You can see why having a romantic relationship, a job and maybe some children can make this feel difficult to impossible. But like every relationship in your life, it's quality over quantity. Make some plans together, whether it's a catch-up over coffee or a night away. The main requirement is that you both feel happy and that the giving and reciprocity feels equal to you both. In terms of spending time together, that is a personal preference, it only become an issue when it isn't mutual.

It might sound daft to say that having too many friends can be a problem, but what if there isn't enough of you to go around? Or what if you haven't learned how to say no and stretch yourself to the brink of your time and energy threshold? Ask yourself if you have too many people hanging on to you who drain you and don't give enough back. If this sounds like your friendship situation, you need to take stock and choose the friends that feel right for you. Choose the uplifting, energy-giving friends who make you feel rejuvenated.

You should also question why you have so many friends and ask yourself: can I be alone? Does that word terrify you? If so, you might be busying yourself to distraction, which is something I see a lot among my clients. If you are harbouring an abject fear of spending time on your own with your own thoughts, that isn't good. It's so healthy and important to like being in your own company. I understand that for many people, the mental anguish of the noise in their minds isn't a nice place to be. I understand why people distract themselves. In the short term, you might get away with it, but at some point your body will rebel, often in the form of anxiety or panic attacks. You need to address the fear of being alone, then you can ensure your friendships are healthy and mutually fulfilling.

A common form of unhealthy friendship is with the needy friend. A friend in constant need may not be a friend you need. Friendship has to be reciprocal; it is not therapy. There has to be a balance. One word: boundaries. How do you create and define boundaries when your time and energy lines have been crossed? Please stop, have respect for the non-infinite amount of energy you have. I have seen too many clients who are burnt out, exhausted and unhappy. And another word: self-care. This is essential in all your relationships, to preserve your own health and wellbeing.

Another word I might throw out there unabashedly and ask you to give it a go is 'no'. Try it and see how you get on. What is the worst that can happen? Be honest with your friends. If you don't have the time or energy and you say 'yes', then you are not being fair or honest to the friendship. The slightest annoyance will then make you feel resentful, which is somewhat passive-aggressive. There is no other way around this, boundaries and self-care are about respecting your own needs, which is a healthy part of your relationship with yourself. If you're able to say 'no', then when you say 'yes' and you do meet up, you are happy and have chosen to be there. 'No' is a full sentence. Here's a few more. No. No. No.

I have to make a particular note on female one-to-one friendships. The see-saw of friendship will require give and take on both sides, and there will be times when it's not equal, but once you maintain the integrity and interest in how the other person is as well, it will naturally reset. However, you are not your friend's therapist. Please don't try to be. This is an issue I have seen too many times, where you get into the friendship rut of being the friend-counsellor. If you get off the phone and your friend hasn't come up for air and you feel exhausted, the exchange is way off. Like most things in my field, it's all relative, and it's about how long it has gone on. There may be long periods of time when you are in a supporting role as a friend, just don't be in it so long that you qualify for receiving a statue for it.

Which of these two do you think is a key indicator of a good friendship?

1. Being there for your friend when they are having a tough time.
2. Being happy for your friend when their life is on a winning streak.

It can be easier to be there in the tough times. A true measure of the health of a friendship, more specifically of your own inner happiness, is when you have the capacity to be genuinely happy for your friend when everything is going well for them. For adults in this complex and harried world, time and energy are a dwindling, if not extinct, resource. That inner strain and conflict can make it difficult to be generous, not to the friend in need, who might make us feel better about ourselves, but to the friend who seems to be winning on all counts. That's a whole different ballgame.

This skewed perception people have that *everyone else has got their act together except me* is exacerbated by social media. When managing all the adult responsibilities – pressures of work, your relationship, your lack of a relationship, family or trying for a family, finances, illness and life's unexpected curved balls – it can just feel too much. When was the last time you posted online that you were having an epic fail day, or just not feeling good enough? With negative social comparison being so visceral and, thanks to Instagram Stories, in surround sound as well, a scroll through social media influences your mood and how you feel about yourself. Let's be real, I'm not advocating an all-or-nothing tech ban, I'm merely asking you to identify what it was that triggered your change in mood. Did you feel more body conscious or self-conscious? Did you feel your life pales in comparison to someone else's? Once you have identified your triggers, ask yourself is there anything you can do to prevent them? And remember, the posting person is showing you their best self, but they have bad days and self-doubt as well.

In research by Strasburger et al. (2007) the media is referred to as a 'super-peer'. You have your peer group, who you have always looked to for advice, support and re-enforcing your shared values, but with the emergence of the internet and social networks we are also bombarded 24-7 by 'personalised' news feeds influencing us in very powerful ways. In terms of mental wellbeing, the value needs to be placed back on meeting face-to-face rather than virtually.

Do you think you still need that external peer admiration? This shows itself when you care first about what others think about you. This form of extrinsic value leaves you vulnerable to other people's moods and preferences. I often remind my clients that it's called self-worth, not others-worth.

The question is: how can you change it? The goal is to value who you are first, and then it is perfectly fine to get 'likes' externally – as long as it's not a mood changer. If it is, then notice when your mood changed. Downward social comparison affects your mood. Catching it is the answer.

Another common issue is when every conversation with your friend starts with, '*Do you remember when …?*' If this is the case, your friendship might be stuck in a rut. Reminiscing is lovely, but friendships need to grow and change, just as the people within them do. New experiences and new challenges keep friendships alive. You must allow room for you both to change or try different things, without it being a criminal offence.

If you're stuck in a *remember when* rut but you want the friendship to continue, throw out some new ideas or ventures to do or go on together. Other universal friendship ruts are the negative friend, the 'friend' who puts you down and the friendship that only involves drinking, kids and/or work. To break out of a rut you need to try a different venue or something new for both of you. In all your relationships, staleness can set in if you don't hit the refresh button every now and then. Novel experiences are where it's at. It's like coming back to the beginner's eyes in mindfulness, seeing yourself and your friend with fresh new eyes. Plan something to do together, stick it in the Diary and do it.

There are different types of friendship rut, but if you're stuck in the groove of a toxic friendship, the best advice is to break off that friendship and let it go.

What is a toxic friendship? A friendship that has turned or always was toxic makes you feel bad, really bad. While in this person's company or afterwards, you notice your energy and mood have changed for the worse. For all the incredible health benefits a good friend can bring, the opposite also holds true quite consistently of a bad friendship, which brings increased blood pressure and blood sugar, IBS and lowered immunity. A bad friendship is likened to a bad marriage, and can be just as damaging.

What other red flags should you look out for? Competition, deception, betrayal, brutal honesty, exclusion and criticism can come under the guise of *'I'm just trying to be a good friend'*. I do feel constructive criticism plays an incredibly important role in all relationships, but integrity and truth are two words that need to stick together. You can be kind in your words. Even when the message is hard to hear, you'll know when it's buffered with good intent. Toxic words just hurt.

It takes a lot of courage, but toxic friendships need to go. How do you do it? You could have an honest conversation, or send a card/letter/email if you know it will end very badly face-to-face. But let them know, be honest and cut ties. Sometimes the decision is the hardest part. Another popular way is to ghost them by ignoring or not responding to their effort of connecting, but the pain of that is intense for the 'ghosted' person.

The break-up of a friendship – whether it's toxic or not – can be an excruciating experience. When friendships break up it shouldn't really come as a surprise, which often people find is the most unpleasant part. When sociologist Gerald Mollenhorst went back to re-interview his research group about their friendships seven years on, the majority had replaced half of their friends, with only 30% remaining close friends. Talk about the seven-year itch!

The social and physical pain of rejection hurts, so how do you do it, or get over it?

Feelings of embarrassment and shame are felt strongly by people when they have been 'dumped' by a friend. The initial sting is felt as *'what is wrong with me?'* When others ask, 'how's your friend?', that sense of personal blame and shame is often internalised. Liz Pryor, author of *What Did I Do Wrong? What to do when you don't know why the friendship is over*, says this is more centric to female friendships, where she found two very different stories of why it ended. The dumped friend was often in a state of shock, blind to the build-up of tension and anything being wrong, while the dumper felt they had let things slide for too long. This is why I encourage women to be more direct and assertive in telling friends what has upset them. In fairness to the friend, they don't have the opportunity to change if you don't tell them, and the ensuing tension and resentment are a bad friendship combination.

The problem with unfinished business is that the story didn't end the way you wanted it to. Often when you are on the receiving end of the friendship dump, you can agonise over all the why's and unanswered questions of *'what happened?'* The uncomfortable and yet inevitable truth lies in accepting the situation as it is, not as you want it to be. Talking it through with friends, family or a professional can help give you a different perspective and a clearer headspace to vent, release and heal.

KEY THEORIES

We looked at the research that showed people fit into one of four friendship categories: accepted, rejected, controversial and neglected (Coie et al., 2000). In non-psychology speak, these groups may be more clearly demonstrated by the popular 1985 film *The Breakfast Club*, where 'a brain, a beauty, a jock, a rebel and a recluse' are sent to detention. If you'd like to find out which category you fall into, you can take Mitch Prinstein's online quiz at www. mitchprinstein.com.

We've seen how your friendship status is affected by various factors. As with everything else, your attachment type plays a big role in this. In a study by Grabill and Kerns (2000) that examined three types of intimacy in friendship – 'self-disclosure; responsiveness to a partner's disclosure; and feeling understood, validated and cared for by a partner during conversations' – it found that people with a secure attachment may have a bias in their schema when someone is disclosing something intimate that allows them to tune into this, which can lead to increased intimacy in the friendship. Someone who has an avoidant attachment may feel worried or anxious and not that open to taking social risks and may have a negative bias in terms of how a conversation is going.

Attachment style holds quite consistently across relationships, although perhaps somewhat less within the friendship role. All the mitigating factors and your experiences create your social expectations. It is very useful to be aware of your ongoing friendship narrative that you carry – *'I am popular/unpopular'* or *'I am liked/disliked'* – and to break the old schemas and belief systems that you hold around this. By doing so, you can then respond to the social opportunities that present themselves every day.

The lifelong thread of being connected, feeling accepted and belonging is something you continuously strive for in all your relationships. As social beings we are wired to connect, and the strongly positive health predictors are encouraging factors in overcoming the 'time cost' of creating and maintaining friendships. Friendship can create a shared meaning and understanding of each other's life contexts. It requires you to disclose some of the private *I* and asks you to share your stories of hope and vulnerability. The reward for this is trust and intimacy.

Jane: *'I've been feeling pretty down lately.'*

Nora: *'I'm really sorry to hear that, Jane.'*

Jane: *'It's been a shock. I've been having panic attacks that seemed to come out of nowhere.'*

Nora: *'Oh, trust me, I know all about them.'*

Jane: *'What? You never said a word.'*

Nora: *'I suppose I was really embarrassed and I just couldn't admit it.'*

Jane: *'I am so sorry to hear that, when did you have them?'*

Nora: *'Last year, for about six months. I went for therapy and I have it under control now.'*

Jane: *'I'm really sorry I couldn't be there to help you, I really get it now. Not being selfish, but it's really good to hear someone as normal as you had this as well and you are doing better now.'*

Nora: 'Normal!'

Both laughed.

....

It is in that mutual space, protected by a sense of safety where another person 'gets you' and accepts you as you are, that friendship blossoms. That sense of belonging and being liked and accepted impacts so many of your daily micro social interactions. These small and yet important interactions can strengthen or weaken relationships. At a basic level, it is chatting with the barista who makes your coffee each day. The 'accepted' person may chat away happily, may know their name and how many kids they have, where they are going on holiday and so on. People from the three other categories may not interact at this micro level and have the perfunctory greeting and thank you, but they may actively not engage or purposely disengage by looking at their phone. Are you are open to talking to people or do you prefer not to engage?

It also sets your biases in terms of how you perceive and react to situations and people. Our biases work as a shortcut to the quickest route of how we expect situations to be. The remnants and scars of unpopularity can create a 'hostile attribution bias', whereby the person sees others' intent as hostile, even if this is not the case (Werner, 2012). This is tested when psychologists ask children to interpret stories, such as: 'You are sitting at lunch when someone walks behind you holding his drink. The next thing you realize is that there's milk all over your back.' Most children will interpret this ambiguous statement as an accident, but a child who has been rejected will often see it as intentional. It becomes a problem if you don't grow out of this bias because then it bleeds into your inner lives, as partner, co-worker, neighbour and parent, leading you to view others' actions as purposely hostile or difficult towards you – *'they're trying to annoy me on purpose'.*

Your friendship category bequeaths you a certain way of looking at the world, and that can be helpful or unhelpful. An extensive global study (Prinstein et al., 2016) showed that adults who recalled feeling popular in childhood felt they had:

- happier marriages;
- better work relationships;
- were a flourishing member of society.

Sadly, the exact opposite was expressed by people who felt they were unpopular in childhood. They had a higher risk of:

- substance abuse;
- obesity;
- anxiety;
- depression;
- illness;
- problems at work;
- suicide.

The findings showed that popularity affects the wiring of the brain, your social perceptions, your emotions and how your body responds to stress, right down to changing your DNA. It was like both sets of people – perceived popular and perceived unpopular – had lived in two different worlds, where each group's perceptions of the world and how they would be treated affected every aspect of their lives.

Dale Carnegie's famous book *How to Win Friends and Influence People* was published in 1936 and has sold over thirty million copies, making it one of the bestselling books of all time. This staggering sales figure reflects the fact that people are fascinated by being liked and how they are perceived. Let's face it, everyone is curious about what people think about them. You are neurally wired to want acceptance and belonging, and that need never changes, only the dynamics of the relationships change. Bringing that back to how you formed an opinion of yourself first may the best place to start.

As we saw in Chapter 2, during your formative years, the parent-child relationship moulded much of how you view yourself. The secure child-turned-adult may feel less upset by the opinion of someone who doesn't matter too much to them. A person with self-esteem issues, however, may find it easier to accept, and expect, that people may think badly of them. Each time you think of the primary threads, see how you can challenge them now. I encourage you to care less about what an acquaintance says than your best friend. This takes practice, but the lesson is simple: you will care what people think, but don't give everyone equal status.

The research conducted into friendship gives us the great insight that rather than it being about you, it is the experience of being unpopular that is the issue. This creates the vicious cycle of continuing to experience rejection in your everyday social interactions, strengthening pre-existing biases of high sensitivity and hostile attribution. But you can learn from your past history with popularity and change your status by being very aware of how you interact with people now and in the future. This is the grounded hope for change: challenge your preconceptions, be open to being surprised by people, take social risks, like saying hello, and build your social collateral.

From tomorrow onwards, become aware of how you interact with every single person for the whole day. This is the beginning of bringing more friendship into your life. You have complete control over this. Take notes about the good interactions and the bad ones. What made the interactions different? I bet the good interactions flowed smoothly.

When you strike up a conversation, any silence four seconds long or more is awkward and will generate that old feeling that you have been somewhat rejected (Koudenberg et al., 2011). People are very harsh on themselves, internalising the feeling that *it was my fault there was a silence*.

Think about all the great relationships in your life. The beginnings of such relationships were often filled with great conversations, where you experienced flow and synergy of ideas and minds, and they were so fulfilling and enjoyable. The opposite of that is awkward silence. Can you see that when in flow, you feel connected, but when conversation is stilted, it feels the complete opposite, with feelings of rejection and disconnection?

Stilted conversations breed a feeling of uncomfortableness for you and certainly for the other person. If you are popular, keep doing what you are doing. If you see someone in a conversation and you can see they are nervous or ill-at-ease or talking a mile a minute, be kind and inclusive. The art of conversation and friendship-building is something you can help this person with. I see a lot of clients who go into full avoidance mode, but this only makes the situation worse as you won't get your daily practice of chatting. I have heard *'I have nothing to say'* or *'how can I start the conversation?'* so many times, leading to more avoidance.

What's the worst-case scenario? Is it saying the most ridiculous thing and walking away feeling mortified and self-chastising, *'why did I just say that?'* Own it, say *'Sorry, I'm rambling'* or whatever you are thinking in your head. Authenticity is a gift. You know when something happens and you walk away and afterwards you have the 'ah-ha' moment when you think of something that would have been the perfect thing to say? Well, the truth is you have the perfect thing to say, but through social inhibition or past negative experiences, fear keeps you silent. Everybody makes mistakes, but the fact is we like people better who are human and flawed and not perfect, because we can relate to them.

I'm asking you be internally accountable to yourself and to the value of investing in your friendships. It is essential to understand that adult friendship isn't a luxury, it's a human necessity. It is as good for your health as eating and exercising well and, of course, a lack of it is as bad for your health as poor eating and no exercise. You won't be long getting in trouble if you think, *'I must try and go to that mandatory Monday morning meeting at work sometime soon'*. No, you don't, it is written in and you do it. People feel externally accountable to bosses, dates and meetings. So I'd like you to add a friend 'date night' to your working vocabulary and Diary.

The transactional model studies the social interaction between two people. It is the chain reaction between how people behave towards you, and how you respond. It is this daily give and take that creates new behaviours and ways of responding, and the more you practice these interpersonal skills, the higher the likelihood of forming friendships that you value. The model holds that each encounter and transaction is an opportunity to connect socially, change old biases and cultivate new ways of responding to the world.

Here's an example of a good transaction:

Molly heard that lovely crinkly sound that is the cellophane around flowers. She looked up from her desk and came face to face with her favourite flowers, the most beautiful peonies and huge hydrangea. She smiled as she opened the card, it was from her best friend. It wasn't her birthday, but she had been going through a really tough time of late. She was really touched and decided there and then that she needed to get things back on track. She realised how lucky she was to have a best friend like that who knew her so well.

Here's an example of a bad transaction:

Jonathan found speaking with Mark a challenge. He could never really put his finger on it, and it felt petty but he always walked away feeling a bit worse about himself.

Think of all the encounters you have every day, from the briefest to that great conversation with a friend. There is a give and take in each transaction. The transactional model looks at what you give or put out into the world, and the interplay in how the world responds to you. Do you engage and say 'Hi' to everyone, stopping for a chat? Or are you racing, head down, mentally already at your next destination? In terms of 'how to' make more friends and connections, this is it – you must be open to interactions. This may be difficult if you have endured less favourable social experiences, but you need to see the difficulty as a challenge. This is your chance to make a change for yourself and establish a new way of interacting with people, which in turn will make them change how they respond to you.

There is a big 'but' here, however: you can't change the past. And another big 'but': but you can change how you react now and in the future. You must learn to let go of the past negative experiences and throw yourself into the uncomfortable new, allowing yourself to write a different script and storyline for your life, one that has more joy, fun and mental freedom. Think of yourself as a first responder and ask yourself: what can I do to help? What problem can I solve here? How can I make this situation better? Likability isn't something you're born with or without, it's something you can work on and improve throughout life.

Have a look at the two lists below from *Popular* and let it guide you to improve your 'likeable' skills and to change or work on any dislikeable behaviours you may have.

Likeable people are:

- well-adjusted;
- smart, but not too smart;
- good-humoured;
- know how to have a conversation, can talk and listen;
- creative, particularly in difficult or awkward social situations;
- don't disrupt the group.

Dislikeable behaviours:

- aggressive;
- break social norms and rules and aren't sorry;
- selfish;
- over-share;
- seek excessive reassurance.

Have you ever experienced either of these types of situation?

Transactions big and small, meaningful or difficult make up an intricate pattern of experiences of who you are in the world and your expectations of how your social interactions will pan out. They also create positive or negative social contagion. Think of a lovely interaction you had with someone recently. I have no doubt it impacted your mood positively. It's quite likely you did something lovely for someone soon after. This is the 'contagion'. Good actions are catching – it's like a chain reaction. Of course, the same is true of bad experiences, which ripple out and infect others. The best approach is to enjoy and notice the good, and notice and let go of the bad. Acknowledge what has happened, but also mindfully let it pass.

DIARY

◇ What moments in your life have changed how you thought the world was? _____

_____

◇ Name a good social experience. What happened, how did it change how you felt about yourself and why? _____

_____

◇ Name a negative social experience. What happened, how did it change how you felt about yourself and why?_____

_____

_____

Have a look at Jane's two experiences.

Jane was best friends with a girl from school and one day, with no explanation at all, she stopped talking to her. Immediately, Jane began to worry, wondering what she had done wrong. One by one, each of the girls in the group distanced themselves. Jane was cast out of the group, without even a fight to make any sense of it. Jane was deeply upset, and she became hyper-aware and apprehensive about the possibility of people rejecting her.

Four years later, Jane had just started her first real job. She may have looked confident, but she was extremely anxious. Each day a small group of the younger employees went for a coffee at 10.30am. Each day, Rachel invited Jane to join them, but she always refused. She would then chastise herself. The problem was, she felt the rest of the group wasn't as friendly as Rachel and felt like they didn't want her to join. After a month of this, Rachel stopped asking Jane to join them.

One Friday morning at 10.30am, Rachel came over and handed Jane her coat and said, 'Come on, let's go'. Jane stood up and awkwardly put on her coat. She felt she couldn't walk or talk properly. But she did join the group and she did her best to participate. This moment of kindness from Rachel, of seeing through her apprehension, was a complete game-changer for Jane. It healed the pain of the childhood rejection.

As in all things, your perception of events is crucial to how you feel about them. Think about the last time someone was late or cancelled plans on you at the last minute. What was your initial reaction? Was it, *'Typical, I knew they wouldn't come'* or *'I knew we weren't really friends, she probably doesn't even like me'* or *'OK, that's a pity, I'll text her/him to see when would suit again'*? Did you take it personally? Or did you give them the benefit of the doubt? The answer will tell you which world you belong to, or at least have belonged to. It will tell you if it was a world that accepted you, or was it a more threatening, hostile world that gave you umpteen reasons to be cautious and vigilant for the next attack.

The last decade of research has proved very interesting, unveiling the biological basis of friendship and loneliness. Experiments conducted by neuroscientist Naomi Eisenberger have shown that the brain experiences unpopularity as physical distress, which she terms 'social pain'. Eisenberger's study participants were scanned with an fMRI (brain scan) while playing 'Cyberball', a game set up to simulate a negative experience with a peer. The game is basically Catch: you are told the other players are in a nearby room, they are represented as two stick figures, and that you are a 'hand'; the other players do not exist and are part of the simulation. For about ten minutes everyone plays the game, fairly throwing the ball back and forth, and then all of a sudden the other two exclude you and start playing just with each other for another ten minutes. What Eisenberger noticed in the last ten minutes was that the part of the brain that deals with physical pain became activated, most specifically the dorsal anterior cingulate cortex (dACC) and the anterior insula (AI). Obviously the participant wasn't feeling actual pain, but these two parts of the brain interpret serious pain signals, such as the 'sensation of burning and stinging', and instruct you to move away from it as quickly as possible. The study showed that this alarm system activates when you feel unpopular or rejected. Have you felt the sting of rejection like that?

Even more remarkable are the findings of UCLA psychologists Slavich and Cole, who have shown that rejection affects our DNA by changing inflammation and immune responses. They described our DNA as 'exquisitely sensitive to social rejection'. They studied what happens when you feel rejected by a stranger, socially excluded, dumped by a romantic partner or judged by people you care about. These experiences impact our very DNA, with the change becoming visible in the blood 40 minutes after the experience. Out of about 20,000 genes, only a few dozen are affected, and yet this makes a significant difference to your immune system. The activated genes were linked to inflammatory response to fight off bacterial infections and to increase healing time when wounded. The researchers feel this 'pro-inflammatory response' may have been evolutionary in terms of protecting people who were unpopular as they had no one to help them when they faced death from being injured or attacked. Their sensitivity to rejection or attack led to a pre-emptively activated pro-inflammatory response, leading to a quicker healing from a wound and, thus, survival. The genes that were deactivated impacted viral protection. If ancient man or woman had no friends, they gave all their energy to protect bacteria as they couldn't be infected by peers. In modern times, inflammatory responses, especially those chronic in nature, are not your body's friend.

I'm sure everyone can attest to a time when they felt rejected or betrayed, but it's probably a surprise to find out that it impacted your immune system. The key concern is for those who experience such feelings chronically, which can then impact the cells and render them 'hyper-sensitive'. Even a few months of unpopularity could trigger a 'molecular remodelling', as more cells are replaced with the hyper-sensitive DNA. So these findings confirm that friendship goes right to the heart of what makes us human. As the father of psychology William James said: 'The deepest principle in human nature is the craving to be appreciated.' This is why it's so important for you to assess the health status of your friendships and make any changes necessary.

THE PRACTICE

This is where you can examine your friendship history and its ongoing effect on your adult life. If you have concerns or hurts regarding your friendships, working through this section will help you to see how past experience informs the present, and how you can change and improve things for yourself.

DIARY

◇ What makes you a good friend? _____
_____
_____

◇ What are your friendship strengths? _____
_____
_____

◇ What is the nicest thing a friend has ever said to you? _____
_____
_____

◇ What are your friendship weaknesses? _____
_____
_____

◇ What was the most upsetting thing that happened in a friendship? _____
_____
_____
_____
_____

◇ What did you learn from it? _____
_____

◇ Did it change the friendship? _____
_____

Those questions were just to limber you up! What follows is a much more comprehensive look at your friendships across your lifetime. The aim here is to establish your core friendship circles.

List your friends based on:

◇ Acquaintances: _____
_____
_____

◇ Friends (outer circle):_____

_____

_____

◇ Friends you call when the **** hits the fan (inner circle): _____

_____

_____

◇ List the qualities of these friends: _____

_____

_____

Who would you call for:

◇ A coffee? _____

◇ A party? _____

◇ When you are in trouble? _____

What type of friend are you?

◇ What type of friend do your friends think you are? _____

_____

_____

◇ What did friendship mean to you in your childhood? _____

_____

_____

◇ What did friendship mean to you in each decade of your life – answer for each decade under these three headings: the challenges, the joys, the life curve balls. _____

_____

_____

◇ How do you fight with your friends? _____

_____

◇ Is your fighting style consistent in all your relationships? _____

_____

How do you feel when you are hurt by a friend? Do you:

✧ Go quiet, but silently fume? Go on the attack? Go on the defensive? Talk to everyone but the person you are fighting with? Try to see it from their side and talk it out together? Are you a texter or talker? _____

_____

_____

How do you resolve an issue? If you want to make up with your friend, here's how:

- Say sorry.
- Listen to what your friend has to say, understand it from their point of view.
- Explain how you feel and why.
- Don't blame, be specific about what you are annoyed or upset about.
- If you are losing emotional control, take a deep breath or take a break from it.
- Don't play text tag.
- Make up old style: face to face.

What if you have no friends and no idea how to go about making them? You probably feel very alone in this, but the truth is it's far more common than you might imagine. But loneliness, isolation and feeling like you don't belong are pernicious feelings and, as we've seen, they can really hurt you. You won't want to hear this, but you are going to have to take the risk of interacting with people. Nothing will change until you put yourself out there. Start small, force yourself to have practice conversations at the shop or when you are buying your coffee. Don't use your phone as a human shield.

DIARY

✧ Make a list of your strengths. _____

_____

_____

_____

◇ What type of friendship would you like? _____

_____

_____

_____

◇ Do you like one-to-one friendships or to be with a group of people? _____

_____

_____

_____

◇ Do you enjoy classes or any sports? _____

_____

_____

_____

◇ Are there any possibilities of making friends at work or in any other area of your life? _____

_____

_____

◇ Where do you have to put yourself to meet new people? _____

_____

_____

_____

◇ Write out a few things you could say that are topical, to have 'back-up' conversations. _____

_____

_____

CONCLUSION

Among all the relationships in your life, friendship is unique because it is the one you freely choose and maintain. Many adults give so much time to all of their inner lives that friendship can be relegated as non-essential, but this is a mistake. As we've seen, friendships are enriching and valuable. But like all your relationships, they need time and effort. When you are juggling a jam-packed schedule, your friendships can feel like yet another thing on your to-do list, and one you don't have time to do. It's essential to get away from this way of thinking. Friendship is non-negotiable in terms of being a happy and healthy adult.

The key is making but also keeping friendships. We are all self-absorbed to a certain degree, not even in an egotistical way, but in terms of our worldview. The main way you can see the world is through your own eyes. This lens is filtered by all your experiences, your personality and your procedural memory, all of which are linked to one another. You can see how the circle of life can get interwoven pretty quickly by all the threads of your past and present experiences.

I said at the outset that people worry a lot about what others think about them, and this is not a weakness, in fact a certain amount of it is healthy. It gets you to question if your behaviour is conducive to being in and having better relationships. That's the interesting thing about friends – often they are the ones who have to tell you the truth. Friends can be part of the truth we need to hear. We are all deluded, but a friend can tell you the things you need to hear. A friend will help you know yourself. This is because the ties of friendship are intentional, as opposed to being biological or through marriage. Emotional baggage creates sensitive spots that render us sometimes unable to hear and see what family and partners are saying to us, but a good friendship gives you room to listen and hear objectively.

How many friends do you need to reap the benefits? According to Professor Dunbar, three to five close friends does the trick – this is known as Dunbar's Number. In truth, even one strong friendship can provide a buffer against the stresses and strains of adulthood. As you get older, making friends becomes more of a challenge, but you will not make friends from your couch. Get up, go out, walk, talk, volunteer, sing, eat or dance. My hope is that this chapter has inspired you to join that class, go on that outing, call up a friend and make a date. Friends are your psychological wealth and health.

'Work, Work, Work'

Love and work are to people what water and sunshine are to plants.

Jonathan Haid

INTRODUCTION

Work-life balance. I hate that saying. I much prefer my own version: life-work balance. What is your relationship to work and employment, and what does it mean to you? For many, their work identity may be the public part of their Russian doll that everyone sees first. For some, work is a means to an end, while for others, their work is a wonderful fusion of personal values in action. For yet others, their sole value comes from what they do. As an adult, your relationship with work and what it means to you is inextricably linked with how you define yourself.

This chapter is not about work per se, it's about the relationship you have with work and the relationships you have at work, and how that carries back home and into all your other selves. If you look at your Russian doll in terms of size, would your work self be one of the larger parts of you, and that you give time to? These are two separate things. Your inner selves are often proportionately different sizes and as you carve up your different roles, it isn't possible to give the same time and energy to each one. This is where I ask you to redress the balance, if needs be, to make life come first and work fit into your life. For the many people who derive meaning from their work, it is integral to your wellbeing. It doesn't mean hypothetically 'you'll never work a day in your life', but it does mean there is a deep sense of purpose

209

to your goals and passions. In my experience, however, it is the opposite – admittedly, people come to my clinic because they are not happy, which might skew what I am seeing. But what I do see is many people who are experiencing huge inner conflicts, often stemming from conflicted roles and a lack of meaning, from either boredom or overwork, that hits a crisis nerve.

There's an awful lot of nonsense surrounding the notion of work, but I'm just going to call it what it is. The fact is, no amount of free cake and coffee or tug-o'-war team days can pay back the time and energy asked of you at work throughout your career. And yet, we all need to earn a living. For this reason, wellbeing, and a sense of purposeful meaning needs to be at the heart of the organisational culture and a cohesive part of the work agenda – and your personal agenda.

COMMON ISSUES

I try and not take any calls at home as my kids laugh at my 'work voice' and mimic it really well as I run out of the room, phone pressed tightly to my ear. It's not our voice that changes at work though, is it? Work allows us to be a version of ourselves that perhaps our friends, partner, kids and parents don't get to see. We often have a work identity, which gives us the freedom to demonstrate our unique strengths, training and expertise. It can provide us with a structure to develop aspects of our work identity.

When the question is asked, '*What do you do?*' and you follow with, '*I am a …*', how much of your work identity is rolled up into your core identity? If your answer is '*I'm a doctor or musician, librarian or traffic warden*', it's safe to assume that people will identify specific qualities they think a person with that occupation is likely to possess, rightly or wrongly, and so will you. It isn't necessarily a problem that your work identity is so important to you, but it does become a problem when your work identity becomes who you are in entirety. This can then easily lead from busyness to workaholism, and then all your other relationships, from yourself to your family, will lose out.

What if you feel like a resistant workaholic, trying desperately to keep a clear and clean work-life balance and yet finding yourself succumbing to hitting the laptop from 10pm to get a start on tomorrow, or trying to finish what you were supposed to get done today? The resistant workaholic is the one I see most frequently in my clinic, and it causes an uncomfortable discrepancy between what the person wants to be doing and what they are doing. It is from these people that I hear they want to pack it all in and get a non-demanding job that finishes at 5.30pm.

For people who are perfectly happy that their job is just their job, this works really well. But for those who feel their job is 'just a job', and they mourn the loss of a career they dreamed of, this is a completely different scenario. It can feel like a battle to drag themselves to work when it isn't meaningful to them. This can elicit an existential crisis, where they wonder, 'what am I doing with my life?' Strong emotions of personal failure, often presented as anxiety and a loss of confidence, will manifest in many different ways to get your attention. Fear, boredom and lack of purpose create a level of low to acute levels of distress. I have often thought of this as the 'backward positive' of anxiety because it drives you to make changes that you are afraid to make.

The antidote is identifying and acting upon what it is you want to do. Sounds too easy, perhaps, but the years tick by if you don't bring about change – and nothing will change until you do. Like so many huge decisions in life, you have to stop waiting for the perfect time, or until you have enough money, or have paid for the mortgage, or … the perfect time doesn't exist. Be aware that the 'golden handcuffs' of a job can deaden your soul. I have seen this first-hand with thousands of people at major crossroads in their lives, facing the agony of 'should I stay, or should I go?', 'will I retrain, how will I pay for that?', 'am I being selfish, we have a young family?' I find it very interesting that regardless of the work context – I have worked with people from state organisations, tech firms, multinationals, many different industries – and regardless of gender, age and skillset, no matter what the career or job, it can make people feel stuck and without options. No one, at any level, is immune to this feeling.

When I look to people who have been 'successful', there are a few common denominators: they work really hard, I mean really hard, they faced failure many times, but they got back up each time, they are resilient, determined and tough-minded. Is this you? When you look to your inner work self, you have to ask where you are now and where you would like to be. What would be the right fit for you? In order to decide this, you have to identify your key character strengths. You can do this using your Values in Action (VIAs), which classifies twenty-four character strengths across six virtues: Wisdom and knowledge; Courage; Humanity; Justice; Temperance; and Transcendence (see Psychological Toolbox, p.245). One study of 1,031 adults found that signature strengths specifically impacted better 'performance, organizational citizenship behavior and lower counterproductive work behavior', while the character strengths of 'zest and hope' had the highest unique contribution to work meaningfulness, engagement and job satisfaction (Littman-Oviada et al. 2006).

Identifying and using your top four signature strengths is correlated with being three times happier in life and six times happier at work. A workplace study showed that having a strong signature strengths fit with your job was highly correlated with workplace wellbeing, which was measured in having 'positive emotions, engagement, positive relationships, meaning and achievement' (Harzer et al., 2017). This means using your VIAs in your work promotes a purposeful, engaging and meaningful work life. You will get to experience flow and synergy and you will flourish. The key features of a good working relationship are where you are using your strengths, you feel inspired and engaged, coupled with a sense of connection to an idea and a sense of belonging to an organisation that you value.

Of course, this can be very difficult for people whose workplace and tasks are boring or routine. In one company that was closing down, I went in to help with the psychological fallout from the redundancies. It was Christmas time and the people working at the factory had families, mortgages and presents to buy. I still have vivid memories of how it felt to be there. As soon as I walked in the door, the first feeling that struck me was a horrible weight of despair. It was that gut feeling of dread and fear that whispered, *'how am I going to tell my wife?', 'how will I pay the mortgage?', 'how will I be able to buy that bike for Lucy?'* It was emanating from the stressed employees, and it was a feeling of being stuck. Some had only ever worked there, having started at the company straight from school, but the problem was that twenty years had passed since then. When you feel your options are limited by experience and expertise, going back out into a competitive work market is a seriously daunting task. It compounds that awful feeling of being trapped.

Fear and uncertainty were the psychological fallout at that company, as they always are in such situations. The danger is that it can slip into a feeling of hopelessness. From my perspective, one of the most damaging aspects of the recession psychologically was that it closed down people's sense of options. It culled creative thinking and problem-solving. These are the very psychological weapons you need when facing uncertainty and job loss.

The problem, of course, is that most people have to work. There's no choice from the outset – you need to earn a living. I read an interesting article that asked: why do we work? It gave an overview of the hedonistic partying the Victorian era engaged in, when work was done on the farm and the end of chores signalled the start of a bit of a free-for-all. Then came the Industrial Revolution, and it changed the face and time aspect of work from that point forward. Instead of work being local, seasonal and guided by the light of day, it became structured into units of time. The work process was divided into distinct parts, and you were assigned your little cog in the ever-turning industrially charged wheel. There were no fancy induction weeks, no meet-and-greet with your new team lead, it was just 'work, work, work'.

This paradigm shift has started to come at least half-circle now, with the modus operandi of the modern world of work being challenged and upgraded by the potential to work anytime and anywhere. The punch in-punch out clock of the industrial era has been replaced by an 'always on' generation. The pre-digital era enjoyed the unencumbered joy of walking out of the office with a cheery, *'see you tomorrow'*. There wouldn't be enough holes for all the post-work work that is punched out by twenty-first-century workers. This is where the long arm of digital connectivity can rob the quality of your home life and social life.

This is one of the most pressing issues of modern work: boundaries. It is important to explore, question and challenge your work boundaries. I have seen too many workers performing well at work but at a huge cost to their important relationships. This is now a gender-neutral concern, with both men and women feeling guilty and torn. It is often said that the best thing you can give in a relationship is the gift of time. What happens when you want to give that time but it feels like there isn't enough inner you to go around?

Social media has thrown up a lot of problematic issues in terms of boundaries. To friend or not to friend?, that is the question. If you receive a friend request from a colleague, or a boss, should you accept, ignore or reject? I wish I could say I had a definitive answer to this very modern dilemma, but I'm afraid I don't. The answer lies with you. Where do you want to draw the line? Do you want your boss seeing you out on the town with your mates? Do you feel that would blur the lines of work and personal life, and would you rather keep those lines rigid? You have the right to choose, that doesn't make it easy, but you do have that right.

Who you are at work will likely be appropriate to that job and that environment, and it might be inappropriate or unhelpful to share all the other aspects of your inner selves, whether that's you at that amazing party or being a playful dad with the kids or your love of cat videos. What you 'like', watch and follow clearly provides a profile of your predilections. It is your choice whether to invite or accept Billy from two floors down who you literally only say 'hello' to but have never spoken to properly. If you want to leave work at work, then don't invite them into your social media home.

Among your co-workers, no doubt there are some you call friends, some you call colleagues and some who drive you around the twist and what you feel about them can't be printed here! You can't choose your family, but biology helps with bonding. That doesn't apply to your work 'family'. Work colleagues and friends can provide great support and good humour, and add to that sense of belonging that is so integral to feeling engaged and happy at work. However, one unfortunately common issue with colleagues is bullying. I hear about this in my clinic far too often. The damage it can cause is not to be underestimated. If we remember back to the idea of rejection being felt like the sting of physical pain, known as social pain, bullying also impacts every aspect of a person. I can't cover much of this immense problem here, because a single chapter could never do it justice, but it is important to recognise that it is a major problem and must be tackled and solved. The following list is argument enough:

Stress-related diseases and health complications from prolonged exposure to the stressors of bullying:

- Cardiovascular problems: Hypertension (60%) to strokes, heart attacks.

- Adverse neurological changes: Neurotransmitter disruption, hippocampus and amygdala atrophy.

- Gastrointestinal: IBD, colitis.

- Immunological impairment: More frequent infections of greater severity.

- Auto-immune disorders.

- Fibromyalgia (21%), Chronic Fatigue Syndrome (33%).

- Diabetes (10%).

- Skin disorders (17%).

- Some physical indications of the above stress might include:
    ◇ Nausea
    ◇ Tremors of the lips, hands, etc.
    ◇ Feeling uncoordinated
    ◇ Chills
    ◇ Profuse sweating
    ◇ Diarrhoea
    ◇ Rapid heartbeat
    ◇ Rapid breathing
    ◇ Elevated blood pressure
    ◇ Chest pain
    ◇ Uncontrollable crying
    ◇ Headaches

(Source: WBI 2012 Impact on Employee Health Survey)

The definition of workplace bullying is the repetitive and systematic engagement of interpersonally abusive behaviors that negatively affect both the targeted individual as well as the work organization (Askew et al., 2013). In practice, it often begins subtly. The subtlety is manipulative in nature, making the victim feel like they are being 'petty'. It is the incessant nature of each back comment or put-down that builds over time and causes stress. And then there is the bully who openly engages in bullying tactics. This is the one that frustrates me the most as it seems to be rewarded in organisations. I wonder how many readers who have been bullied have been 'moved' to another department while the bully maintains their position? If you find yourself in this position at work, it is essential to talk to someone, get help and put your wellbeing first.

Of course, a bully isn't the only colleague who can cause you stress. What do you do when you work with people you find difficult? When you work with someone who has a very different personality from you, different ways of seeing and doing things, facing them day after day can be a major challenge and wear on your nerves. The first course of action, as always, is to think about how you can change your response to them or the triggering situations. Ask yourself what you find difficult about this person, and why. What do they bring up or trigger for you? Take out your Diary and do some work: *'When Anna says "let's get this over the line", it makes my blood boil.'* Identify the emotions that are coming up for you and see if you can accept the situation and person as they are. You may never be office buddies, and that's OK, you may not ever like them, this is about being aware of when your mood changes and what you can do about it. Breathe, release and let go. Accepting your frustrations and how you feel can be a powerful antidote. You can't change them, but you can change your response (see Mind the Gap, Psychological Toolbox, p. 243.)

One colleague relationship I would gently caution against is the office affair. You may think you are being masters of camouflage, but in the jungle of work, those first tentative looks and heightened sense of attraction are noticed easily. The truth is: either everyone knows or everyone will know. It is almost impossible to keep it secret. Affairs are a messy business, and while they may seem sexy and thrilling at first, they have a tendency to end in a whole heap of pain.

A caveat: this advice is for people who are married or in committed relationships. An office romance between two single people can work out. You spend a lot of time together, and you can really get to know each other.

You need to be mindful if one of you is in a senior position, as that could put you both in a questionable position, especially when management finds out, but for many it does work out and good matches can be made.

While the digital age of work brings its own unique problems, it also brings a huge wealth of opportunities. We've moved on from 'earning a crust' to the idea of work as an integral part of our identity, and that can be empowering and liberating. The idea of a 'job for life' is nearly extinct. The modern workforce feels a lot less restricted by location and frowns at a résumé that's sparse on varied experience. The one-size-fits-all model is, thankfully, changing as one size does not fit all. There are new theories and thinking surrounding the idea of the work self and the psychological benefits of work, and that helps us all to tap into those benefits and try to avail of them.

KEY THEORIES

Brian Dyson, former CEO of Coca-Cola, gave a speech that has since become famous as the 'five balls speech'. He advised people to imagine their life as a game in which they had to juggle five balls.

The game of life balls are:

1. Work
2. Family
3. Health
4. Friends
5. Happiness/spirit

The work ball is made of rubber. You figure this out when you drop it and it bounces back to you. The other four balls, however, are made of glass. Drop any of them and at best, you will damage them and they will never be the same, at worst, you will destroy them. His inspiring speech beseeched us to value the time we have with the important relationships in our lives and to be present with them when we are. This is becoming more and more difficult for people as they succumb to a phone-in-the-hand life, where they are always connected, always accessible. The reality of work for many is a feeling of being digitally scattered. What I find striking, though, is the lack of annoyance at this – it seems the intrusion of work into home life is not questioned and has become normalised.

You might find Mary's story familiar:

Mary has just started into the dinner preparations, her peeler is flying through the various veg and spuds as she chats with her children about their day. She has been working flat out from home all day. She's trying really hard to get her kids to focus on their homework.

Ding dong.

Mary answers the door and standing there is Fred, her boss. Mary is somewhat mortified as she's wearing unicorn slippers.

'Hi Mary, sorry, I know it's nearly six o'clock, but I've just a few more things I need you to do before tomorrow. Won't take more than five minutes.'

Mary closes the door. She feels it was a bit much for Fred to come all the way out to her house just for that.

Mary goes back inside. The kids are now fighting among themselves and the homework is still far from done. Mary feels irritated; her fuse shortens, she snaps at the kids.

She responds to the request from her boss and presses 'Send'.

Ding dong.

Guess who? It's Fred again.

As Mary opens the door, Fred says, 'Thanks Mary, that's great, just one more small change here and it's all good.'

This is tongue-in-cheek, of course, but the unfortunate part is that 'Fred' does intrude into your home. He comes into your house and interrupts your dinner, as you shush your kids so you can take that 'quick' work call. Fred sits down between you and your partner on the couch as you finally get to watch a bit of TV. Truth is, I know a lot of you take Fred to bed with you too. The sad part is that Fred makes you feel harried and irritated, which makes you a bit grumpy with the people you love the most when you should be enjoying their company. The plain fact is: Fred shouldn't be there. He doesn't belong in your home. He's in the way.

If this strikes a chord with you, think about it, think about your boundaries and try to instigate this simple rule: work hard, be fully present at work; then come home and be fully present. The acceptance of work intrusions into your home via any digital device needs to be questioned, and the expectation of an immediate response needs to change. If you let this become your work norm, it will take over your life.

Even worse is when you are a Fred yourself. It feels so hard to not reply to that email request, often pushed to action by the subject line screaming 'urgent'. I say with hand on heart that I am not good at this. But I am going to change. I am looking around for good role models, and there are many and they know what they are doing. Good role models are specific to each person, so you need to look around your own office or industry for them. The things to look for are people with clear work boundaries, an ability to get ahead, and be highly successful, but also to nurture their other relationships outside of work. This is real leadership in action.

People find it difficult to change this aspect of their lives and set boundaries because busyness has become a status symbol. But I think what many are finding out is that it is a dysfunctional status symbol that is leading to exhaustion and burnout. As a society, we need to place value on living a good life with real balance. The key to this, as we saw above, is setting healthy boundaries. Using Dyson's very neat 'five life balls', ask yourself honestly what priorities did you update in your relationship today? Or would you pass an ISO for how you parented today? Surely that was on your agenda? It wasn't, oh. Guess what? It's not on Fred's agenda either. Organisations are profit-driven, and your family and life are not on their agenda.

When you are at home, you cannot just be physically be at home, you must be mentally and emotionally there as well. As philosopher Simone Weil so beautifully puts it: 'Attention is the rarest and purest form of generosity.' You need to commit energy, time and love to your four other balls, the glass ones that have a warning on them: *breakable, handle with care*. The problem with glass is that once broken, it's gone forever. The issue with time is that once it's gone, it's gone forever. There will always be more work to do. If you break down how much time you put into your work, can you say that you put the same time into your most treasured relationships? This is not to add to any guilt or regret, it is to drive change, to make you realise that you need to prioritise you and your relationship needs and keep these times as you keep your contracted work times.

When work stresses accumulate, it can lead to decompensation. This occurs when your usual defences in managing your mental health break down and make normal daily functioning very difficult. Past mental health issues may have been managed up to that point, but can deteriorate and impact your ability to function in a day-to-day manner, from being able to work to managing housework, personal hygiene and stress. It is important to recognise the signs of decompensation and seek professional help.

Joe was on the senior management team in his organisation. He was well liked by his colleagues and known as an old-school 'strong and silent' type. But everyone knew that Joe was the man to get the job done. If you wanted to know, you asked Joe.

Joe was decompensating at 90 miles an hour at work, he was doing and being the same guy he always was, 'good old Joe, dependable and calm'. But behind the calm façade he felt like he was just about keeping his head above water. His chest was tight and heavy. He was falling behind on projects, he found it harder to concentrate and by the time he got home, all he was fit for was the couch. He had experienced periods of depression before and had been managing it for a few years, but he could feel that he was slipping back into that black hole very quickly. He had always had a close relationship with his wife, but he felt very alone in his thoughts and didn't want to let her down. This in turn affected their connection and she felt alone as well.

Eventually, his wife insisted he go to the doctor. She diagnosed anxiety. Much to Joe's shock and embarrassment, the tears came.

'Please don't tell my wife, she'll be so worried. I'm fine, really, I'm fine.'

'Joe, how long have you been feeling like this?' his GP asked.

'Years, on and off, and I always managed to get back on track, but this time I can't. I just feel spent.'

Joe was referred for CBT (cognitive behavioural therapy), where he began to see that his personality strived for perfection. The years of putting every project first, or taking that extra job or staying that little bit later just to get it off the list had gradually worn away at him and his confidence. He could do it while at work, but at the expense to his other life balls. The panic started to set in when it wasn't even working at work, the anxiety triggering faster than his ability to get the job done. Joe was surprised by how negative his thoughts had become. He started to see how the perfectionism drove his constant 'people pleasing' behaviours.

Through therapy, Joe was encouraged to see the collateral damage that his lack of boundaries was having and how it was spilling into all of his other relationships, mood, health and general happiness. The biggest revelation to Joe was that he realised nothing was ever enough. His perfectionism was like an insatiable monster. He truly believed that when he got that next project over the line, he'd feel great, but it never came. He saw how relentless he had been on himself. When asked would he treat any of his colleagues like this, horrified, he said, 'no, never'.

He worked on creating healthier expectations and room for reality to change those timelines. He could see that every small add-on and extra task took far longer than he ever imagined. It was really tough for Joe because so much of his work and social identity was tied into being easy-going, always there to lend a hand. Through the CBT process, he began to see that to have real compassion for others, he first had to have it for himself. He worked on ways to consolidate that in a manner that matched his personality. He learned that 'no' wasn't aggressive and mean and that he could say, 'I can't get to that today, this month, or ever' with a gentle smile.

I have seen so many 'Joes' in my clinic that I can spot them as soon as they walk into the room. They have an unassuming manner, soft voice and kind face and eyes. Their enthusiasm and conscientiousness for their job is beautiful, but perfection is a beast.

Psychologist Alison Gopnik's research casts a different light on the idea of creative problem-solving at work. She found that pre-schoolers outperformed older children and adults in their natural flair for problem-solving. This led Gopnik to describe toddlers as 'the R&D of the human species while adults are production and marketing'. This is because adults tend to overthink, while toddlers are impulsive, imaginative and reactive. It makes sense as our reliance on heuristics and mental short-cuts boxes our thinking into *'this is the way something is'* or *'this is how it looks'*, making it harder to literally think outside of the box.

This is where teamwork can be of great benefit, where you try and see it from one of your colleague's point of view. Another creative way to think is to use your imagination, thinking about it 'as if' it was already done or achieved. Children use their limitless imagination, often without any restraints of reality, and just dream, and it is in these states that the brain can come up with new ideas and possibilities. Another strategy brings us back to the idea of a role model or mentor. While your kid may be inspired by a superhero, who inspires you? Then ask, *'what would … do in this situation?'* Sometimes our limitations are stuck within the idea of who we are, not who we can become.

There's a new buzzword in the research on work and the self: EE. It refers to your energy expenditure and is a strong indicator and measure of your mood, how your day went or your general wellbeing. Do you leave work feeling fantastic, having had a really productive and synergistic team meeting that made you feel engaged, and like you belonged to something that you liked being a part of? Or, did you leave feeling tired, drained or exhausted? Let your 'energy expenditure' be your guide to decide if you have the time to say yes to that other request or project. Ask yourself: is the amount of energy you have given proportionate to the work outcome? If you already feel spent, do you need a rethink on this? Maybe to discuss it with your boss or team? Could you get some help or change the deadline? Keep your mind curious and creative to see what options are available to you.

We have already looked at the work *me*, the identity that you inhabit while at work. This public self is often rational, capable and directed towards problem-solving, which are hugely helpful traits. They can be helpful in other areas of your life as well. I like how people are professional and rational at work. If you were doing something wrong in your job or you realised it wasn't working, you would most likely take action and change it. Whereas the private *I* might continue with the same mistake many times and in many different ways before making a concerted effort to change it. This is why I often ask clients to bring their professional self into areas of their private lives, so they can be more objective, clear-cut and actionable when things are not the way they need to be. I'm fully aware that changing a project or work decision can be less uncomfortable than, say, changing your partner, but the objectivity that people bring to work can serve them well in their home or personal life. Engaging in behavioural change is immensely uncomfortable and tricky, and often has a lot of baggage that you are not even aware of, but there can be a depersonalisation in your work self that makes getting stuff done a little easier.

Impostor syndrome

Of course, not everyone feels competent or rational or capable at work. Sometimes, this feeling of public competence declines as your private self is wracked with 'impostor syndrome'. This is a doubly painful dichotomy of public perception and private self-doubt. The fear of being 'caught' or 'found out' is a genuine worry for people, even more so for those who feel they are perceived as being really good at their job. For that person, the margin for error can feel very small to minimal. This is where unrealistic personal expectations of having to be perfect can take hold and take over.

So many people feel this that the term impostor syndrome was coined in 1978 by clinical psychologists Pauline Clance and Suzanne Imes, who said it referred 'to high-achieving individuals marked by an inability to internalize their accomplishments and a persistent fear of being exposed as a "fraud". So, contrary to the evidence of their exemplary and stellar work performance, high-achievers still wrestle with silent fear, self-doubt and huge insecurities as they wait to be exposed. One of the main time triggers for impostor syndrome is when you have just completed a very important project or you have won an award or been recognised for your work.

Why does this happen? At base, it is the fear of being exposed as a fake. The reason for this is that you depersonalise your hard work and effort and attribute your success to something outside yourself, such as good luck. You find it difficult to take credit or praise as you have a fundamental lack of self-belief and confidence. Valerie Young, author of *The Secret Thoughts of Successful Women,* identifies five competence types who suffer with low confidence and impostor syndrome.

1. The perfectionist.
2. The superman/superwoman.
3. The natural genius.
4. The rugged individualist.
5. The expert.

THE PERFECTIONIST

Perfectionism and impostor syndrome are an unfortunate good fit. The perfectionist sets incredibly high, sometimes impossible goals for themselves. They find it extremely difficult to delegate and feel *'it would be quicker* (read: better) *if I did it myself'*. Ask yourself one simple question: when you have completed a huge achievement at work, how do you feel afterwards? Are you thrilled, delighted with yourself or is this when the fear creeps in? This is one sign of the perfectionist, another is that you will often procrastinate until it is the 'perfect time' to start. Once finished the task, you will conduct a dissatisfied post mortem: *'it could have been better'*, *'if I only had more time it would have been perfect'*. Perfectionism linked with impostor syndrome is a nasty and often lifelong affliction. Use your level of discomfort as a good sign that you are making difficult but really important changes.

THE SUPERMAN/SUPERWOMAN

Beneath the superhuman façade lies a fear that you aren't talented or skilled enough. So you have to engage in three times the work that everyone else does because you 'know' they actually belong there, whereas you feel like you don't. Get to the core of your insecurities: have you always felt like this, or did something happen that impacted your confidence? Chart it back and write it down. When and what is 'enough'? Most 'superheroes' ignore this until they are flattened by exhaustion, illness, reduced ability to deal with stress and negative impact on their mental health. What validation will be the one that will make you believe in yourself? How about you try to do this for yourself? End each day by writing down three things you are giving yourself credit for that day. Try and focus on internal achievements of changing your relationship with the relentless and impossible pursuit of achievement: *'Today I handed the project in, it's wasn't perfect, it was so uncomfortable, but I did it.'*

THE NATURAL GENIUS

This is the student who got straight As. When faced with a new task, if they don't get it immediately, they think they're no good at it. The danger is they may give in and internalise if they don't score perfectly: *'I am bad at accounting'*. They see working hard at something as a sign that they don't have the ability in the first place. Where is this coming from? How was achievement rewarded at home? Barbara Frederickson's 'broaden and build' theory holds that each new learning forms more new learning from which you can build upon. Revise your attitude so that each new task is a completely new challenge, your discomfort is a positive sign and confusion or 'not knowing' is simply learning and growth.

THE RUGGED INDIVIDUALIST

How does asking for help make you feel? Is this a sign to you that you are an impostor because you should know this stuff already? Being unable to embrace the vulnerability of asking for help is something I know many people suffer from. Often this is a learned response, probably from home or school. You might find yourself saying often, *'I don't need any help'*, but we are interdependent on each other for learning and growth. Being fiercely independent serves no one really.

THE EXPERT

Some people are very 'creative' on their CVs, but the expert may not even apply for the job if they feel they don't meet every single requirement as it would be a lie, and then they would be caught out. The simple fact is, you can't know everything. If you find yourself endlessly upskilling, you have to ask yourself: when will I feel qualified or experienced enough? Naming this fear will reduce a lot of its power over you.

Have you asked any of your work colleagues if they have ever felt like this? If you haven't, you will be very surprised: it is the very people you wouldn't expect to have impostor syndrome who will admit to it. You need to value your skills and contribution. When someone pays you a compliment, don't brush it off. Listen to the good feedback. Try and assimilate the positive feelings to your inner self. It sounds crass, but *fake it until you make it* is good advice. The thing about confidence is that you only get it after you've done the scary deed. If you had experience, it wouldn't be as scary.

As with any act of confronting yourself and striving for change, it's hard and challenging, and it's so much easier not to do it. In today's world, we have a wealth of distractions to keep us from doing this kind of work on ourselves. Political philosopher Matthew Crawford has described distraction as a 'kind of obesity of the mind'. The media have become masters at packaging stimuli in ways that our brains find irresistible, just as food engineers have become expert in creating 'hyper-palatable' foods by manipulating levels of sugar, fat and salt.

There is an interesting connection between the pioneering work of Dr David Kessler and how technology has been engineered to be 'hyper-palatable' to the end user, which is you and me. Kessler, a former FDA commissioner, took the tobacco industry to court. (He is the reason why 'Smoking Kills' is written on cigarette boxes.) Kessler then turned his attention to the obesity crisis after watching a morbidly obese woman on *Oprah* crying because she couldn't understand why she was eating herself to death. He set himself a goal to find out why. His research led him to identify hyper-palatable foods, which are specifically engineered to make certain foods irresistible. These foods are the ones that contain the triple threat of high salt, high fat and high sugar. In Crawford's view, he sees technology as being engineered to appeal to our brains in a way that is also irresistible. The key point here is that while putting cigarettes, obesity and distraction together may seem like an odd line-up, the common thread is that each is engineered to make these things hyper-palatable to your brain.

Crawford's book, *The Case for Working with Your Hands*, recommends working on something manual, or at least tangible, to combat the constant distractions. When you are focused on a specific task, you are in a state of flow and lose yourself in what you are doing. In a digital society, your attention is being demanded and grabbed from myriad sources and it bounces all over the place, but this is not good for your brain. You can only focus on one task at a time. Working with your hands is a good antidote. When you are making something, you are fully present, engaged and in the moment. It is an excellent skill to cultivate in yourself.

The value now placed on knowledge workers and expertise has degraded the value of manual or trade work. And yet, I have spoken with many tradespeople who will point out how much they love their job. Doing a day's work, seeing something real at the end is something they describe as deeply rewarding. Perhaps you've heard of the IKEA effect. Harvard psychologists showed that a cognitive bias occurs when a person makes something, even partially, themselves. They apply a disproportionately high value to the item, and think others should share their view.

From a clinical point of view, I have seen so many people struggle with that sense of not finishing the day with a tangible or tactile sense of '*I made this*', or any sense of doing or achieving something real and/or tangible. Maybe our post-industrial surreal and invisible work has contributed to an increase in what may present at my clinic as anxiety and panic attacks. Not too far under the surface, a dull heavy ache of existential angst asks: '*what is the purpose of what I am doing at work, and what am I getting out of it?*' The quest for purpose is often underlain by a much deeper human yearning to discover what life is all about. Just remember that there is no reason why you can't fulfil these hopes and dreams outside of work – that may be in the form of volunteering, walking the Camino or giving time to hobbies that give you a sense of personal satisfaction. You can create the life-work balance that works for you.

THE PRACTICE

We have established that boundary-setting is a key theme of this chapter, but don't forget the 'emotional labour' that you pay by losing yourself in the role of the company man/woman. You may be given a name badge at work, but you need to mind that you don't lose your true identity there. Coined by Arlie Hochschild in her book, *The Managed Heart: The Commercialisation of Human Feelings*, emotional labour can often be seen in the caring profession, where the needs of others always come first. As a result, you are more prone to burnout by the very fact that you care, especially if you are very conscientious.

Does that mean that you need be less caring? No, not at all. It means that you need to establish and be aware of your own work boundaries and to redress the balance by engaging in active self-care. Here's a little trick: if you are asked to do something at work and you experience an immediate sense of discomfort or unease, check in with yourself, sit with the feeling and ask yourself:

- What is the feeling?
- Has a time boundary being crossed?
- Has a competence boundary been crossed?
- Is this actually your job?
- Do you have the energy to carry out the task today?

Work values your expertise, but you need to value your time. Remember: 'Value has a value only if its value is valued' (Brian Dyson).

Being fully present at home is almost a lost luxury for many people. From a clinical point of view, I see a definite increase in work-related stress issues and it's a cause of much concern. Your employer knows they have a duty of care to you, but you need to extend that duty of care to yourself, whether you are employed or self-employed. Using this template, complete your own duty of care.

The juggle	The struggle	The goal	How to achieve it
Work	Feeling like you don't belong, boredom, angst, work feels pointless	Engagement, purpose, meaning	Write down your top four VIAs . Can you incorporate any or some of them in your role? If you can't, do you want to change jobs/career? What do you need to do that? Start with the end in mind. See the type of work environment, time scales, etc. Write 'Engagement, Purpose, Meaning' at the top of a page, list underneath what they mean to you, and then what you can do to bring them about.
Family	Stress, feeling overwhelmed, low quality time together	Connection, belonging, meaning	Identify your stressors on paper. Next write what you can control and what you can't. What actions can you take on the things within your control? Can you accept the things that are outside of your control? Write 'Connection, Belonging, Meaning' down and under each list where, how and with whom you can get these. Self-care.
Health	Lifestyle habits, time, pressure, not a priority	Minding physical & mental health	Write the specifics of what you want to change in your health, list them under 'Physical, Emotional and Mental'. What needs to happen for this to occur? Get your calendar out and start scheduling.
Friends	Too busy, so gets crossed off the to-do list	Fun, a release, connection, support	Write out the last fantastic time you had with friends, list what you got out of it. Make and keep some plans with friends.
Happiness	Undefined and not on the priority list	Sense of peace, contentedness	What is happiness to you? With this as your starting point. How are you going to bring this into your life?

DIARY

In order to clarify your own feelings and thoughts about your work self, answer these questions.

◇ What would your ideal job be? _____

_____

_____

◇ How would that ideal job look and what would you be doing? _____

_____

_____

◇ What does your day involve? _____

_____

_____

◇ What aspects of your job do you really like? _____

_____

_____

◇ What type of work environment works for you? _____

_____

_____

What is your biggest turn-off at work? _____

_____

_____

◇ What can you do about it? _____

_____

_____

◇ What does your work mean to you? _____

_____

_____

_____

◇ Do you derive a sense of purpose from work? _____

_____

_____

_____

The digital question is a pressing one now, and will probably become more so. The world has shrunk to a village as we all log on and connect 24/7. But humans have a distinct circadian rhythm and it's not wise to ignore it. Digital use is having a direct impact on when and how we sleep. Are you aware of the extent of this impact on your mind and body?

- Do you check your phone before bed?
- Is your phone turned on and in the room where you are sleeping?
- What wakes you up in the morning – is it the gentle light of the new day with the birds' chorus or is it some awful chiming ringtone to frighten you awake?

Did you answer yes to all three? Me too! In time, I predict smartphones will carry a health warning. Put an app on your phone that monitors your daily social media use. This is your baseline of the amount of change you need to make. What would it be like to take social media off your phone? I am not asking you to do it, but how did the thought of that make you feel? Can you make some new work rules, whereby you don't check e-mails after a certain time? These self-directed work rules would be of great benefit to you, your relationships and ultimately to your work productivity. There will always be exceptions, the problem is when the exception becomes the norm.

Why do you work? That remains our fundamental question. There's the obvious answer – that we need to work to live, to pay the bills – but it's often so much more than that. You might work to live, but you might also live to work. Only you know what the truth is for you. If you live to work, this can be a really tough one because it's very difficult to get workaholics to change. Ask yourself how you feel at work and then compare to how you feel at home. Sometimes there can be quite a discrepancy when your competent and in-control work self meets the avoidant and uncertain you at home. Avoidance can come in the form of conversations, intimacy, fear of vulnerability, over-reliance on yourself, which may relate back to your primary attachment style. Is there something you are avoiding at home?

We have mentioned above that it is important to retain yourself within your work self. The Russian doll needs each of its dolls slotted into place to be complete. It's important to be aware of your work self, and how it's complementing or impacting your other selves.

DIARY

◇ Who is your work self, e.g. professional, focused, efficient? _____
_____
_____
_____

◇ What is your work identity, e.g. *'in control'*, *'know what I'm doing'*? ___
_____
_____
_____

◇ Name three strengths of your work self, e.g. completer, good team worker, flexible. _____
_____
_____
_____

◇ Name three things you would like to strengthen or change about your work self, e.g. your response to stress, procrastination or not standing up for yourself and not being heard at meetings. _____
_____
_____
_____

One way of aligning your personal and work goals is to actively use your VIAs. These are important for your work self because they will add a level of congruence between your personal and work self. Everyone has weaknesses, the trick is to work on your core strengths and improve and develop workable goals that fit with your VIAs.

◇ Write down your top four VIAs. _____

_____

◇ How do you use these in your job? _____

_____

We examined the problem of distraction above, and the antidote to the frustration of constant interruptions and distraction, particularly in open-plan offices, is flow. In his marvellous book, *Flow: The Psychology of Optimal Experience*, Mihaly Csikszentmihalyi explains that people who experience more 'flow' in their life are more contented. Basically, you experience 'flow' or a 'peak optimal experience' or 'being in the zone' when you:

- are challenged by a task, but it's not too challenging;
- are fully absorbed in it, so much so that time either slows down or speeds up;
- are really clear about what you are doing and are fully focused on the task;
- lose self-consciousness by being absorbed in the task;
- feel there's an intrinsic motivation or reward in that you enjoy doing it for the sake of doing it.

When you watch any expert or athlete, you'll see that they have 'flow' and make it look effortless. Of course, they have trained immensely to go from novice to expert. Csikszentmihalyi describes it like this: 'The best moments in our lives are not the passive, receptive, relaxing times ... The best moments usually occur if a person's body or mind is stretched to its limits in a voluntary effort to accomplish something difficult and worthwhile.'

◇ What brings flow into your life? _____

_____

◇ When do you experience flow at work? _____

_____

◇ What do you lose yourself to, when do you do this, where do you do it? __

_____

_____

Ask yourself this: when was the last time you really experienced that feeling of total immersion in a task? The state of flow is a luxury, akin to the luxury of time that I fear will happen less and less in the age of distraction. Work can provide a wonderful opportunity to lose yourself temporarily in a task or project. Alternatively, work can be one interruption after another. Your brain does not work well in this sort of disrupted system. Systematically set aside time where you can be absorbed in the task at hand.

So, how can you create flow at work? Try these tips.

1. Set aside predetermined days and times in the week for 'flow work'.
2. During these times, turn off email notifications, put the phone in a drawer, and ensure you have no meetings scheduled.
3. If need be, have some sort of sign on your desk or an email notification to let people know you are in the zone and that they may not enter the zone. You could use headphones to indicate this too. No matter how quickly you think you can reply to someone, it takes you so much longer to get back on task and into the zone again, so don't allow those distractions.
4. Practice. It might not come easily, but if you focus on it and practice it, you will be able to increase your flow work. It's worth it because flow gives a wonderfully satisfying feeling of being absorbed and productive.

Work life is full of challenges, and challenge is a game-changer. It is a hugely positive experience as adversity makes you aware of strengths and virtues you didn't even know you possessed. It is the perception of the challenge that makes it either stressful or something you view with relish. Resilience is a key skill, and you would do well to add it to your Psychological Toolbox. Stress, uncertainty and change will always be there, but amidst that chaos you can learn how to change your reaction and choose to respond in the way that serves you best. Rising to challenges means learning to be aware of what the negative emotions are telling you and using them to drive new, healthier behaviours to become more mentally fit. It pays to see challenges and adversity as good training for your brain.

There are many inspiring people who use challenge to help them grow through adversity. Face down your challenges, look them straight in the eye and ask: What am I going to do to change this or make it better? The first step is to accept the reality of the situation, which is useful because you can then focus on what needs to be done to change it. Once you have achieved mindful acceptance, you can manage the challenge.

John came for a consultation. While he felt his presence was a sort of failure, his ability to see his situation clearly was actually a huge strength.

'My boss is a complete asshole,' John said. 'I think his goal in life is to make me miserable. If it weren't so bad, it would actually be kinda funny. He must sit awake at night dreaming up new ways to embarrass and humiliate me. But I've had enough. I'm not sleeping, I am in a constant bad mood, when I wake in the morning I have this immediate sick feeling in the pit of my stomach. If I told you some of the things, you'll think I'm over-reacting, but I actually can't take it anymore. I can't believe I'm here today, I am such an idiot, and I'm not this guy.'

The venom with which John said this about himself was indicative of the chronic stress, anxiety and bullying he had been experiencing at work, which had slipped into depression.

'What do you want to do, John?'

'Not this,' he said as he put his hands up in disgust, pointing to himself.

'That's a good place to start.'

One part of happiness is the ability to take risks. Risk and challenge work well as a team because they open you up to new experiences and give you the courage to take the next step. This allows you to grow and experience a more fulfilling life. This isn't about Las Vegas-style risks, but if you want to be happier at work, relationships or life, you need to walk towards new challenges and experiences, to reach the state of Eudaimonia.

Aristotle came up with the concept of Eudaimonia, from the Greek word *daimon*, meaning 'your true nature'. Eudaimonia is considered the gold medal in human flourishing, but like anything that is worth achieving, it requires grit, tenacity and effort. It isn't just about happiness or pleasure, it's about what the good life and the meaningful life means to you. It is in this authenticity that you hope to experience your true self. I know this is not what is promised in the world of instant self-help, but if you really want to help or change yourself, you must first recognise that everything you have ever changed before took a lot of hard work, effort and tenacity. Your brain gets bored of 'easy' very quickly. When you stretch yourself, you become something new.

John's case included bullying, but for many people who feel that constant dread about their unfulfilling, soul-deadening job, the mortgage and adult responsibilities can make it feel like they should just get on with it. They try to minimise the experience and their feelings about it by telling themselves, *'it's not that bad, others have it worse'*. It's a very comfortable uncomfortableness.

As adults, we do have responsibilities, but this doesn't mean the end of options and choices. Finding meaning in your work is the antidote to a job that has no meaning to you. If this is not possible, finding it outside work through a hobby is another viable option. It might entail a risk, but you owe it to yourself to figure out what it is that you would really love to do, and then aim to do it.

DIARY

✧ If money was no object, what would you do? _____

_____

_____

_____

> ✧ Is there any way you can do this in stages, or in some partial way? _____
>
> _____
>
> _____
>
> _____

We have seen that flow is an energising and deeply satisfying experience, but when you are in a negative, self-critical place it is impossible to reach the state of flow.

It is unrealistic to think you could love everything about your job, but I think we have become unrealistic in terms of the amount of time – physical, mental and emotional – that people put into jobs they hate. A lot of people are serving life sentences for the crime of not taking a risk and for doing something that is incongruous with their VIAs and intrinsic work motivation. Prioritising the extrinsic motivation of 'succeeding' or the politics of playing the game and moving up the career ladder is no good if you come home spent.

For those of you who work in an office, what name springs to mind when you hear the words 'the office'? Like many of you, I suspect, I see David Brent, sitting in his chair with two thumbs and index fingers cocked at you as he says, 'pow, pow'. Have you worked for a David Brent character? Brent is the epitome of the so-called Dunning-Kruger effect, named from their paper 'Unskilled and Unaware of It'. This provides the science behind what you already know about your own office.

The Dunning-Kruger effect is a cognitive bias in which people of low ability have illusory superiority and mistakenly assess their cognitive ability to be greater than it is. The David Brents of this world believe they are really good at their job, extremely competent and excel at leadership. They have greatly overestimated their skill level, but lack the meta-cognitive ability to see this gross overestimation. There are many names for this cognitive bias:

* The above-average effect.
* The superiority bias.
* The sense of relative superiority.
* The illusion of superiority.

As philosopher Bertrand Russell puts it: 'The trouble with the world is that the stupid are cocksure and the intelligent full of doubt.' But before we get too comfortable with pointing the finger at 'David Brents', the fact is that most people judge themselves to be more moral, honest, kind, trustworthy and in happier relationships than others. This is known as the 'better-than-average (B-T-A) bias', and it affects us all.

Self-awareness is key. Although self-awareness often comes with pain, especially when it lights up one of your blind-spots. Feedback can feel like criticism. Words can sting and stay with you long after they have been uttered. The whole Russian doll comes to work with you, so other selves can come into play and be affected. Your frame of 'feedback' will look different to you if you have always or mostly been in the 'accepted' group, whereas it may be heard as criticism if you have a high rejection sensitivity bias.

The cruel irony of the Dunning-Kruger findings is that those who are most incompetent are happily oblivious to their level of incompetency. The participants who scored the lowest in tests on 'humour, grammar and logic grossly overestimated' how well they did in the test and their own ability. They estimated themselves to be in the 62nd percentile, when they actually were in the 12th percentile. At the other end of the scale, those who are lowest in self-esteem grossly underestimate their abilities and competencies.

DIARY

Thinking about your own work situation, answer these questions:

◇ Who is the David Brent in your office? _____

_____

_____

◇ What do they not see about themselves? _____

_____

_____

_____

◇ Have you ever been surprised by something someone has shared with you about yourself? _____

_____

_____

_____

◇ Did it change your behaviour, or were you hurt, or both? _____

_____

_____

_____

◇ Who do you think your colleagues think you are? _____

_____

_____

_____

◇ What do you think would surprise them to learn about you? _____

_____

_____

_____

◇ Would you consider asking a colleague for some honest feedback? ____

_____

_____

_____

Life is too short to do things every day that you hate, and it really is bad for your health. You always have options. Brainstorm options, leaving reality aside, because that allows you to be open and creative. How do your options look now? Remember you always have choices, you just need to choose to see that you do.

CONCLUSION

Know this: there will always be more on your to-do list. Work can and will be many things over the course of your working life, but the key is to bring 'you' home every day. Not a shell of you that is overwhelmed, harried or burned out, unable to connect with the people you want to love and cuddle. It works both ways, because if you are a more balanced, healthier, happier person, you will also be a more engaged employee or boss. You will be more innovative, energised and able to do a better job that gives you meaning. It's all about balance, but only you can put that balance in place.

- You need to build at work, love and repair at home.
- You need to allocate time to self-care, more so when you don't feel like it.
- Stop burning the candle at both ends – recognise that you have limits and accept them.
- Connect with your family, be present, have a laugh, eat dinner together, get out for your weekly soccer match or class. Family and social life isn't a luxury, it is a necessity.
- Work 'you' into your schedule, which means committing to do things for you, on a consistent basis, across all of your health: sleep, diet, exercise and physical and emotional wellbeing.

Companies are big on mission statements, and they can be extremely useful. They distil the aims and philosophy of the organisation into a clear, workable set of guidelines. I recommend you do this for yourself and write your own, personal work mission statement. Your mission statement will change over time, but it will help guide your choices and decisions.

Here's a sample mission statement for you to consider:

Having freshly finished her surgical internship, Rosa felt equally inspired and scared. It was her dream job, but she could see how the doctors around her had become burnt out, cynical and exhausted. She thought long and hard about why she was doing what she was doing and set out her own mission statement;

'I will honour my Hippocratic Oath and endeavour each and every day to 'do no harm' to any of my patients. I am including myself in this

protective oath and aim to listen to myself as I do my clients. I will take breaks, rest and mind myself, as I know I can't help anyone until this is done.'

....

Now it's your turn.

DIARY

✧ My work mission statement: _____

_____

_____

_____

_____

_____

_____

_____

_____

_____

_____

_____

_____

_____

_____

_____

_____

_____

_____

Afterword

GROUNDED HOPE

This ending contains the hope of your new beginnings. I recommend that you now create a psychological contract with yourself, showing yourself 'how' to honour this amidst the chaos and joy within all the inner lives in your adulthood. The thread through this whole book is you, each inner self impacting and influencing the other.

DIARY

⬦ Your psychological contract with yourself: _____

_____

_____

_____

_____

_____

_____

_____

_____

_____

_____

_____

_____

_____

_____

_____

_____

_____

Your Psychological Toolbox

This is your Psychological Toolbox. It is filled with the work of the psychologists I admire most and whose work has been validated by my own clinical experience. The aim of the Toolbox is to promote your mental wellbeing by giving you tools to manage emotions, stress and difficult situations. It is based on four main suppositions.

1. You are responsible for your mental wellbeing.
2. You need to invest time and effort into maintaining it.
3. You need to be consistent.
4. This applies even when you are feeling good, but especially when you are feeling bad.

Tool	What is it?	How to apply it
Mind the Gap (Viktor Frankl)	Think of the stimulus (anything that triggers a reaction) and no matter what challenges are thrown at you, you always have the freedom to choose your response. There is a gap between stimulus and response. Don't just react, *choose* your response.	**Stimulus:** Deadline **Gap:** Choose to change your reaction to the stress **Response:** 4 x 4 breathing (breathe in for four – hold for four – breathe out for four) Think of the train announcement to 'MIND THE GAP'. Think about what types of situation you would like to change your response to, e.g. your thoughts, stress, relationship triggers.

Tool	What is it?	How to apply it
Shame, Vulnerability and Connection (Brené Brown)	We are programmed as human beings to connect, but this can prove difficult when people hide their vulnerability due to shame and fear Brené Brown's ethos on this is to live wholeheartedly. In order to do this, you have to open up to connect.	Be courageous when you feel fear, or vulnerable about people seeing the authentic you. Open yourself to uncomfortable conversations and dare to be who you want to be. Use your vulnerability as a sign that you are growing. This can be seen in how you relate to people, from home to work. What makes you feel vulnerable? Are there certain situations, triggers or people who bring this up for you? What do you feel shame about? What experience(s) made you feel most connected? Can you write out times when sharing the private, vulnerable part of you led to feeling connected?

Tool	What is it?	How to apply it
Emotional First Aid **(Guy Winch)**	Treat your emotions as you would a physical injury. Do emotional triage: 1. Assess the damage. 2. What do you need to do next? 3. Allow time for healing.	Don't get plastered! Pay attention to the emotional pain. Don't minimise your emotions with 'just get over it' – they are alerting you to the fact that you need to take action. Connect to what your emotional wounds are telling you. Make a list of how you would like to react differently next time. Ask yourself, is this what you would say to a friend? Make a list of three things that improve your mood. Become aware of how you have grown through adversity. Seek to find the meaning in the negative experiences. In what ways have the emotional scars changed you? What strengths did you learn that you didn't have before? If you are wrong, say sorry. You need to forgive yourself, learn and move forward. Listen to what your emotional wounds are telling you. Do you get angry? Do you ignore them? Do you numb them with alcohol, drugs, food or technology? Do you go silent?

Tool	What is it?	How to apply it
Values in Action **(Martin Seligman and Christopher Peterson)**	Values in Action (VIA) is a questionnaire to identify your top character strengths.	Take the VIA questionnaire here: www.viacharacter.org How can you apply them to your life? Write down your top four VIA character strengths. Do you use any of your top strengths in your daily life? If so, where? If you don't, how could you introduce them into your life?
Tool	**What is it?**	**How to apply it**
Growth Mindset **(Carole Dweck)**	When you have a growth mindset, you believe you can always change and improve. This is so powerful. You can change your life by adding the word 'yet' to the end of your sentences.	Fixed mindset: *'I'm no good at maths.'* Growth mindset: *'I'm not good at long division, yet.'* **What do you want to add *'yet'* to?** Think of a recent setback. How did you manage the following: • Challenges? • Obstacles? • Effort? • Criticism?

Tool	What is it?	How to apply it
Soften, Soothe, Allow **(Kristen Neff)**	An exercise in kindness and self-compassion to help you process feelings when you are upset. Allow yourself to sit with the discomfort, which allows you to acknowledge your feelings and soothe the upset that comes with them.	Close your eyes: Think of a situation that you are or have been upset by. Notice how your body reacts to those thoughts. As you acknowledge those feelings, imagine sitting next to them. How does that feel? Is it difficult? Imagine it softening. Watch your reaction. Do you want to cry, move away from the feeling or both? Even though it is hard, try to breathe into the feeling. Place your hand where the feeling is coming up. It may be your throat, chest or head, or anywhere you feel it. Imagine soothing the feeling, as you would for an upset child. Allow yourself to feel the feelings. When you are ready, take a deep breath and open your eyes. Do you avoid thinking about difficult experiences? If so, does the avoidance work? Ask yourself then if this would help to process the experience?

Tool	What is it?	How to apply it
Boundaries	Boundaries are like the lock on your front door. You have a right to say 'no'. Give yourself permission to say 'no'.	People can't read your mind, so don't expect them to. Tell the person directly where your boundary lies ... it can be said with a kind smile. It can be really hard to practice this in reality because you will feel three big feelings – fear, guilt and self-doubt. What are your personal boundaries? Set them and stick to them. When boundaries have been crossed they can bring up feelings of resentment and discomfort – has this happened to you and if so, how did you feel? Be direct and trust your gut instinct. Be self-aware. Family dynamics – are you the 'good daughter' or 'good son'? How does this affect you? Self-care starts with you – outline how you can do this.

Tool	What is it?	How to apply it
Compassion	Compassion is the foundation of a good relationship. It can only start with self-compassion.	Adults are so busy. Dare I say too busy? Be kind to yourself and remember each day that: *'I am enough.'* *'I have enough.'* *'I do enough.'* Be aware of your inner critic. Would you talk to a stranger how you talk to yourself? How can you be encouraging to yourself in your daily thoughts and deeds? Practice mindfulness and kindness (to yourself and others). Allow for your vulnerabilities and others' – we all make mistakes. Keep a self-compassion log for a fortnight.

Self-compassion Log

This is a good way to see how you treat yourself and how you treat others. It may provide a starting point if you lack self-compassion. This is a skill to grow and develop. Practicing self-compassion will help it become part of your life.

Day	Others-Compassion	Self-Compassion
Monday		
Tuesday		
Wednesday		
Thursday		
Friday		
Saturday		
Sunday		
TOTAL		

Acknowledgements

I have three super girls, for this we know how lucky we are. As one of four sisters, my childhood 'norm' was that I would be a mum of four. I'd watch as my mum's face would light up with pride when she would tell people she had four girls. After our youngest got the flu at ten months and was seriously ill, we decided to count our three lucky stars.

Today, though, I feel that my fourth has been born. This 'baby' has also been a childhood dream. As a book lover, I always thought: *what amazing thing to do, to make change with words.* The power of that is immense. I offer this book to you as a psychologist. I am not a writer, and hopefully my 'book pregnancy' will turn me into an author.

I had many people who helped bring this 'baby' into the world and I want to thank you all from the bottom of my heart.

I'll start with my three little stars, Alannah, Hayley and Brooke. These three light up our lives and have helped with great wisdom beyond their years and laughter when forced to listen about 'the book' from the car to the kitchen.

To Thomas, who will probably kill me for writing this, but you are the best and I love you so much. I loved you the moment I met you and always will.

To my mum and dad who are also the best, you are always fully there, and your support is and always has been unconditional. I love you both so much and I know how lucky I am to have parents like you. The practical help from minding the girls to cooking dinners was never a problem. Your help was not only appreciated but it was so generous. I am so lucky to have your support, kindness and love, and I love you so much.

My sisters, Sarah-Jane, Carol Ann and Barbara, who I threw 'the book' at in between trying to work, be on the school run and generally just being super mums and great sisters. To Barbara, who sat through edit one with me and was a great sounding-board and my first test at what the book would mean to a reader, thank you so much. To Carol Ann, thanks for all your help, for the fantastic next-door dinners that I am so grateful for, and for all your help that was given without a question. To Sarah-Jane, thank you for always been there when my 5.28 pm call came in to give me a dig-out for those extra minutes, it made all the difference. And to you all for the endless questions and hypothetical ideas that I threw your way. You also did some serious magic and made twenty pages disappear in the Psychological Toolbox, this was an impressive feat. I am immensely lucky to be surrounded as an adult with the security blanket that is my family.

My whole family patiently listened and kindly gave thoughtful feedback on the many edits that you all went through that were so helpful. Dad, I loved your first review of the final edit.

To my friends, old and new, who I pestered with psychology questions and picked your brains, I love you all, you know who you are. Maybe this is a book we'll actually read!

To 'the girls'.

To Carol, for all the beautiful 'how are you, my friend' check-ins.

To Sarah, for you warm support, thank you.

Deborah, love you like a sister, thanks for everything, always.

To Cecelia Ahern, thank you so much for your advice and amazing support, you have mentored and championed me and I am truly grateful.

In true modern style, a twitter DM from Sarah Liddy at Gill Books came through and she asked me did I want to meet up to have a chat about some book ideas. This ended with a personal dream of mine coming true. Your support and ease of getting what this book was all about led to an instant connection as ideas sparked, thank you so much. It has been a pleasure to work with you.

To all the team at Gill, thank you so much, what an amazing team and group of people. To Sarah Liddy and Sheila Armstrong, whose expert eye on the edit

ACKNOWLEDGEMENTS

was much appreciated. A big thanks to Rachel Pierce for the super support in the edit, it was really helpful and collaborative. I really enjoyed working with you as we burned the midnight oil. Your questions were so helpful in guiding me. To Teresa Daly, for your enthusiasm and encouragement, you are a joy to work with. To Paul Neilan and Avril Cannon, it was a pleasure and thank you for all your help.

To Kate Gaughran, for the wonderful cover design.

To Faith O'Grady, my literary agent, a true lady whose passion for books and lovely nature facilitated me on my maiden book voyage, thank you for all your help.

To the bWell team who put these theories into action every day with warmth, compassion and expertise.

To Catherine Bolger, my fantastic supervisor who guides and helps me so much, a huge thank you for your wisdom, kindness and generosity of spirit.

To my clients, who have always inspired me. I learned so much from you and I have been so privileged to watch the strength of people coming through adversity. This book is to you all and to everyone who wants to be that person they know they truly are inside. As you look at each of your inner lives, I thank you all for letting me into that privileged space in yours.

Thank you,

Allison x

References

INTRODUCTION

Brown, C. B. (2010) *The Gifts of Imperfection: Let Go of Who You Think You're Supposed to Be and Embrace Who You Are.* Center City, MN: Hazelden.

Dweck, C. S. (2008) *Mindset: The New Psychology of Success.* New York: Ballantine.

Mead, G. H. (1967) *Mind, Self, and Society from the Standpoint of a Social Behaviorist.* Chicago: The University of Chicago Press.

Park, N., Peterson, C. & Seligman, M. E. P. (2004) 'Strengths of character and well-being.' *Journal of Social and Clinical Psychology,* 23(5): 603–619.

Winch, G. (2014) *Emotional First Aid: Healing Rejection, Guilt, Failure and Other Everyday Hurts.* New York: Plume – Penguin Group.

CHAPTER 1

Dr Seuss (1969) *My Book about Me, By Me Myself.* New York: Beginner Books.

Eurich, T. (2017) *Insight: Why We're Not as Self-Aware as We Think, and How Seeing Ourselves Clearly Helps Us Succeed at Work and in Life.* New York: Crown Business.

Germer, C. K. & Neff, K. D. (2013) 'Self-compassion in clinical practice.' *Journal of Clinical Psychology,* 69(8): 856–867.

McCorry, L. K. (2007) 'Physiology of the autonomic nervous system.' *American Journal of Pharmaceutical Education,* 69(8): 856–867.

Wegner, D. M. (2002) *The Illusion of Conscious Will.* Cambridge, MA: MIT Press.

Winch, G. (2014) *Emotional First Aid: Healing Rejection, Guilt, Failure and Other Everyday Hurts.* New York: Plume – Penguin Group.

CHAPTER 2

Ainsworth, M. D. S. (1973) 'The development of infant-mother attachment.' In B. Cardwell & H. Ricciuti (eds), *Review of Child Development Research* (Vol. 3, pp. 1–94). Chicago: University of Chicago Press.

Bowlby, J. (1969) *Attachment and Loss, Vol. 1: Attachment.* New York: Basic Books.

Brown, B. (2010) *The Gifts of Imperfection – Let Go of Who You Think You're Supposed to Be and Embrace Who You Are.* Center City, MN: Hazelden.

Bullemer, P., Nissen, M. J., & Willingham, D. B. (1989) 'On the development of procedural knowledge'. *Journal of Experimental Psychology: Learning, Memory and Cognition,* 15(6): 1047–1060.

Colman, A. M. (2006) *Oxford Dictionary of Psychology.* New York, NY: Oxford University Press.

Dweck, C. S. (2006) *Mindset: The New Psychology of Success.* New York: Random House.

Fournier, G. (2018) 'Social Norms.' *Psych Central.* Available at: https://psychcentral.com/encyclopedia/social-norms/.

Hackney, C. H. & Sanders, G. S. (2003) 'Religiosity and mental health: A meta–analysis of recent studies.' *Journal for the Scientific Study of Religion*, 42: 43–55.

Kaufman, S. B. (2011) The will and ways of hope.' *Psychology Today*. Available at: https://www.psychologytoday.com/blog/beautiful-minds/201112/the-will-and-ways-hope.

Kondo, M. (2014) *The Life-Changing Magic of Tidying Up: The Japanese Art of Decluttering and Organizing*. London: Vermillion.

Lieberman, M. D. et al. (2007) 'Putting feelings into words: affect labeling disrupts amygdala activity in response to affective stimuli.' *Psychological Science*, 18: 421–428.

Lyons-Ruth, K., Bronfman, E., & Atwood, G. A. (1999) 'Relational diathesis model of hostile-helpless states of mind: Expressions in mother-infant interactions.' In: Solomon, J., George, C. (eds). *Attachment Disorganization*. New York: Guilford Press, pp. 33–70.

Main, M. & Cassidy, J. (1988) 'Categories of response to reunion with the parent at age 6: Predictable from infant attachment classifications and stable over a 1-month period.' *Developmental Psychology*, 24: 415–426.

Main, M. & Solomon, J. Procedures for identifying infants as disorganized/disoriented during the Ainsworth strange situation. In: Greenberg, M., Cicchetti, D., Cummings, E.M. (eds), *Attachment in the preschool years: theory, research and intervention.* Chicago: University of Chicago Press; 1990. pp. 121–60.)

McCulloch, A. *et al.* (2000) 'Internalising and externalising children's behaviour problems in Britain and the US: relationships to family resources.' *Children & Society*, 14: 368–383.

Nelson, J. K. (2005) *Seeing Through Tears: Crying and Attachment.* NY: Routledge.

Simpson, J. A., Rholes, S. W. & Phillips, D. (1996) 'Conflict in close relationships: An attachment perspective.' *Journal of Personality and Social Psychology*, 71: 899–914.

Snyder, C. R., Lopez, S. (2005) *Handbook of Positive Psychology.* Oxford: Oxford University Press.

Tessina, T. (2014) *It Ends with You: Grow Up and Out of Dysfunction*. California: Muffhaven Press.

Waters, E., Cummings, E. M. (2000) 'A secure base from which to explore close relationships.' *Child Development*, 71: 164–172.

Zeanah, C. H., Danis, B., Hirshberg, L., Benoit, D., Miller, D., Heller, S. S. (1999) 'Disorganized attachment associated with partner violence: A research note.' *Infant Mental Health Journal*, 20: 77–86.

CHAPTER 3

Boer, F., & Dunn, J. (1992) *Children's Sibling Relationships: Developmental and Clinical Issues.* Hillsdale, NJ: Lawrence Erlbaum.

Boutle, G. 'Brothers and Sisters: An ambivalent relationship'. *All About Psychology*. Available at: https://www.all-about-psychology.com/brothers-and-sisters-an-ambivalent-relationship.html.

Cicirelli, V. G. (1989) 'Feelings of attachment to siblings and well-being in later life.' *Psychology and Aging*, 4(2): 211–216.

Dunn, J. (1993) *Young Children's Close Relationships: Beyond Attachment* (Vol. 4, 1st ed.). Newbury Park, CA: Sage.

Dunn, J., Creps, C. & Brown, J. (1996) 'Children's family relationships between two and five: Developmental changes and individual differences.' *Social Development*, 5: 230–250.

Dunn, J. & Plomin, R. (1990) *Separate Lives: Why Siblings are So Different* (1st ed.). New York: Basic Books.

Grose, M. (2003) *Why First-borns Rule the World and Last-borns Want to Change it.* Australia: Penguin Random House.

Kluger, J. (2011) *The Sibling Effect: What the Bonds Among Brothers and Sisters Reveal About Us.* NY: Riverhead book.

Levenson, S. (2016) *Everything but Money: A Life of Riches.* New York: Open Road Media

Bank, S. & Kahn, M. D. (1997) *The Sibling Bond* (15th ed). New York: Basic Books.

Marar, Z. (2012) *Intimacy: Understanding the Subtle Power of Human Connection.* Durham: Acumen.

McGuire, S., Manke, B., Eftekhari, A. & Dunn, J. (2000) 'Children's perceptions of sibling conflict during middle childhood: Issues and sibling (dis)similarity.' *Social Development,* 9: 173–190.

Nhất Hạnh, T. (2008) *The Miracle of Mindfulness.* Boston: Rider Books.

Prinstein, M. (2017) *Popular: The Power of Likability in a Status-Obsessed World.* London: Vermillion.

Schachter, F. F., Shore, E., Feldman-Rotman, S., Marquis, R. E. & Campbell, S. (1976) 'Sibling Deidentification.' *Developmental Psychology,* 12: 418–427.

Sulloway, F. J. (1996) *Born to Rebel: Birth Order, Family Dynamics, and Creative Lives.* New York: Pantheon Books.

Waldinger R. J., Vaillant G. E. & Orav, E. J. (2007) 'Childhood sibling relationships as a predictor of major depression in adulthood: a 30-year prospective study.' *Am J Psychiatry,* 164: 949–954.

Additional reading:

Lehmann, J-Y., Nuevo-Chiquero, A., Vidal-Fernandez, M. (2016) 'The early origins of birth order differences in children's outcomes and parental behaviour.' *Journal of Human Resources,* 0816–8177.

CHAPTER 4

Ainsworth, M. D. S., Blehar, M. C., Waters, E. & Wall, S. (1978) *Patterns of Attachment. A Psychological Study of the Strange Situation.* Hillsdale, NJ: LEA.

Bowlby, J. (1969) *Attachment.* New York: Basic Books.

Firestone, R. W. & Catlett, J. (1986) *The Fantasy Bond: Structure of Psychological Defences.* US: Glendon Association.

Firestone, L. (2013). 'How your attachment style impacts your relationship'. *Psychology Today.* Available at: https://www.psychologytoday.com/blog/compassion-matters/201307/how-your-attachment-style-impacts-your-relationship.

Frankl, Viktor E. (1984) *Man's Search for Meaning: An Introduction to Logotherapy.* New York: Simon & Schuster.

Hazan, C. & Shaver, P. (1987) 'Romantic love conceptualized as an attachment process.' *Journal of Personality and Social Psychology,* 52: 511–524.

Hazan, C. & Shaver, P.R. (1990) 'Love and work: An attachment – theoretical perspective.' *Journal of Personality & Social Psychology,* 59: 270–280.

Johnson, S. M. (2013) *Love Sense: The Revolutionary New Science of Romantic Relationships.* New York: Little, Brown and Company.

Marar, Z. (2012) *Intimacy: Understanding the Subtle Power of Human Connection.* Durham: Acumen.

Preston, N. 'What is your relationship attachment style?' *Psychology Today.* Available at: https://www.psychologytoday.com/blog/communication-success/201507/what-is-your-relationship-attachment-style

Winch, G. (2014) *Emotional First Aid: Healing Rejection, Guilt, Failure and Other Everyday Hurts.* New York: Plume – Penguin Group.

CHAPTER 5

Arnold, J. E., Graesch, A. P., & Ragazzini, E. (2012) *Life at Home in the Twenty-first Century: 32 Families Open Their Doors.* Los Angeles, CA: Cotsen Institute of Archaeology Press.

Farrell, A. (2017) The impact of stress at different life stages on physical health and the buffering effects of maternal sensitivity. *Health Psychology* 36(1) 35–44

Frankl, V. E. (1984) *Man's Search for Meaning: An Introduction to Logotherapy.* New York: Simon & Schuster.

Gopnik, A. (2016) *The Gardener and the Carpenter: What the New Science of Child Development Tells Us About the Relationship Between Parents and Children.* New York: Farrar, Straus and Giroux.

Gretchen, R. (2017) *The Four Tendencies: The Indispensable Personality Profiles That Reveal How to Make Your Life Better (and Other People's Lives Better, Too).* London: Two Roads.

Kazdin, A. E. & Rotella, C. (2013) *The Everyday Parenting Toolkit: The Kazdin Method for Easy, Step-By-Step Lasting Change For You and Your Child.* Boston: Houghton Mifflin Harcourt.

Oliver, J. (2006) *They F*** You Up: How To Survive Family Life.* London: Bloomsbury.

Oliver, J. (2015) *Jamie Oliver's Everyday Super Food.* London: Penguin Books.

Additional reading:
Seligman, M. E. P., Reivich, K., Jaycox, L. & Gillham, J. (1995) *The Optimistic Child.* Boston, Mass: Houghton Mifflin.

alankazdin.com; yaleparentingcenter.yale.edu; drkaylenehenderson.com/free-resources; happyyouhappyfamily.com/; racheous.com

CHAPTER 6

Anderson, G. O. (2010) *Loneliness among Older Adults: A National Survey of Adults 45+.* Washington, DC: AARP Research.

Berne, E. (1961) *Transactional Analysis in Psychotherapy.* New York: Grove Press, Inc.

Bhattacharya, K. et al. (2016) 'Sex differences in social focus across the life cycle in humans.' *Royal Society Open Science,* 3(4): 160097.

Burton-Chellew, Maxwell N., Dunbar, R. I. M. (2015) 'Romance and reproduction are socially costly.' *Evolutionary Behavioral Sciences,* 9(4): 229–241.

Carnegie, D. (2009) *How to Win Friends and Influence People.* New York: Simon & Schuster.

Chopik, W. J. (2017) 'Associations among relational values, support, health, and well-being across the adult lifespan.' *Personal Relationships,* 24(2): 408–422.

Coie, J. D., Dodge, K. A. & Cappotelli, H. (1982) 'Dimensions and types of social status: a cross-age perspective.' *Developmental Psychology*, 18(4): 557.

Coie, J. D. & Kupersmidt, J. B. (1983) 'A behavioural analysis of emerging social status in boys' groups.' *Child Development*, 54(6): 1400–1416.

Downey, G. & Feldman, S. I. (1996) 'Implications of rejection sensitivity for intimate relationships.' *Journal of Personality and Social Psychology*, 70(6): 1327–1343.

Dunbar, R. I. (2010) *How Many Friends Does One Person Need?: Dunbar's Number and other Evolutionary Quirks.* London: Faber and Faber.

Dunbar, R. I. (2018) 'The Anatomy of Friendship.' *Trends in Cognitive Sciences*, 22(1): 32–51.

Eisenberger, N. I., Lieberman, M. D. & Williams K. D. (2003) 'Does rejection hurt? A fMRI study of social exclusion.' *Science*, 302(5643): 290–292.

Grabill, C. M., & Kerns, K. A. (2000) 'Attachment style and intimacy in friendship.' *Personal Relationships*, 7: 363–378.

Haber, S. N. (2011) Neuroanatomy of reward: A view from the ventral striatum. In: Gottfried J. A (ed.), *Neurobiology of Sensation and Reward.* Boca Raton (FL): CRC Press/Taylor & Francis, Chapter 11.

Holt-Lunstad, J., Smith, T. B. & Layton, J. B. (2010) 'Social relationships and mortality risk: a meta-analytic review.' *PLoS Med*, 7(7): e1000316.

Holt-Lunstad, J. et al. (2015) 'Loneliness and social isolation as risk factors for mortality: A meta-analytic review.' *Perspectives on Psychological Science*, 10: 227–237.

Jo Cox Commission Report (2016) *Trapped in a Bubble: An Investigation into the Triggers for Loneliness in the UK.* UK: Co-op and British Red Cross.

Joiner, T. E. Jr., Metalsky, G. I., Katz, J. & Beach, S. R. H. (1999) 'Depression and excessive reassurance-seeking.' *Psychological Inquiry*, 10(4): 269–278.

Koudenburg, N. et al. (2011) 'Disrupting the flow: how brief silences in group conversations affect social needs.' *Journal of Experimental Social Psychology*, 47: 512–515.

Lemerise, E.A. et al. (2006) 'Do provocateurs' emotion displays influence children's social goals and problem solving?' *J Abnorm Child Psychol* 34: 555.

Melton, G. D. (2018) 'One teacher's brilliant strategy to stop future school shootings – and it's not about guns.' *Reader's Digest*. Available at: https://www.rd.com/advice/parenting/stop-bullying-strategy

Mollenhorst, G. (2009) 'Half of your friends lost in seven years, social network study finds.' *Science Daily* (Netherlands Organization for Scientific Research).

Paresky, P. (2017) 'Meet the teen who discovered the secret of social capital.' *Psychology Today*. Available at: https://www.psychologytoday.com/blog/happiness-and-the-pursuit-leadership/201711/meet-the-teen-who-discovered-the-secret-social.

Perissinotto, C. M., Cenzer, I. S. & Covinsky, K. E. (2012) 'Loneliness in Older Persons: A predictor of functional decline and death.' *Archives of Internal Medicine*, 172(14): 1078–1083.

Piaget, J. (1932) *The Moral Judgment of the Child.* New York: The Free Press.

Prinstein, M. J. (2017) *Popular: Why Being Liked is the Secret to Greater Success and Happiness.* London: Vermillion.

Prinstein, M. J., Nesi, J. & Calhoun, C. D. (2016) Recollections of Childhood Peer Status and Adult Outcomes: A Global Study. (*In preparation*, University of North Carolina at Chapel Hill.)

Saphire-Bernstein, S. & Taylor, S. E. (2013) 'Close relationships and subjective well-being.' In I. Boniwell & S. David (eds), *Oxford Handbook of Happiness* (pp. 821–833). UK: Oxford University Press.

Schneider, F. W., Gruman, J. A. & Coutts, L. M. (eds) (2012) *Applied Social Psychology: Understanding and Addressing Social and Practical Problems* (2nd ed.). Thousand Oaks, CA: SAGE Publications.

Slavich, G. M. & Cole, S. W. (2013) 'The emerging field of human social genomics.' *Clinical Psychological Science*, 1(3): 331–348.

Strasburger, V. (2007) Super-peer theory. In J. J. Arnett, *Encyclopedia of Children, Adolescents, and the Media* (Vol. 1). Thousand Oaks, CA: Sage Publications Ltd.

Underwood, M. K., Kupersmidt, J. B. & Coie, J. (1996) 'Childhood Peer Sociometric Status and Aggression as Predictors of Adolescent Childbearing.' *Journal of Research on Adolescence*, 6(2): 201–223.

Werner, N. E. (2012) 'Do hostile attribution biases in children and parents predict relationally aggressive behaviour?' *Journal of Genetic Psychology*, 173(3): 221–245.

CHAPTER 7

Alicke, M. D. & Govorun, O. (2005) The better-than-average effect. In M. D. Alicke, D. A. Dunning & J. I. Krueger (eds), *Studies in self and identity. The Self in Social Judgment*, pp. 85–106. New York: Psychology Press.

Askew, D. A., Schluter, P. J. & Dick, M. L. (2013) 'Workplace bullying – What's it got to do with general practice?' *Australian Family Physician*, 42: 186–188.

Biswas-Diener, R. & Kashdan, T. B. (2013) 'What happy people do differently.' *Psychology Today*. Available at: https://www.psychologytoday.com/articles/201307/what-happy-people-do-differently.

Buunk, B. & Van Yperen, N. W. (1991) 'Referential comparisons, relational comparisons, and exchange orientation: Their relation to marital satisfaction.' *Personality and Social Psychology Bulletin*, 17: 710–718.

Clance, P. R. & Imes, S. A. (1978) 'The imposter phenomenon in high achieving women: dynamics and therapeutic intervention.' *Psychotherapy: Theory, Research and Practice*, 15(3): 241–247.

Crawford, M. B. (2015) *The World Beyond Your Head: On Becoming an Individual in an Age of Distraction*. London: Penguin.

Crawford, M. B. (2010) *The Case for Working with Your Hands: or Why Office Work is Bad for Us and Fixing Things Feels Good*. London: Penguin.

Csikszentmihalyi, M. (1990) *Flow: The Psychology of Optimal Experience*. New York: Harper & Row.

Frankl, Viktor E. (1962) *Man's Search for Meaning: An Introduction to Logotherapy*. Boston: Beacon Press, Chicago.

Fredrickson, B. L. (2001) 'The role of positive emotions in positive psychology: the broaden-and-build theory of positive emotions.' *The American Psychologist*, 56(3): 218–226.

Fuocco, M. A. (1996) 'Trial and error: They had larceny in their hearts, but little in their heads.' *Pittsburgh Post-Gazette*.

Gopnik, A., Griffiths, T. & Lucas, C. (2015). 'When younger learners can be better (or at least more open-minded) than older ones.' *Current Directions in Psychological Science*, 24: 87–92.

Harzer, C., Mubashar, T., & Dubreuil, P. (2017) 'Character strengths and strength-related person-job fit as predictors of work-related wellbeing, job performance, and workplace deviance.' *Wirtschaftspsychologie*, 19(3): 23–38.

Hochschild, A. R. (1983) *The Managed Heart: Commercialization of Human Feeling.* Berkeley: University of California Press.

Kessler, D. (2009). *The End of Overeating: Taking Control of the Insatiable American Appetite.* New York: Emmaus.

Kim, J., Dear, R. D. (2013) 'Workspace satisfaction: The privacy-communication trade-off in open-plan offices.' *Journal of Environmental Psychology*, 36: 18–26.

Kruger, J. & Dunning, D. (1999) 'Unskilled and unaware of it: How difficulties in recognizing one's own incompetence lead to inflated self-assessments.' *Journal of Personality and Social Psychology*, 77(6): 1121–1134.

Littman-Ovadia, H., Lavy, S. & Boiman-Meshita, M. (2016a) 'When theory and research collide: Examining correlates of signature strengths use at work.' *Journal of Happiness Studies*, 18(2): 627–648

Mark, G., Gudith, D., & Klocke, U. (2008) 'The cost of interrupted work: More speed and stress.' Paper presented at the 26th annual SIGCHI Conference on Human factors in computing systems, Florence, Italy.

McGinnity, F., Grotti, R., Kenny, O., & Russell, H. (2017) *Who experiences discrimination in Ireland?* Report for Irish Human Rights and Equality Commission by the Economic and Social Research Institute.

Morris, E. (2010) 'The anosognosic's dilemma: something's wrong but you'll never know what it is' (Part 1). *The New York Times*.

Norton, M. I., Mochon, D. and Ariely, D. (2012) 'The IKEA effect: When labor leads to love.' *Journal of Consumer Psychology*, 22(3): 453–460.

Peterson, C. & Seligman, M. E. P. (2004) *Character Strengths and Virtues: A Handbook and Classification.* Washington, DC: American Psychological Association.

Young, V. (2011) *The Secret Thoughts of Successful Women: Why Capable People Suffer From the Impostor Syndrome and How to Thrive in Spite of it.* New York, NY: Random House.

Zabelina, D. L. & Robinson, M. D. (2010) 'Child's play: Facilitating the originality of creative output by a priming manipulation.' *Psychology of Aesthetics, Creativity, and the Arts*, 4(1): 57–65.